WORTH DYING FOR

Lewis M. Simons

WORTH DYING FOR

WILLIAM MORROW AND COMPANY, INC.
NEW YORK

Library of Congress Cataloging-in-Publication Data

Simons, Lewis M.
Worth dying for.
Includes index.
1. Philippines—History—Revolution, 1986. I. Title.
DS686.62.S56   1987   959.9′046   87-7857
ISBN 0-688-06940-1

Printed in the United States of America

First Edition

1 2 3 4 5 6 7 8 9 10

BOOK DESIGN BY PATRICE FODERO

ACKNOWLEDGMENTS

I have dedicated this book to my wife because without her I could not have written it. Her optimism, encouragement, and understanding were gifts beyond measure. But she also shared with me her skills as a journalist and editor, her insights into Asia, her patience, and her relentless questioning. I was, I am, fortunate to have her at my side.

There are others to whom I am deeply indebted. Jonathan Krim, my friend and my editor at the *San Jose Mercury News* during the years between the assassination of Aquino and the flight of Marcos, read the entire manuscript and made valuable improvements. Abby Tan conducted several key interviews for me in Manila after I had begun writing. A longtime colleague and friend, she shared generously her extensive sources and her superior understanding of the Philippines and Southeast Asia.

How many Filipinos contributed to this book would be impossible to say. Often, a fleeting exchange with a taxi driver or a participant in a street demonstration proved as insightful as an hours-long interview with a cabinet minister or a general. Many of those who were most helpful are named in the text. Two who are not are Joan Orendain and Antonio Gatmaitan. Over the years they offered information and interpretation and, more importantly, friendship that I will always treasure. My understanding of people and events would have been immeasurably poorer without them.

Others who helped me find my way through the Philippine business and political maze were Cesar Buenaventura, Emanuel Soriano, David Sycip, Jesus Estanislao, Eduardo Alunan, and Rex Arnaldo. I also want to thank Nancy Pelletreau, one of my oldest and dearest friends, for her introductions and good advice.

It is the nature of journalists to compete rather than to cooperate. But some are always willing, even pleased, to share their knowledge, and I have benefited from their good will. Tiziano Terzani of *Der Spiegel* first suggested that I do this book, and his enthusiasm was contagious. Bruce MacDonell of NBC-TV was exceptionally generous during the hearings of the Agrava Fact-Finding Board. Some other colleagues to whom I am grateful are Conrado Andres of *Business Day*; Anthony Barbieri of *The Baltimore Sun*; Thomas Breen of *The Washington Times*; David Briscoe of The Associated Press; Michael Browning of the *Miami Herald*; Noel de Luna of *Business Day*; Jim Laurie of ABC-TV; Ryoichi Nishida of *Yomiuri Shimbun*, and Guy Sacerdoti of the *Far Eastern Economic Review*. Harvey Stockwin of the *South China Morning Post* is a special friend whose vast knowledge of the Philippines and of all Asia he has shared unstintingly for twenty years.

My editors at the *San Jose Mercury News*, Robert Ingle, Jerome Ceppos, Robert Ryan, and Victoria Loe, could not have been more generous with their encouragement and support and in granting me time away from my reporting duties.

Harvey Ginsberg and Paul Lerner, my editors at William Morrow, deserve all the thanks I can give them, and something extra, for their patience and expert guidance, as does Robert Ducas, my agent, who understands the idiosyncracies of foreign correspondents who would be authors.

Justine, Rebecca, and Adam Simons receive my special thanks for their many suggestions and for putting up with an insufferable grouch during the time of writing. Goldie Simons gave me a mother's unwavering confidence. And, to Lu and Herb Adler, my fondest appreciation for sacrificing the room with the view in Camden, Maine, where I wrote much of this book.

My final word of thanks is for Father James Donelon, whose devotion to the people of the Philippines, whose erudition and gentle good humor have helped me keep what I hope is a fair and honest perspective of his adopted country.

AUTHOR'S NOTE

As a journalist I have relied to the fullest extent possible on my own reporting from the Philippines as the basis for this book. During the years that I covered the events I've written about, I interviewed hundreds of people—Filipinos, Americans, and others. Wherever possible, I have named them in the text. Some, however, such as foreign diplomats and individuals in sensitive positions, have asked not to be identified, and I have abided by their wishes.

Since no one journalist, no matter how well intentioned and hard-working, could cover everything of importance going on in any country for nearly three years, I have helped myself freely to the work of many others. In some cases I have used their reporting to fill in periods when I was away from the Philippines, in others to augment my own coverage. Those to whom I turned with most regularity were Sandra Burton and Nelly Sindayan of *Time*; Melindia Liu and Richard Vokey of *Newsweek*; Steve Lohr and Seth Mydans of *The New York Times*; William Brannigan of *The Washington Post*; Anthony Spaeth of *The Asian Wall Street Journal*; and Guy Sacerdoti and Rodney Tasker of the *Far Eastern Economic Review*.

A specific instance in which I relied on others' work was the hearings of the Agrava Fact-Finding Board, which were covered daily, without fail, by a five-member team of correspondents for *Asiaweek* magazine and written with sensitivity and charm by editor-in-chief

9

Michael O'Neill. An article in *Manhattan, inc.* magazine by Jonathan Greenberg and John Taylor helped with details on the Bernstein brothers in regard to the Marcoses' New York properties. Some of the details on Roman Cruz, Jr., and his relationship with Imelda Marcos came from a firsthand account by Barbara C. Gonzales, a former friend of Cruz's, in *West* magazine. The reporting of Alfred McCoy, Gwen Robinson, and Marian Wilkinson in the *Australia Times on Sunday* was valuable in fleshing out interviews Abby Tan and I conducted among the principals in the military rebellion and those with whom they interacted.

Pete Carey and Katherine Ellison, my colleagues at the *San Jose Mercury News*, were sources to whom I turned frequently, particularly for developments in the United States related to the "hidden wealth" of the Marcoses and their associates. Carl Cannon and Frank Greve of the Knight-Ridder Washington bureau provided detailed information on developments inside the Reagan administration.

Unavoidably, other journalists will find their reporting mixed with mine and feel that they should have received credit. I concur and I apologize, but the omissions were purely unintentional.

It was my good fortune that a number of books on the four-day rebellion against the Marcos regime were produced with remarkable speed, and I used some of them to augment and check my own reporting. These were: *Bayan Ko!*, which contains pictures of the military rebellion by a large contingent of international photographers and concise written accounts by Lin Neumann and Guy Sacerdoti; *People Power*, edited by Monina Allarey Mercado with written segments by Francisco S. Tatad; and *Breakaway*, by Cecilio T. Arillo.

For background on Benigno S. Aquino, Jr., I turned to *The Aquinos of Tarlac*; by Nick Joaquin, and to *Ninoy Aquino*, by Asuncion David Maramba. Material on Salvador Laurel and his relationship with Benigno Aquino came from *Doy Laurel in Profile*, by Nick Joaquin.

Marcos of the Philippines, by Hartzell Spence, *The Untold Story of Imelda Marcos*, by Carmen Navarro-Pedrosa, and *The Conjugal Dictatorship of Ferdinand and Imelda Marcos*, by Primitavo Mijares, were of great value in providing material on the Marcoses' early years.

A source for the history of the Communist movement was *Philippine Society and Revolution*, by Amado Guerrero.

CONTENTS

I have asked myself many times: Is the Filipino worth suffering, or even dying, for?

Is he not a coward who would readily yield to any colonizer, be he foreign or homegrown?

Is a Filipino more comfortable under an authoritarian leader because he does not want to be burdened with the freedom of choice?

Is he unprepared or, worse, ill-suited for presidential or parliamentary democracy?

I have carefully weighed the virtues and the faults of the Filipino, and I have come to the conclusion that he is worth dying for.

—Benigno S. Aquino, Jr., in a speech before the Asia Society, in New York City, August 4, 1980, three years before he was shot to death at Manila International Airport, minutes after returning to his homeland

PROLOGUE

THE DURIAN LOVER

Among Southeast Asia's curiosities is a fruit called the durian. About the size of a pineapple, it is spiky and tough on the outside, creamy and soft inside. What is oddest about the durian is the contrast between its taste, which aficionados consider heavenly, and its smell, which is putrid. Eating durian has been likened to consuming strawberries and cream in a public lavatory. Some find the durian nauseating; others, quite literally, kill for it. Supposedly endowed with aphrodisiac powers, the fruit is the subject of much ribald humor.

I have never acquired a taste for the durian, despite my twenty years in Asia. Yet it continues to intrigue me, with its myths and anomalies, with the sentiments and the passions it arouses. So, too, am I continuously intrigued by Ferdinand E. Marcos, the fallen dictator of the Philippines, a man of mercurial contrasts who aroused emotional extremes among his countrymen.

As it happened, Marcos was a true durian lover, enamored of its rich flavor and its allegedly strength-enhancing qualities. And, like the fruit, Marcos appeared tough and forbidding. But after his surface was cracked, what was inside was found to be soft and malodorous.

The end came in February 1986, when he fled into the night in an American helicopter, disappearing so quickly that some refused to believe that he had really gone. After his twenty years on the presidential throne, the man and the place had become synonymous. Marcos and the Philippines. Marcos of the Philippines. But the rottenness that everyone suspected was buried somewhere inside was brought to the surface by a handful of events strung together over two and a half years: The man Marcos most feared was murdered; his soldiers were accused of the killing; he was found to be bleeding the country white; he was challenged by the widow of the murdered man; finally, his bishops and generals deserted him.

Right up until the end, Marcos postured, boasting that he would single-handedly fight it out with rifles from his palace. But he had no heart for a fight.

As the durian leaves behind its stench, so Marcos and his wife left behind their own residue. Their abandoned palace yielded piles of black underwear and more than a thousand pairs of shoes, racks hung with more dresses than are displayed in many department stores, gallon jugs of perfumes that sell for a hundred dollars an ounce, tasteless trinkets, and boxes full of receipts for the most extravagant of indulgences. More importantly, they left behind a plundered economy, where once there had been the greatest promise for prosperity in Southeast Asia; a disheartened and politicized military force, where once there had been professional soldiers committed to a constitution and flag; and an increasingly threatening Communist insurgency, where once there had been little more than a defeated gang of ideologues. In the end, Marcos was just one more dictator, turning to America for protection in return for two decades of favors, running away from the nation he had driven into penury.

1

ASSASSINATION

He had to know they were going to kill him.

In his last few moments, after the uniformed men located him in his seat on the plane, the emotions flickering across his face showed that he knew. Surprise. Realization. Fear. Resignation.

They led him down the stairway and, seconds later, a bullet crashed into the base of his skull. A fragment of the ruptured metal burst out through his chin. He died instantly, falling heavily to the tarmac. Blood spread quickly, forming a slick around his body.

A fusillade of automatic-rifle fire erupted. Another body fell, one they would say later was that of the assassin.

The shot that killed Benigno S. Aquino, Jr.—Ninoy Aquino— succeeded in eliminating the man most feared by Ferdinand Marcos, then in his eighteenth year in power and sick with a chronic kidney ailment. Those most concerned with prolonging his stay in the Spanish-colonial splendor of Malacañang Palace, his wife, Imelda; his military commander, General Fabian C. Ver; and his so-called cronies, felt that Marcos and, therefore, they were safe. They could not have foreseen that a single shot could backfire so dramatically, that just thirty months later they would have to flee the palace and the country for their lives. Never in their worst nightmares could they have anticipated that Marcos would be replaced as president of the Philippines by Aquino's soft-spoken, self-effacing widow, Corazon.

Certainly, no one could have predicted that the assassination of

Aquino would capture the imagination of the world. Even now, it seems impossibly melodramatic—the forces of good against evil, the downtrodden poor against the bloated rich, the emergence of an unlikely and unwilling champion, the tense confrontation between innocent women carrying rosary beads and flowers and soldiers armed with deadly weapons, the glory of a bloodless victory won by the masses.

Aquino himself never would have dreamed of these developments as he boarded China Airlines Flight 811 in Taipei, August 21, 1983, for the final leg of his painstakingly orchestrated trip home. Even so, no one, other than Marcos, understood Philippine politics better than Aquino; and no one fathomed the ruthless, slavish loyalty to Marcos of the top military commanders better than Aquino did. And if he had any doubts, he'd been warned specifically that his safety couldn't be guaranteed if he returned to the Philippines. Marcos had told him himself. So had Imelda Marcos. So had Defense Minister Juan Ponce Enrile. So had Cardinal Jaime Sin, the nominal head of the country's Roman Catholic Church.

Why, then, did Ninoy Aquino return home? Why didn't he stay in the comfortable Boston suburb of Newton, Massachusetts, where he and his family had been living for three years since his triple-bypass heart operation in 1980? Certainly, his wife and five children were content in the United States; Cory Aquino said those three years were the happiest of her life. Ninoy had prestigious teaching fellowships at Harvard and Massachusetts Institute of Technology. He'd made influential friends in Washington, among them Senator Edward Kennedy and Representative Stephen Solarz. Nor was he isolated from Philippine affairs. Aquino was a beacon for millions of his countrymen living in the United States and for anti-Marcos visitors from back home. The hundreds of Filipinos who wait patiently every day for a chance to plead for a visa to the United States would have sacrificed heavily to be in his place. At fifty, Aquino was a free man and welcome in a free country after spending nearly eight years in one of Marcos's military prisons, much of that time in solitary confinement, under a death sentence.

In the days immediately following his assassination, amateur psychologists in every Manila coffee shop analyzed Aquino's motives for returning. One of the more titillating theses was that he had a "death wish.'' Another was that his heart condition had taken a turn for the worse, and, thinking he didn't have long to live anyway, he decided to take a chance.

There seemed to be some basis for the ''death wish'' theory. His mother, *Doña* Aurora Aquino, a grande dame who was tough and politically savvy, said that in his last letter to her, Ninoy had written, ''Mommy, Boston has become our second home. All my needs for intellectual pursuits are met here. Life here is comfortable and beautiful. But, I'm leaving all this for home, even if it means jail, the firing squad, or death.''

Felix Bautista, a relative of the Aquinos' and a close friend and speech-writer of Cardinal Sin's, who put most of the canny prelate's more stinging words in his mouth, subscribed to the ''death wish'' line of thinking. Bautista said of Aquino: ''He wanted martyrdom. But, there is no question that he loved this country, he despaired of what Marcos was doing to it, and he felt helpless in the United States. He was a master strategist. He felt that by coming home, he'd put Marcos in a no-win situation—he'd be martyred, of sorts, if he was jailed; he could be effective if he was put under house arrest; and, if they killed him, of course he'd become a true martyr.''

Aquino's murder as a catalyst for dramatic change in the Philippines has important historical precedent. In 1896, a Spanish firing squad executed José Rizal, who'd been exiled four years earlier, for agitating for Filipino participation in the Spanish *Cortes*, or parliament. The execution made Rizal a revolutionary martyr and stirred Filipinos to launch a full-fledged fight for independence. Two years later, the United States helped the Filipinos overthrow the Spanish, without a shot, only to take over as the Philippines' next colonial master. Between 1898 and 1902, Filipino guerrillas led by the passionate patriot Emilio Aguinaldo waged a little-known but bitter war against the U.S. Army. The struggle ended with Aguinaldo's capture and U.S. control continued, with a three-year interlude of Japanese rule, until the end of World War II.

America's historical role was of paramount importance, setting much of the background for the drama surrounding the Aquino killing and its sequel. In the years between the end of World War II and the Aquino assassination, State Department officials enjoyed telling themselves that America's little brown brothers had absorbed their lessons well during the relatively benign forty-year colonial period and were building a U.S.-style democracy that could be emulated by the rest of developing Asia. This became a particularly sensitive issue after South Vietnam fell to the Communist North in April 1975. If the Philippines could make a success of democracy, then perhaps the dominoes might not fall.

But what Filipino politicians acquired from their exposure to U.S. rule was only a thin veneer of democracy. Behind the surface glitter was the reality of some 350 years of Spanish colonialism, during which the ruling class had learned how to enrich itself by keeping the underclasses in check. Even more fundamentally, the underlying layer of indigenous Malay culture, the bedrock of Filipino culture, excuses virtually any misbehavior in public office for the sake of family loyalty. This conduct is so deeply rooted that the poor themselves not only accept high-level corruption, they expect it and would be shocked if their leaders behaved in any other way. But there are limits.

New myths about Aquino were nurtured in the months after he was assassinated. One was that he believed if Marcos would listen to him for just one hour, he would be persuaded to leave office voluntarily in order to repair his image for posterity. In an interview in Boston shortly before departing, Aquino told Teodoro Benigno, the veteran Manila bureau chief of Agence France-Presse, "For this single opportunity I am putting my life on the line. Just a chance to talk to him one on one. I know he doesn't trust me. He thinks I'm most unreliable. Maybe he hates me. But, all I'm asking in exchange for my life, for my freedom, is one hour to talk to him. After talking to him, after making my presentation, it's up to him. But at that point, I can rest peacefully."

His confidence that he could convince Marcos to step down was, in part, an outgrowth of an intensely religious experience he had undergone while a prisoner at Manila's Fort Bonifacio. Aquino told friends that during the early days of his imprisonment he had found God. Though a lifetime Catholic, he had realized that he'd been practicing his faith more out of habit than conviction. In a letter dated June 19, 1973, he wrote Francisco Rodrigo, like himself a former senator who had been held prisoner by Marcos, how his rebirth had come about. He'd been kept in a "sweatbox" for "thirty harrowing days," and his weight had dropped from 190 pounds to 148. All his clothing and possessions, even his glasses, had been taken from him. He "suffered terrible headaches." He slipped into black pits of depression. As Cory Aquino would later reflect, "Marcos must have studied Ninoy well. He chose the right punishment for Ninoy. He could have tried, convicted, and executed him in the first year of martial law when, frankly, quite a lot of people gave Marcos the benefit of the doubt and were prepared to pay the price of tolerating his rule with the lives and liberties of those who opposed him on principle. Marcos instead put Ninoy in solitary confinement. In that way, he stripped Ninoy of what he loved most: the talk and company of people, the liberty to mingle and work with them. God had shaped Ninoy for action. Now, all his outward-flowing energies had only the blank walls of his cell to receive them. It was hard for Ninoy to learn, as he finally did, to turn into himself. He would fall into despair occasionally and ask me, 'Are there people who still remember me, or who even think of me once in a while?' "

It was during this period, he wrote Rodrigo, that a voice came to him and said: "Why do you cry? I have gifted you with consolations, honors, and glory which have been denied to millions of your countrymen. I made you the youngest war correspondent, presidential assistant, mayor, vice governor, governor, and senator of the republic, and I recall you never thanked me for all these gifts. I have given you a full life, a great wife, and beautiful, lovable children. Now that I visit you with a slight desolation, you cry and whimper like a spoiled brat!"

With that, Aquino's letter continued, "I went down on my knees and begged His forgiveness. I know I was merely undergoing a test, maybe in preparation for another mission. . . . I therefore resigned myself to His will."

Whatever religious experience he might have undergone, there is no question that Aquino's chief motive for returning remained political ambition. He'd been in jail from 1972 until 1980, then in the United States until 1983, long enough to be forgotten by a generation of young Filipinos. Following Marcos's state visit to the United States in September 1982, Aquino was convinced, correctly, that the Reagan administration was solidly behind the dictator. Administration officials had been dispatched to Boston prior to Marcos's arrival to warn Aquino not to do anything that might embarrass Reagan. In addition, his fellowships were coming to an end, his visa had nearly expired, and he realized that he had little room left for maneuvering in the United States. Most importantly, he believed that Marcos was sick, perhaps dying, and that this was the moment for him to strike.

Luis Beltran, a columnist and editor and an old friend from Aquino's newspaper days, recalled his last conversation with Ninoy in New York, exactly a year before he flew home. "In typical Ninoy fashion, he gave answers even while he was asking questions. There was no doubt in his mind that Marcos was really sick. He had talked to American doctors who had told him the extent of the medical problems."

Aquino, like Marcos, lived for politics. Although Marcos was older by sixteen years, their shared traits outweighed their differences. They had both been brilliant young men who had made their marks early. Aquino broke into journalism at the age of seventeen and was elected mayor of his hometown, Concepcion, at twenty-two. He was soon the governor of Tarlac province and then a senator. Marcos won, in rapid succession, a series of command positions in the two houses of the national congress and was elected president at forty-seven. One was as ruthless as the other.

If Marcos was sharply criticized for condoning brutality, people who knew Aquino when he was running Tarlac said violence was commonplace in the province. Both men understood the incredible complexities of leadership required in the 7,000-island nation. Both were destined to lead. It was inevitable that they would clash.

On September 22, 1972, Marcos imposed martial law. Had he not done so, he would have been barred by the constitution from running for a third four-year term. Aquino, then a senator, almost certainly would have been elected his successor. He had the charisma, the wealth, the backing, and the ambition. But Marcos had the power, and he used it to discard the constitution and to perpetuate his reign. Martial law was required, he told the nation, because the government was being threatened by a rightist-leftist conspiracy. What was being planned, Marcos said, was his overthrow and eventual liquidation by the military. The Communists would then follow up by ousting the military and establishing a Maoist state. In turn, Muslim rebels on Mindanao would claim sovereignty over all the southern islands, and the Philippines would be split asunder.

Bizarre though this alleged conspiracy sounded, Marcos used it as all the excuse he needed to round up his political enemies. Aquino was arrested in the first few minutes after midnight while attending a meeting at the Manila Hilton, probably the first of the president's opponents to be picked up. He was charged with subversion, murder, and illegal possession of firearms.

A long, drawn-out trial, lasting nearly five years, ensued. On November 25, 1977, a military court sentenced him to death by firing squad. Two days later, his mother filed a petition claiming that her son had been denied the opportunity to present evidence. Marcos responded by ordering the military court to reopen the case. The trial resumed but quickly bogged down, and Aquino remained in Manila's Fort Bonifacio for another two and a half years.

Aquino spent much of his time in prison reading. On a two-week "furlough," over Christmas of 1979, he told friends that he'd read something like three thousand books during the preceding seven or so years. His tastes were eclectic: philosophy, religion, history, politics, ideology, economics, science, technology, fiction, drama, poetry. Gregorio C. Brillantes, a writer, recalled that Ninoy had mentioned one book that "tells you how to build a castle, step by step, from the drawbridge to the spire of the highest tower. And you have to do it all in your mind, in stages, day after day, for weeks on end. Where to place each stone or tile, each plank of wood, everything." It seemed like the kind of book a person would read solely to keep his sanity.

On other Christmases and New Years, his young family visited him in his cell. Ninoy and Cory and the five children would be locked into the cramped cubicle where they'd have makeshift dinners on the floor. The parents fretted about the effect of these prison visits on their youngest child, Kristina, who was just two years old when her father was arrested. The older children could recall happier times, but the baby of the family knew only holidays in jail. For her sake, Cory would transport stacks of gifts to the cell. Ninoy had invented a character he named Putris, and he got one of his guards to play the role, knocking on the cell door at midnight and bringing in the presents. After unwrapping the gifts, the entire family would sleep side-by-side on the floor.

Prison life ended for Aquino early in May 1980. He had suffered a heart attack and was taken to the Philippine Heart Center for Asia. This was an elaborate but underutilized facility built by Imelda Marcos in 1973 at a cost of $50 million. Filipinos who could afford to use the center normally chose to go to the United States for treatment. A preliminary examination showed that Aquino would require multiple-bypass surgery. Arrangements were made hastily, and he left for Baylor University Medical Center in Texas on May 8, immediately after the Philippine Supreme Court approved his request to go abroad. In order to win the high court's assent, Aquino signed a statement promising "to immediately return to my detention quarters . . . after my operation or whatever would be the result of my Stateside consultations . . . four weeks at the utmost." The death sentence still stood.

Since Marcos controlled the Supreme Court, as he did the entire Philippine judiciary, its approval for Aquino's journey was tantamount to the president's own nod. Why would Marcos permit Aquino to leave the country? If, as is widely accepted, he viewed Aquino as the politician who could cause him the most harm, why didn't he leave him in prison or even at the Heart Center, where he could have died from natural causes?

More to the point, why did Marcos keep Aquino in jail for eight years, under sentence of death, yet never carry out the execution? One possible answer is that the Damoclean threat was intended as a warning to other Marcos opponents. Aquino was the last member of a major "oligarchic" family held in prison. Two others, Eugenio Lopez, Jr., and Sergio Osmena, Jr., both sons of eminent, multimillionaire families whose properties had been confiscated under martial law, had escaped from Fort Bonifacio in 1977 and fled to the United States. Friends of the Osmena and Lopez families believe that Marcos may have permitted the two men to break out. Marcos's reputation for plotting ingenious means of outwitting and outmaneuvering his enemies was such that his countrymen simply accepted that he could never be bested. Aquino worried that the president wanted to send him to the United States so that he would become identified politically with the soft life of the self-exiles, who were referred to laughingly by people back in Manila as "steak commandos."

Another reason for Marcos's action was to place himself in better standing with the administration of President Jimmy Carter, which was already pressing him to improve human rights. Through Assistant Secretary of State for East Asian and Pacific Affairs Richard Holbrooke, Marcos was being asked to release political prisoners. U.S.

presidential elections were set for November 1980, and although Marcos was betting on Reagan, he couldn't be sure that Carter would be defeated.

When Aquino was gunned down at the airport, the first suspect in the minds of millions of Filipinos was the president. Indeed, Cory Aquino never hesitated to insist publicly that Marcos was behind her husband's murder. But many Filipinos believed then, and still do, that Marcos did not want Aquino to die, either by an assassin's bullet or by a heart attack. Aquino himself, shortly before he was killed, mused that he believed Marcos "might not like me, but . . . I was a sparring mate for him, and he would be lonely without me."

Aboard his final flight Aquino claimed not to understand why Marcos would consider him a threat, suggesting that they were like two brothers. In fact, they had belonged to the same fraternity at the University of the Philippines and, as is the custom, always addressed each other as "brother" or, in the shortened Filipino form, *brod*.

A good part of Aquino's last year and a half in the United States was occupied in sparring with Marcos over the question of his returning to the Philippines. When Marcos wanted him to come back, Aquino refused; when Aquino wanted to return, Marcos warned him away.

In February 1982, Marcos said he would "officially ask" Aquino "to come home and face the court cases against him." If Aquino "is any man worth his salt, who maintains his word of honor, I think he should therefore come back and face the Supreme Court." Aquino dodged: "I've always said I'll return. I have no intention of seeking permanent residence in the United States or anywhere else."

Two months later, on April 22, the military tribunal that had passed the death sentence against Aquino in 1977 reaffirmed it and ordered that he be arrested and returned to Fort Bonifacio. Many interpreted this as Marcos's warning to Aquino not to come back.

In May, Aquino replied to the verdict in a letter to veteran Foreign Minister Carlos Romulo that accompanied his application for a renewed passport. He wrote that he did not respect the judgment of the military tribunal, since he was a civilian, and that the Supreme Court had given him permission to leave the country. Following his bypass surgery, he had cabled Marcos of his willingness to forgo six to eight weeks of physical rehabilitation ordered by his doctors if the president wanted him to live up to his signed promise to return after the operation.

"Within thirty-six hours," Aquino wrote, "I received a reply from the president through his then senior military aide, Major General Fabian C. Ver, who . . . informed me that the president has given me the permission 'to take your time and go through with the physical rehabilitation therapy and you can stay in America indefinitely.' It was my distinct impression that President Marcos did not want me back in the Philippines."

But by May 1983, Aquino had second thoughts. Parliamentary elections seemed certain, and he sniffed blood. If Marcos truly was sick and dying, Ninoy had to get back to Manila before the failing president maneuvered his politically powerful wife or one of his close associates into position to succeed him. It was, as Aquino saw things, a now-or-never situation. He wouldn't seek a seat for himself, but he and Salvador H. Laurel, another old pro in the Aquino and Marcos mold with long-smoldering ambitions of his own, had been discussing plans to organize the fragmented, ineffectual opposition.

The relationship between Aquino and Laurel was an uneasy one. They had known each other since boyhood and gave the appearance of being allies, but they would have been at each other's throats if and when the opportunity arose for one of them to run for the presidency. The tenuousness of their relationship became apparent two years after Aquino's assassination when Laurel and Cory Aquino came close to destroying the opposition because neither would concede to the other the right to head the ticket against Marcos.

As Marcos saw things, May 1983 was also time for him to change direction again. He didn't want Aquino back in the Philippines during the election campaign. He knew very well that Aquino would hurt him and his ruling New Society Movement, whether Aquino was actively stumping for the opposition or if he was back in Fort Bonifacio. Laurel he could handle; Aquino was another matter.

On May 21, Imelda Marcos, at her husband's behest, summoned Aquino to the penthouse of the Philippine Center on Fifth Avenue in Manhattan. They spoke for three and a half hours. Afterward, when she was testifying about the assassination, Mrs. Marcos claimed that Aquino told her he wanted to return home because "he was sick, his days were numbered, one of his heart bypasses was clogging up." Mrs. Marcos said she "pleaded with him" to postpone his trip; that his heart condition would only be worsened by Manila's oppressive heat and humidity and that not even air-conditioning could be counted on since the city's power supply was often hit with brownouts, the result of old equipment and costly fuel.

When Aquino did not seem persuaded, she told him, "as instructed by President Marcos, that there were threats against his life and it would be prudent to postpone his return to the country until 'the area is sanitized.' " She testified that before meeting with Aquino she had called the president in Manila and, as she put it, "maybe the president is sort of a clairvoyant, but definitely, he said, if he can please postpone his visit, if he has plans of going back to the Philippines, because of these threats . . . to give them time to really clear and make the place safe for him to come home."

When Aquino mentioned that his fellowships were about to expire, Mrs. Marcos said she told him that he needn't have any financial worries, that "whatever he needed in terms of support and help, I was ready . . . to help him in all different ways that he would like to be supported and helped. He was a friend. For humanitarian reasons also, I would do everything, whether for a friend or a foe, I will do it. But I never considered him a foe."

The First Lady was prepared, it seemed, to do quite a bit for her friend. In a letter to his mother, Aquino wrote that Mrs. Marcos had offered him a loan of $10 million so that he could stay in the United States and go into business.

But despite—or possibly because of—the proffered generosity of his "friend," Aquino became more determined to go back to Manila. For the next couple of months, he and his attorney in New York, Ernesto Maceda, a self-exiled Filipino, stepped up efforts to obtain a new passport. In response, Marcos instructed all consulates not to issue one. In mid July, Aquino set a deadline for his return—August 1— and informed the government of his plans. Marcos intervened directly, sending a strange telex from Malacañang Palace to Aquino, informing him: "Intelligence reports confirm that there are certain groups that plan to assassinate you when you come to the Philippines. Since the government will be blamed for anything that happens to you in the Philippines, it prefers to assume a prudent approach by requesting you to stay in the United States in the meantime . . . until such time that it can identify and neutralize these groups who are engaged in revenging the killing of their relatives by you and your men."

Aquino predictably ignored the warning and immediately replied that he still planned to return around the first of August. The world slowly began to tune in and watch and wait for this new drama to play itself out.

The president turned the heat up a notch, instructing Philippine Airlines offices not to issue tickets to Aquino or to allow him to board any flight without a passport signed by the consul general. Marcos then ordered the consulate in New York to remind Aquino that the Manila military court had found him guilty of half a dozen "executions" and "liquidations" and added, "these are only some of the cases that need to be mentioned to remind Mr. Aquino that his enemies are numerous and determined and that it is to his advantage that we take necessary precautions."

A letter from Maceda to the consulate, written on July 21, neatly summed up Aquino's reaction to Marcos's argument: "While we appreciate Malacañang's concern for the personal safety of our client, I would like to inform you that no amount of threats can dissuade him from returning home."

For the next week or so, some light sparring ensued, with Aquino unable to get a passport and the government scrambling to close off various avenues of return, including other airlines.

Then, on August 2, Defense Minister Juan Ponce Enrile sent an impassioned message to Aquino, advising him "that we are convinced beyond reasonable doubt that there are plots against your life upon your arrival in the Philippines. It is not merely to comply with our public duty to protect you but also to satisfy our conscience. We request you therefore to suspend your return to the Philippines for at least one month. After a long and intensive study of your case, your avowed intention to answer the call for national unity and reconciliation will not be advanced by any attempt against your life which would exacerbate the present situation."

This was the only government plea to make any impact on Aquino. He compromised. He agreed to postpone his trip for two weeks and told the consulate in New York that he was going to leave Boston on August 12 and would arrive in Manila on the twenty-first. He refused to say where he'd be in between.

Why Aquino paid heed to Enrile is curious. The defense chief certainly was no friend. He'd been in Marcos's cabinet from the start and, probably more than any other minister, had grown hugely rich as a result. He had a well-deserved reputation for cunning and had knowingly participated in a faked assassination attempt on himself in order to help Marcos justify imposing martial law. Indeed, he'd once told Laurel that he and Marcos had drafted the martial law declaration themselves, in secrecy, and only they had known about it in advance. Aside from Marcos, it was Enrile who was most directly responsible for holding Aquino in Fort Bonifacio for nearly eight years.

After the assassination, Enrile's own ambitions would emerge; he would quietly court foreign journalists, telling them that he had tried to resign from the cabinet the preceding April, of his growing disdain for Marcos, and suggesting strongly that he had plans to run for the presidency. He had tried to attend Aquino's funeral, but Cory had angrily rejected him. Although there would be other surprising, emotional signs of a stricken conscience, there was nothing to prepare the public for Enrile's military break with Marcos that would sweep Cory Aquino into office in February 1986. But in the first week of August 1983, Enrile, as far as the world knew, was still very much Marcos's man.

Even though he was unable to get a new Philippine passport, Aquino began his journey home, carrying two forgeries. One was an outright fake he'd bought during a trip to the Middle East. He had it made out in the name of Marcial Bonifacio, the first name for martial law and the second for the place where he'd been imprisoned. The other was a blank that an acquaintance in the government had gotten for him and that he'd filled in with his real name.

Armed with these documents, he flew aboard China Airlines on August 14 to the tiny island republic of Singapore, whose tough, brilliant prime minister, Lee Kuan Yew, was a critic of Marcos. He was met there by the son of the sultan of Johore, the southernmost state of neighboring Muslim Malaysia, who took him across the causeway to his home. Aquino and the young prince had become friends at Harvard. The sultan was to become king of Malaysia in another six months, and Aquino was calling on him as well as on leaders of Middle Eastern Islamic countries to help resolve the Philippines' bitter struggle over the movement for secession, or at least political autonomy, by the country's Muslim minority, most of whom lived on the southern island of Mindanao. Settling the Muslim problem, which had taken

some sixty thousand lives over eleven years of fighting between guerrillas and the armed forces, would have enhanced Aquino's standing
in the Philippines, to the consternation of Marcos and his supporters.
Furthermore, relations between Malaysia and the Philippines had long
been touchy, largely as the result of a territorial dispute over Malaysia's
northern Borneo state of Sabah. Thus, Aquino's dalliance with the
members of the wealthy Johore royal family was viewed from Malacañang Palace not just with disfavor but with a measure of alarm, a
sign that the neighboring country was backing Marcos's enemy in his
effort to dislodge the president.

While in Malaysia, Aquino met also with top government officials
from Indonesia and Thailand. These countries, along with the Philippines, Malaysia, and Singapore, are all part of the Association of
Southeast Asian Nations, a group of pro-Western governments in the
region. (Brunei joined in 1984.) ASEAN was formed during the Vietnam War, and it achieved unexpected unity after the fall of Indochina
in 1975. At that time, the Philippines was regarded as the most promising of pro-Western nations in the region.

Now, as Aquino discussed his plans, the prosperity of the Philippines had been surpassed by that of the other ASEAN countries.
Their economies were on the rise, the Philippines' was declining; their
citizens were enjoying better lives while Filipinos grew poorer. The
traditionally conservative regional leaders were fearful of the possible
effects that Aquino's return might have on the stability of the Philippines and on their own governments, their own delicately balanced
racial, ethnic, and religious compositions, their own long-smoldering
and potentially explosive Communist insurgencies. They heard him
out but made no commitments. Aquino went back to Singapore before
beginning an evasive game of hopscotch to Hong Kong and Taipei,
shuffling his two passports as he moved.

In Taipei, he checked into the aptly named Grand Hotel, a copy
of a classic Chinese palace, with gleaming tile roof and towering
crimson-lacquered pillars. The next day, August 20, the foreign journalists who were to accompany him on the flight into Manila arrived
at the Grand, and Aquino spent most of the day and night being
interviewed and chatting with the correspondents. Among them were
Ken Kashiwahara, who was married to Aquino's sister, Lupita, and
who worked for ABC-TV in San Francisco; Jim Laurie, ABC corre-

spondent in Tokyo; Max Vanzi of United Press International; Sandra Burton, *Time* magazine correspondent in Hong Kong; Katsuo Ueda of Japan's Kyodo news agency; Togo Tajika of Tokyo Broadcasting System; and Kiyoshi Wakamiya, a free-lance.

As a onetime reporter, whose brief but splashy career with the *Manila Times* included a stint as an eighteen-year-old war correspondent in Korea, Aquino valued and enjoyed the company of journalists and had long maintained good relations with them. Aquino was good copy, and he was the kind of figure reporters found irresistible, a smart, shoot-from-the-lip joker, laugher, drink buyer.

When he was imprisoned in Fort Bonifacio, Cory kept up his contacts with foreign correspondents, inviting them to dinners where they would be exposed to the views of opponents of the Marcos regime. This was a service newsmen appreciated at a time when Marcos thoroughly controlled the mass media, and in return the reporters kept Aquino's image alive.

Even while they were in his hotel room, the correspondents were playing a valuable role for Aquino. Vanzi showed him a story from the UPI wire reporting that General Ver was warning him not to return. Aquino scanned the dispatch. His mood, which had been excited and effervescent, suddenly turned serious, and his reaction was dramatic. "Oh, my God!" he said, and explained to the newsmen that Ver was "a dangerous man." Distressed to learn that Ver was taking a direct hand in trying to keep him out of the country, he referred to a story that had long circulated in Manila that illustrated Ver's blind loyalty to Marcos. If the president were to ask him to jump out of a window, the story went, Ver would snap to attention, salute, and ask, "From which floor, sir?"

Aquino had other very practical reasons for inviting these journalists to accompany him into Manila. With the media, particularly American TV cameras, focused on him, he reasoned that his safety, at least initially, would be assured. Even if he were arrested on his arrival, the newsmen would get the story out. And if the story of his arrival and arrest were reported around the world, Marcos would be forced to listen to him, if only for that one hour that he believed could alter the fate of the nation.

Kashiwahara wrote: "Ninoy finally went to his bedroom about 12:30 A.M., exhausted. He lay face down on his bed, hands outstretched, fingering his rosary beads and praying. He was subdued that last night. 'You know,' he said, 'I'm so tired. Maybe it's better if they take me straight to prison so I can rest for a while.' Ninoy slept only about four hours. Up by 5:00 A.M. Sunday, he said his rosary again and called his wife, Cory, in Boston for the last time. She read the Bible to him. He spoke briefly with his children and cried. He then sat down and wrote each of them a letter.''

The TV cameras recorded Aquino as he went through the boarding process for China Airlines Flight 811 at Taipei's Chiang Kai-shek International Airport. On the largely unoccupied Boeing 767, the newsmen asked Aquino to move to the rear so they could film another interview.

At this time, with an unconvincing laugh but uncanny prophecy, he told the correspondents, ''You have to be ready . . . because the action can become very fast. In a matter of three or four minutes it could be all over, you know. I have my bulletproof vest, but if they hit me on the head, there's nothing we can do there.''

Later, just before the plane began its descent into Manila International Airport, Aquino turned to Kashiwahara and said, ''I think it's a victory if we just land. Everything else is a bonus.''

The ''bonus'' amounted to about twelve minutes. The plane landed at 1:03 P.M. and parked at Bay Number Eight of the sleekly curved, concrete-and-tinted-glass terminal building. The spacious, modern airport was a typical Marcos project, an unnecessarily luxurious facility for a poor, underdeveloped country, used by a scant fraction of the population. It was built primarily to benefit Marcos and his cronies through kickbacks and overbillings, and secondarily to enable Imelda Marcos to show the world that she was her people's benefactress. Metropolitan Manila is dotted with such grandiose buildings—a conference center, hotels, theaters, hospitals—built at enormous expense, mostly under her direction. In time, these structures led to bitter jokes about ''Imelda's edifice complex.'' One joke, somewhat more biting than the rest, was told by Ninoy Aquino in the National Assembly when he was attacking Mrs. Marcos during a session in 1970. In a teasing play on words, something that Filipinos tend to be very good at, he called the extravagant and pretentious Cultural Center on Roxas Boulevard ''Imelda's Panty-on.'' According to an assemblyman who was present, the irreverent aside ''made the First Lady cry.''

After the plane had parked, the captain was instructed by the ground controller to keep the passengers seated "until the boarding party is on board." As they waited, impatiently, a flexible "jetway," or tube, was rolled into place against the passenger door of the plane. The door was opened, and three uniformed soldiers entered the aircraft. The three, identified by name tags on their chests, were Sergeant Arnulfo de Mesa, Sergeant Claro Lat, and Constable First Class Mario Lazaga. Their presence was ominous. In the stratified society of the Philippines, people like Aquino, who come from wealth and power, are treated with deference, even by their enemies. Thus, when he was in Fort Bonifacio, after being "sweated," he was allowed to receive home-cooked meals and permitted an occasional "furlough" as well as conjugal visits in prison. (Though Cory was always uncomfortable, knowing the room was bugged, Ninoy laughingly used to toss a blanket over the spying TV camera.) A man of his status should have been welcomed by senior officers, not by enlisted men.

One young officer, Lieutenant Jesus Castro, stood quietly at the end of the passenger compartment and watched as Lazaga walked past the seated Aquino, not recognizing him. The second soldier, de Mesa, spotted Aquino and approached him, as did Lat, who shook his hand and, in Tagalog, the dominant language of the central Philippines, opened the following stilted exchange: "Boss, you are being invited here . . . Armed Forces." Aquino asked, "Where are we going?" "Here, please come with me." Aquino then asked, "May I take this with me, *Brod?*"

As Aquino bent forward to pick up one of his carry-on bags, de Mesa stooped to pick up a second bag and, as he did, ran his free hand down Aquino's bent back.

He could feel the bulletproof vest.

Aquino stood. Lat took his bag from him. The three soldiers turned him toward the door, and a TV camera caught the fleeting shadows of emotion on his face.

He knew.

Instead of taking him through the exit tube and into the airport concourse, the way passengers usually leave an airplane, they suddenly turned him to the left, toward a narrow door in the tube and a narrow steel stairway used by maintenance crew members. At the doorway, they were joined by three more soldiers, Sergeant Filomeno Miranda,

Sergeant Armando de la Cruz, and Constable First Class Rogelio Moreno. These three all wore civilian clothing.

They passed through the door, into the brilliant sunlight and sweltering heat, with Aquino sandwiched tightly between Lat and de Mesa, Moreno and Miranda immediately behind them, Lazaga and de la Cruz taking up the rear.

As they started down the steep, narrow, metal stairway, men's voices came tumbling one over another in jittery confusion, shouting in Tagalog: "Here he comes, I'll do it, I'll do it, I'll do it, here it is [or "Here he is"], let me, ooph, shoot!" (The last word, for "shoot," was shouted not in Tagalog, but in Cebuano, a dialect from the central islands of the Visayans. The word was *pusila*.)

Cameramen and reporters struggled with uniformed soldiers and security men in civilian dress at the door, trying to force their way past, to follow Aquino down the stairs. But they couldn't get through the human wall. A few managed to shove cameras over the heads of the soldiers, shooting film blindly and, for the most part, recording nothing but blue sky. Someone shot a still photo through the legs of the cameramen and soldiers. He got the backs of the soldiers following Aquino down the stairs.

From the last glimpse anyone inside the plane had of Aquino at the top of the stairway until the single shot cracked at about 1:15 P.M., eleven seconds had elapsed. Later, this was precisely determined by timing audio- and videotapes. That it was eleven seconds and not more was to become a crucial issue. It would establish beyond a reasonable doubt that Aquino had not yet reached the tarmac when the bullet was fired into his head. This would mean that he could not have been shot by anyone other than one of the soldiers escorting him down the stairs—a man walking behind him who easily could take careful aim at the base of his skull.

Inside the plane, confusion and bedlam erupted. Screams. "What happened? What happened? Oh, no! He's . . . Oh, no!" Roughly scrambling for places at the little portholes, reporters and photographers sought any way they could to get a glimpse of what was happening outside. A mother's instinctive cry: "Watch out for the children!"

Outside, within seconds, five shots, these louder than the first, barked in quick succession. One or more of these killed a man dressed in blue, whom authorities would later identify as Rolando Galman.

Then a pause of seventeen seconds. Then another salvo of perhaps twenty shots. These were fired into the already inert body of Galman. The next night Marcos would say this man was Aquino's assassin and suggest that he was a Communist agent.

Action spun out swiftly. Two blue-uniformed security men, those who'd fired at Galman, snatched Aquino's body from the tarmac and heaved it into a blue van. The door to the jetway was slammed shut on the cameramen as a man's voice was heard, in Tagalog, shouting, "*Tama na, tama na,*" meaning "that's enough, that's enough." Ironically, when Cory Aquino was running for president against Marcos more than two years later, she used these same words again and again to tell voters that the time had come to get rid of him—"*tama na.*" Seen on videotape at normal speed, the entire tableau of horror lasted just over eighty seconds. Members of an investigative panel, who were to spend a year minutely picking apart and reconstructing what took place that afternoon on the tarmac, had to run the tape over and over again, at super-slow speed, to make any sense at all of the events.

2

*N*OT ALONE

If there was any sense to be drawn from what had just taken place it was this: A man who, had he been allowed to live, might have been a political threat was transformed instantly into a martyr and a national hero. A long yellow-and-black banner hanging from an office building on the day of his funeral stated succinctly what his assassination had accomplished overnight: NINOY AQUINO—ONCE A NAME, NOW A LEGEND. His name, "Ninoy! Ninoy! Ninoy!" would be taken up by hundreds of thousands and shouted from one end of the archipelago to the other. His death unleashed the pent-up anger of millions of Filipinos who for two decades had been made to suffer in a hundred different ways. It allowed Filipinos to focus upon someone who came from wealth and power but with whom they could identify. At his funeral Mass, his mother, *Doña* Aurora, said prophetically, "Ninoy accomplished more in death than he would have in life."

Aquino's family rallied quickly after the murder. Cory, in Boston, gave an interview to the Japanese news agency Kyodo just minutes after the news cleared the wire-service printer. Two years later, people would recall her calm and see in it a hint of the strength she would use in her challenge of Marcos. The blood-encrusted, battered body was claimed by relatives from the military hospital at Fort Bonifacio and taken to his home in Quezon City, technically the capital of the Philippines because it is where the National Assembly building is located, although it is, in fact, a suburb of Manila. The single-story bungalow at 25 Times Street had been vacant while Cory and Ninoy were living in Newton. They had built it after they were married in 1954, and it was, by the standards of wealthy Filipinos, modest. Because Ninoy was then working for the *Manila Times,* and some other staff members built neighboring houses, the street was named for the newspaper.

The body was put on display in the living room, and the huge crowds coming to pay their respect stood in a line that snaked out the door and down Times Street. When Cory and her children arrived from Boston on August 24, they were stunned by the turnout. "I could not believe my eyes," Cory recalled. "I was overwhelmed by this extraordinary display of love and devotion." Aurora Aquino told of waking at about two o'clock one morning and going out into the room where the body was. She was startled to see a few men, wearing T-shirts and shabby trousers, standing over the coffin. They told her they were taxi drivers and this was the only time they could take off from work.

Touching though such incidents were, the family was coldly calculating about how best to use the body for political advantage. It was embalmed and placed in a coffin with a glass top, but Aurora insisted that it not be touched up by a mortician. She wanted the brutality of the assassination to shock everyone who saw the body—the rough hole in the chin where a bullet fragment had exited, the heavy bruises on the eyelids and forehead caused when the body fell, the white bush jacket stiff with dried blood. Even on his burial day, when she finally permitted the body to be dressed in a fresh safari suit and thick pancake makeup applied to the face, she insisted that the wound and the bruises be recreated.

No one who saw Aurora Aquino or spoke to her in those days could help but be struck by how tough she was. She was seventy-three years old and had had seven children; Ninoy was the second. Petite, her gray-streaked hair neatly arranged, her expression sanguine, her speech well-modulated, she wore stiff, black mourning dresses, their high collars fastened by an antique cameo brooch. She was accustomed to being treated with deference; the outmoded Spanish honorific, *Doña,* appended to her name showed that. Laurel recalled that she had told him as he and two soldiers were carrying the corpse from the military hospital on a stretcher, "Don't let them touch him, clean his face, or

change his clothes. I want people to see what they did to my son.''
She had cried softly when Laurel lifted a sheet from his face. ''But
there was no hysteria,'' he said. ''She was always calm, controlled,
dignified.''

The body was displayed and paraded around for ten days. During
that time, it was taken to Tarlac, the family's home province seventy-
five miles from Manila, and the neighboring province of Pampanga.
Massive crowds walked alongside the hearse, decorated with Aquino's
portrait on the windshield and his nickname on a banner across the
hood. They were orderly, shouting only ''Ninoy! Ninoy! Ninoy!'' and
breaking into a refrain that was to be heard constantly in street demonstrations for more than a year—''you are not alone.'' After a weekend in the provinces, the corpse was returned to the house on Times
Street and then taken to Santo Domingo Church, a huge cruciform
structure in Quezon City. In one of the countless, tiny ironies that
would mark events, directly opposite the main entrance of the church
on Quezon Boulevard was a small, working-class restaurant with a
sign above the door advertising it as Imelda's Place.

By now, after a week in ninety-degree weather, the corpse had
decomposed badly. The face had turned green and black and was
grossly swollen. Several women fainted when, after waiting for hours
in line, they reached the casket and saw the figure inside. It was
shocking and very effective. In keeping with the professional management of the wake, Lupita Kashiwahara, Aquino's sister, flew in
from San Francisco to handle the press, which she did with detachment
and aplomb.

''We have come here because Ninoy is a symbol of our lost freedom,'' said a gray-haired man in Santo Domingo's packed churchyard
as he and his wife shuffled in a serpentine line toward the interior of
the dimly lit rotunda. They had been waiting nearly two hours and
had at least another hour to go. ''He was our last hope to unite our
people for change. If this man was ready to give up his life, then we
must show our respect by coming here to honor him.'' When asked
for his name, the man, wearing a gray-striped shirt and necktie despite
the sweltering humidity, shook his head sadly and replied, ''That's
the whole point. There is an atmosphere of fear in this country. If this,
this outright murder, can happen to a man of the national and international status of Ninoy Aquino, then what can happen to ordinary

people like me, like the rest of us? So, you will find that our people are afraid to even give you their own identity.'' A crowd had gathered around us as he spoke, and when the man finished his impassioned commentary, they burst into applause.

Assessing the mood in the streets from inside Malacañang Palace, the Marcoses were keenly aware of the impact being made by the long, public wake. But there wasn't much they could do to offset it. The president was very sick, that much had been obvious during his brief appearance on television to blame the assassination on the Communists, and he was unable to appear in public. Indeed, he hadn't been seen in person or on the air for a month or so before Aquino returned.

Finally, on the night of August 29, Imelda Marcos appeared unannounced at the beautiful, government-owned Manila Hotel. This was the impromptu headquarters of the foreign press corps, and she knew that a stroll through the lobby would give her TV exposure in the United States and elsewhere. It was a way of showing the flag, to tell the world without much effort that all was well with the First Family. The signal that the First Lady was coming, as always, caused frantic scurrying among the white-uniformed bellboys in the ornate, neocolonial lobby. They unrolled huge reels of red carpet, stretching from the heavy mahogany-and-brass doors across the beige marble floor for perhaps fifty yards to the white-wicker-furnished coffee shop. Ever since she had directed the restoration in 1976 of the Manila Hotel, which had been General Douglas MacArthur's headquarters during the early days of the war in the Pacific, an elevated table in the coffee shop was always kept free for Mrs. Marcos. A waitress said that, even if the place was full, ''we are under orders never to allow anyone other than the First Lady or a designated member of her staff to occupy that table.''

She arrived beneath the glass canopy in a motorcade comprising a dozen limousines and a large blue-and-white bus bearing license number 777-777. Seven, in any combination, had long been Marcos's lucky number—for example, he won the nomination to run for president with 777 votes. Numerology is a popular form of superstition in the Philippines, as well as in other Asian countries, and the fact that Aquino had returned on the twenty-first, a number divisible by seven, was marked as significant.

Surrounded by muscular young men in civilian shirts and trousers, with revolvers bulging in their waistbands, Mrs. Marcos, in an unadorned black dress, swept regally into the hotel, as its manager and staff members bowed and applauded and TV cameramen switched on their lights. Correspondents struggled with her armed guards to shout questions to her about her views on the assassination. She ignored them, smiling wanly. Later, while she and a dozen members of her personal staff snacked, a stern-faced, gray-haired press relations official came out and told the correspondents, "It would be inappropriate for the First Lady to comment at this time." When asked why, she replied blandly, "We are in mourning."

Filipinos said good-bye to Ninoy Aquino ten days after he returned home. No one in Manila could recall anything like his funeral procession. How many people came out into the gritty, broken streets to say farewell, to wave, to weep, to sing, to stare, even to laugh as Filipinos have always managed to laugh at times of the worst hardship, no one really knows. The local papers, depending on their loyalties, reported the number of mourners as between hundreds of thousands and millions. The numbers were important to Aquino's family and his political supporters because they gave them a basis for saying that it was the largest crowd ever to pour into the streets of Manila, more people than had ever turned out for Marcos. But there was really no way to know the number that day.

More than three thousand people packed Santo Domingo to hear Cardinal Sin eulogize Aquino as a man who "personified Filipino courage in the face of oppression." The sanctuary was stifling; sweating men and women waved floral paper fans in front of their flushed faces. The heavy air, further heated by the lights from seventeen TV crews, was redolent with incense and candle wax. The glass-covered coffin was placed at the foot of the white marble altar and covered with the Philippine tricolor. Two blue-uniformed security guards from a private firm flanked the coffin, standing self-consciously stiff at parade rest. Guards like these, armed with shotguns and pistols, can be found at the entrances to offices, restaurants, hotels, and shops all over Manila, and their presence at the funeral Mass served as another reminder, as if one were needed, of the violence that has long scarred life in the islands.

But, conversely, there were touches of tenderness and humanity. During the previous night, people had left little farewell gifts along the altar's edge—a stick of Juicy Fruit gum, a pen-and-ink drawing of Aquino, three pesos and seventy-five centavos in coins, a string of rosary beads.

Among those crowded into the front pews were diplomats from a dozen countries, including U.S. Ambassador Michael H. Armacost. The ambassadors from the ASEAN countries did not show up, a clear sign that their governments would not take a public slap at Marcos. Their absence was a disappointment to the Aquino people. But the U.S. ambassador was another matter altogether. The American envoy, successor to a string of governors-general, has always held a special place in the Philippines, courted and consulted by those in office as well as those who would like to be. Communists and others who opposed the relationship consistently stated that the Philippines was under the thumb of a "Marcos-U.S. dictatorship." By showing up at the funeral Mass, Armacost was telling Marcos and the people of the Philippines that the United States deplored the assassination.

By dawn, the entire square block ringing the church was packed. The funeral route wound eighteen miles from Santo Domingo past the Manila Hotel and the U.S. embassy along Manila Bay, in a vast horseshoe to Manila Memorial Park cemetery. The procession crept forward so slowly it could barely be seen to move. People walked or rode on trucks, bicycles, motorcycles, in air-conditioned Mercedes-Benzes, and jeepneys—outrageous adaptations of the U.S. Army jeep with which Filipinos fell in love during World War II.

Thousands more stood at their doors or windows, on balconies, and on rooftops. Work in offices, shops, even hospitals, came to a standstill as personnel paused to participate in the extraordinary event. From the windows of the Court of Tax Appeals and the Philippine Institute of Volcanology on Quezon Boulevard, hundreds of government workers stood at their windows and chanted, "Ni-noy! Ni-noy!" Many were nervous, fearing that there would be trouble. Given the deep passions that the murder had stirred, the funeral procession could easily have degenerated into chaos. But city authorities had had the good sense to order all but a handful of police away from the route. Those who did appear carried no weapons. Because the abusive (albeit underpaid) policemen, in the same tight-fitting military-style uniforms that are favored in many Spanish-influenced, underdeveloped countries, were living symbols of the Marcos regime, their absence eliminated a potentially major provocation. When an NBC-TV helicopter fluttered noisily over the procession, people shook their fists and booed, believing it was the police. Eventually, Filipinos would become accustomed to the extravagances to which American news media would go to follow a story.

More importantly, though, there was an unspoken but instinctively acknowledged agreement among everyone in the streets to keep this procession peaceful. Cardinal Sin set the tone during the Mass when, despite his attack on the regime for creating "the atmosphere of oppression and corruption, the climate of fear and anguish [which] have resulted in a truly tragic condition," he appealed for peace. "Can man liberate man without recourse to violence? Our answer to that is an unequivocal yes."

The pageantry and symbolism of the Mass—Cardinal Sin in rich purple-and-gold vestments backed by a score of priests in simple white cassocks, the chanting, the sprinkling of holy water, the ringing of bells and swinging of incense braziers—were relieved when the Aquinos' youngest child, twelve-year-old Kristina, rose. A tiny, bespectacled replica of her father, she spoke with a faintly American accent about the happy days in Newton, helping her father shovel snow and rake leaves. Then she recalled giving a speech when she was seven years old and her father was still imprisoned. "I told my mom that I took after him the most because I loved being surrounded by crowds," the child said, and the church erupted into applause.

All five Aquino children spoke, but when Cory was introduced as "the better half of Ninoy Aquino," the applause was thunderous, and everyone stood to honor the slight woman whose pale face looked even more ashen against her black dress. Her performance was a precursor of what would happen time and again when, more than two years later, she would campaign for the presidency. Speaking in a flat, nasal, girlish voice, she recited an account of her final conversations with Ninoy, of the shock and grief she and the children felt when they heard by telephone from a Japanese diplomat that her husband had been assassinated, of her surprise and gratitude at the massive outpouring of sympathy. Her speech was altogether unremarkable. What was inspiring was her composure, her serenity. These she would carry with her, and audiences would never fail to be impressed.

Cardinal Sin closed the Mass by sending Ninoy Aquino on his way with the simplest of farewells, "Good-bye, my friend." Then the bells began tolling.

In place of a hearse, which would have been lost in the river of people undulating through the mean streets of a city Imelda Marcos in her bizarre grandiloquence had called the City of Man, the Aquinos had mounted the coffin atop a huge, ten-wheel trailer truck. Draped in black and banked high with yellow chrysanthemums, the truck could be seen from blocks away. The yellow of the floral embankment was reflected throughout the procession: yellow T-shirts, headbands, placards, dresses, umbrellas, hats.

Yellow had quickly been adopted by the Aquino people as their predominant symbol; and in time, Cory Aquino's followers would be referred to by political analysts as "Yellows," as Communists are termed "Reds." As is so often the case among Filipinos, with their penchant for "Stateside" ways, they had picked up the idea from the song "Tie a Yellow Ribbon 'Round the Old Oak Tree" and the ribbons that Americans had hung out to symbolize their hope for the return of U.S. embassy personnel from Iran. Ribbons alone, though, were too sedate for the effusive, entrepreneurial Filipinos. Thousands of T-shirts had been produced, blazing yellow with dozens of images and messages printed on their fronts and backs—black outlines of Aquino's inert form sprawled in a pool of blood, portraits of his smiling, round face with distinctively heavy eyeglass frames, slogans like NINOY IS MY HERO; WE LOVE YOU NINOY; NINOY YOU ARE NOT ALONE; NINOY IS FREE, FREEDOM IS DEAD.

It seemed as though the hundreds of thousands, or millions, accompanying the coffin were transformed into a sea of yellow as they extended their thumbs and forefingers to form the letter L for *laban*, which in Tagalog means "fight." Not coincidentally, *Laban* was also the abbreviation for a movement known as *Lakas ng Bayan*, or "Strength of the Nation," which was started in 1978 to help Aquino campaign from prison against Imelda Marcos for the National Assembly. Vast numbers were singing what was to become the anthem of the Aquino movement, a plaintive melody entitled "Ang Bayan Ko," or "My Country," which tells of a caged bird yearning to fly again.

A few handfuls of "Reds" stood out in the funeral procession. Aside from their obvious red-and-gold banners bearing characteristically wooden slogans like NO RECONCILIATION UNDER THE FASCIST

DICTATORIAL REGIME, they were distinguished by their orderliness and strict discipline. In the period between the Aquino assassination and the collapse of the Marcos regime, it would become evident that the outlawed Communist Party of the Philippines and its armed wing, the New People's Army, were the best-organized political institutions in the country. The Communists were quick to align themselves with pro-Aquino sentiments but were careful to contain their public expressions within well-defined parameters. Had they made themselves appear to be too close, they could have frightened off moderate Filipinos and given Marcos ammunition to tar the dead man, and later his widow, with the same brush as he used on the Communists. In a lengthy statement issued a few days after the assassination, the CPP said in part, "The former senator and we had our differences over how to bring about the downfall of the Marcos fascist regime; we acknowledge that. But our objectives—to end the hated regime—ran parallel to each other. In many ways, his efforts and ours complemented one another as we fought a common enemy of the Filipino people."

The funeral procession was the first of scores of political demonstrations, some calm, some violent, that would take place until Marcos fled the country. At this earliest stage, the participants were almost all the city's dirt poor, its lower-middle-class working people, and college students. The wealthier, though many attended the Mass and some drove independently to the cemetery, didn't take an active role in the procession. To do so wouldn't have occurred to them, nor to those who did participate. Better-off Filipinos just didn't do that sort of thing. The rich kept their noses clean and continued to prosper while confining their complaints about the regime to their own select circles within the walled and guarded splendor of their residential compounds in Forbes Park and their antique- and art-filled executive suites in the financial district of Makati.

Among the few from the privileged class who did take part was Diosdado Macapagal, a former president of the Philippines, who was defeated by Marcos in 1965. He was seventy-two, and he rode in the back seat of an air-conditioned sedan. Ignored for years by the controlled press, he welcomed the opportunity to answer reporters' questions and eagerly rolled down his window to chat. "This huge turnout tells us that the political situation is extremely volatile and unpredictable," he said. "I support the opposition call for Marcos to resign.

But, of course, I don't expect him to." Macapagal added that he had advised Aquino not to come home "because I wanted to preserve him as the rallying point of the opposition."

Typical of the people who wanted to identify with Aquino was a stick-thin cigarette vendor named Ernesto Arinzol, who said of the dead man: "He was a very important person. He is still a very important person, I think. I was his follower even before he was killed. I love him very much." Arinzol, twenty, wore faded green shorts and thin rubber sandals. His sleeveless undershirt was rolled above his concave belly to catch whatever slight breeze might blow. A shiny yellow ribbon tied around his forehead did double duty as a sign of his affiliation and as a way of keeping his long, dusty hair out of his eyes. From a compartmentalized wooden box slung by a strap from his neck, he sold cigarettes to people as poor as himself, one at a time, courteously providing a light to his customers. "I'm here to join in the burial first, and to sell cigarettes second," he said. He lived near Santo Domingo Church, and he walked the entire eighteen miles that day. It took him eleven hours.

Arinzol had little to lose. But others were at risk. Manuel Loretto, for example, was taking a chance, and he knew it. A twenty-seven-year-old government clerk, he declined to identify his agency, fearing publicity could cost him his job, but otherwise he spoke his mind freely and with the acuity of a first-rate political analyst. "There are a lot of us, government workers, who've taken off from work to be here. We're all fed-up and disgusted. This is supposed to be a democratic country with American ideals, but it's not. It's a dictatorship. I'm worried, but at the same time I'm happy because I'm sure today is the beginning of a national awakening to the abuses of our president."

Whether speaking English, Tagalog, or another of the many regional languages, Filipinos tend to be dramatic and fiery. What they have long lacked is the ability to translate words into action and to then sustain that action. A leftist student orator might harangue a crowd of several thousand at one of the capital's open squares and then lead a march to the perimeter of Malacañang Palace, where they would chant unsurprising demands, mostly, "down with Marcos." Afterward, they'd return to their homes, and, if they were feeling particularly indignant, they'd burn old tires in the middle of the road or lead their neighbors in a "noise barrage," a mass banging of pots and pans and

tide. From somewhere, people produced candles, thousands of them, and the surging march became a glittering, endless string of jewels. By now, the marchers were on the four-lane "super highway" leading out of Manila to the cemetery. Cars, buses, and trucks headed in the opposite direction pulled over to the side, and their passengers stood and cheered or joined in the walk themselves. Scores of bonfires were set along the highway's grassy median, throwing long, dancing shadows out into the night. At 9:00 P.M., eleven hours after setting out from the church, the cortege and the black trailer truck bearing the body reached the cemetery.

The burial was anticlimactic. Spotlights played down on a small, simple granite vault. Addressing the giant crowd, Cory Aquino thanked them for coming and appealed to them to "show discipline." A lone trumpeter played the first bar of taps. A priest offered a final prayer. The coffin was slipped into the vault, and the vault was closed. The ceremony took fewer than ten minutes. When it ended, there was silence.

For the hundreds of thousands who had been through the exhausting day and night, there was a sense of exhilaration as well as of sadness. Jesus Gueco, a youthful-looking man of thirty-one with neatly combed hair and a clean white shirt, had driven to Santo Domingo the night before from Concepcion, Aquino's hometown in Tarlac province, to take part in the procession to the cemetery. "I know that thousands of us from Tarlac made the trip yesterday and today," he said. "I think what has happened to Ninoy will finally unite us, all Filipinos, in a common cause. Things won't be like they were before, where people don't mind what's done to them. This is like awakening from a deep sleep."

Hopes that there would be no violence were shattered within hours after the funeral. Hundreds of young people, many of them college students, assembled at the foot of Mendiola Bridge, a short span separating Malacañang Palace and an area of several shabby blocks known as the "university belt," home to several in-town colleges and student dormitories. When the crowd reached Mendiola, they found the approach to the presidential palace blocked by some three hundred uniformed police, armed with wooden truncheons. Not obvious at first were scores of plainclothes officers carrying handguns.

The police allowed the demonstrators to occupy the intersection at the foot of the bridge, absorbing their taunts about Marcos's responsibility for Aquino's assassination. Then, someone in the crowd threw a rock or a piece of broken brick. On command, police rushed the demonstrators, swinging truncheons at their heads. Firing their guns, the plainclothesmen chased after youths who broke from the crowd and ran into the deserted streets, firing their own guns in return. The fighting broke into small, running battles, which continued well into the predawn hours. When it was over, eighteen people were hospitalized with gunshot wounds. One, a twenty-three-year-old student identified by police as Karim Dimacuta, died. Deputy Police Chief Colonel Felicisimo Lazaro said three of the wounded were policemen. He denied that the police had firearms and maintained that they'd been ordered to use "gentleness" on the demonstrators. Other police officers claimed that demonstrators had fired from sniper positions in tall buildings.

Such charges and countercharges by both antigovernment organizations and authorities would become commonplace as demonstrations calling on Marcos to resign became an almost daily feature of Manila life. Newsmen out in the streets covering the events would witness cases of demonstrators deliberately provoking policemen, and of police using unnecessary violence, including firing their weapons at hecklers. On occasion, the newsmen themselves became targets of both sides. More often than not, the accounts issued afterward bore little resemblance to what had actually happened.

The first night's clashes were limited. Worse would come. But suddenly the world's attention swung away from the Philippines. On Wednesday, as Aquino's corpse was being wheeled through the streets of Manila, a Korean Airlines jumbo jet was shot down by a Soviet fighter plane south of Sakhalin Island, killing all 269 persons aboard. The shift in international attention gave the beleaguered Marcos a chance to regain some energy and marshal his defenses. The fact that the KAL flight was number 007 was not lost on many Filipinos. Marcos's luck seemed to be holding.

3

*T*HE YELLOWS

Luck, however, was eluding Marcos's opponents. Simply put, they couldn't get their act together. Only Aquino had possessed the magnetic personality needed to unite the anti-Marcos, anti-Communist moderates, and without him there was no leader. This fact was hardly surprising, considering that during his nearly two decades in power, and particularly during the nine years of martial law, the president had crippled whatever elements of the democratic process had evolved after World War II. Marcos's opponents squabbled and back-bit among themselves so thoroughly that they seemed more like enemies than allies. Indeed, even after Aquino's death, Salvador Laurel would fight his widow for leadership.

Ninoy Aquino and Doy Laurel became friends as children during the war. Both were the sons of men who had collaborated with the Japanese military regime—José P. Laurel as president of the Philippines and Benigno S. Aquino, Sr., as speaker of the National Assembly—and they turned to each other for mutual support after the war, when their fathers were held in Tokyo's Sugamo Prison by General MacArthur's occupation forces and their families were shunned. It is a measure of Filipinos' inability to hold a grudge for long that the sins of the fathers were not visited upon the sons, and both Ninoy and Doy built successful public careers. Laurel earned a doctor of laws degree from Yale, practiced as an attorney, and in 1968 was elected a senator by Marcos's Nacionalista Party. The year before, Aquino had been elected to the senate from the Liberal Party.

Interestingly, the elder Laurel played an important role in the life of Ferdinand Marcos, too. In September 1935, a local politician in Marcos's home province, Ilocos Norte, was shot to death. A few months earlier, the politician, Julio Nalundasan, had defeated Ferdinand's father, Mariano, in a congressional election. After every meal, Nalundasan had the habit of brushing his teeth at a basin in his dining room. He was shot through the heart while engaging in this act of dental hygiene, the bullet coming from a .22-caliber target pistol. Ferdinand Marcos, then eighteen years old, was captain of the rifle team at the University of the Philippines. Four years later, he was arrested, charged with the murder of his father's political foe, and found guilty.

The young man, who had already established a reputation for legal genius, appealed his conviction to the Supreme Court. He defended himself with brilliance before José Laurel, then a justice of the Supreme Court in charge of the hearing. Laurel was so impressed by the twenty-three-year-old Marcos that he reversed the decision of the lower court and threw the case out. The next day, the justice convened a special ceremony at the Supreme Court and presented Marcos with his certificate as a member of the Philippine bar.

In 1978, six years after imposing martial law, Marcos formed the *Kilusang ng Bagong Lipunan,* KBL for short, or "New Society Movement" in English. Marcos claimed that the KBL would be an "umbrella organization," not a political party itself. In fact, by absorbing the Nacionalista and Liberal parties, it became the ruling party, which Marcos built into the most formidable political organization in Philippine history, largely on the basis of "blood debts"—what Filipinos know as *utang na loob*—between himself and a vast pyramid of loyalists among local politicians. Salvador Laurel joined the new organization and, as one of its candidates, won a seat in the Marcos-controlled National Assembly. Although he quit the KBL two years later, Laurel's affiliation with Marcos reminded many Filipinos of his father's association with Marcos as well as with the Japanese.

By the time Aquino came home, Laurel had put together his own twelve-party umbrella organization and called it the United Nationalist Democratic Organization, or UNIDO, with himself as its president. Where Aquino would have fit into UNIDO is open to question. Laurel insisted that Aquino intended to reinvigorate the Liberal Party, but within UNIDO. "Ninoy came home for this," he said, "to strengthen his own party under the UNIDO umbrella." Others believed differently. José W. Diokno, a former senator and a brilliant left-leaning attorney, said that "the only way Ninoy would have remained in UNIDO would have been as its head. So, obviously he and Doy would have fought for leadership."

Although Laurel stressed their long friendship, rumors spread after the assassination that Laurel had pushed Aquino into making his fatal decision to return home, telling him that it was then or never if he was to recoup the vestiges of his political career. Laurel was keenly aware of the insinuations that his intentions may have been malicious. "Many of my friends have warned me that I'm the next target," he said at his suite of law offices in Makati five days after the assassination. "Rumors are spreading that I masterminded the killing and so I'll be killed by one of Ninoy's boys. But he and I were close, we grew up together, and we're the godfathers of each other's kids." Asked if he had indeed urged Aquino to return despite the threats, Laurel turned testy. "What's wrong with him coming home? Why shouldn't he be allowed to return home? Anyway, the decision was his. Even after I warned him, through his sisters, that there was the possibility he'd be killed, he still decided to come home. Besides that, I never suggested that he needed to return in order to regain his popularity. I reassured him during meetings in Boston and New York in June that he was still popular. He wasn't motivated to return by any fear that he was losing support." While Laurel generally succeeded in squelching the uglier gossip, a faint aura of distrust clung to him in the minds of many Aquino supporters.

The absence of an obvious leader plagued the ragtag forces ranged against Marcos and the KBL. Laurel, while coyly hinting that he would answer the call, acknowledged that at the moment no one was strong enough to fill the position that, presumably, Aquino would have taken. "You have to grow into leadership," he said. "I'm not going to ask for it, but I'm not going to turn back, either." Despite his flaws, Laurel had certain strengths—he had organized UNIDO well; he had a natural power base in his family's home province, Batangas, due south of Manila; his name was well known; the large Laurel family was wealthy; and he was extremely ambitious.

Other opposition figures were more seriously flawed.

José Diokno, whose cutting, analytical mind was his greatest asset, was attractive to liberals and civil libertarians. But, by his own admission, he was too opposed to the presence of the two U.S. military bases in the Philippines to be a successful candidate. U.S. support was a vital element in determining Philippine leadership, and Diokno was realist enough to concede it. Beyond that, Diokno, a lifelong chain smoker with a telltale gravelly voice, was to undergo surgery for lung cancer within a year.

Jovito Salonga, a former senator and longtime critic of Marcos, had suffered serious injuries during the bombing of an opposition demonstration in Manila's Plaza Miranda on August 21, 1971, and he was in self-exile in the United States.

Lorenzo Tañada, a Harvard-educated lawyer who had once defended Ninoy Aquino and was a leading liberal politician, remained one of the most fiery and outspoken opponents of the Marcos regime. But he was eighty-four years old.

The search for leadership and coordination dogged the splintered opposition. Agreeing on even the most fundamental course of action posed an insurmountable problem. Some groups led violent outbreaks, others condemned them. The confusion helped only Marcos. Although the assassination had galvanized his opponents, their habitual petty jealousies, personal ambitions, and penchant for legalistic precedent blocked the funnel that was needed to pour all their energies into the same bottle.

New, less formal groups were formed, each with the requisite snappy acronym. There were ATOM (August Twenty One Movement), ROAR (Running Organization for Aquino and Reconciliation—joggers with newfound political consciousness), and many, many more that came and went with dizzying haste. The ultimate, formed with at least a touch of tongue in cheek, when the public had been thoroughly confused by the alphabet soup, was called ACRONYM, for Anti Cronyism Movement.

Acronyms, along with nicknames, were an Americanism that the Filipinos picked up with a vengeance. Hardly a Filipino breathes who doesn't have a nickname: Ninoy and Cory; Ferdy and Meldy (the president was also known as Andy, and his wife occasionally referred to herself and expected others to refer to her as Ma'am); Doy, for Salvador Laurel; Pepe, for José Diokno; Johnny, for Juan Ponce Enrile.

Millions more carry monikers like Baby, Boy, Ting-Ting, Au-Au, Bong Bong, Ding Dong, and Ballsy.

The opposition organizations became known generically as "cause-oriented groups," and they faded in and out of the blurred political picture over the next two years. One of the more resilient and effective was also one of the first to be formed. Known as Justice for Aquino, Justice for All (or JAJA), the group included established opposition people like Diokno and Tañada but also took in younger people with no previous political reputation. Diokno insisted on this. "Lack of organization in the traditional opposition is the reason we're getting nowhere in stirring up significant reaction," he said. "Only new people with fresh ideas can change that. We old people should get out, become advisers, and turn over power to the young."

But the cause-oriented groups could find no one person who embodied the ideals they sought in a leader. They did not think of Cory Aquino.

Nevertheless, the groups made important contributions to the drive for change. Their demonstrations, marches, and pamphleteering kept the opposition alive during extended periods of lethargy. They drew younger, formerly uninterested businessmen and technocrats into the political mainstream. The young, in turn, recruited the vitally needed big-business leaders and top-rank academicians and clergy who had stayed out of the arena because they found all politicians distasteful, or association with them unprofitable. Once these men began participating in earnest, they started a process of reform in Philippine politics that may, eventually, prove truly revolutionary.

The younger people, the white-collar workers, the clerks and secretaries, took to the streets for the first time on September 14, three weeks after the assassination. They demonstrated in the way that middle-class people would, nicely dressed for work, the men in shirts and ties, the women in uniform skirts and blouses issued by their employers—mainly banks and insurance companies—carrying neatly lettered placards, hanging yellow banners from their office buildings, and tossing basketfuls of shredded Yellow Pages telephone directories out of their windows. They massed outside their offices, easily 100,000 strong, and marched through the streets, shouting. Their theme was simple: "Marcos resign!" The initial demonstration took place in Makati, technically an independent town which, in fact, is the financial district of Metro Manila, the populous national capital region run by Imelda Marcos, who carried the title of governor.

What made the demonstration particularly notable was that the wife of one of the pillars of Makati, Beatrice Zobel de Ayala, volunteered a piece of property owned by the family, Ugarte Field, for a rally at the end of the march. Because the field was private property, no permit was required, thus frustrating government attempts to interfere. The involvement of Zobel was a startling signal to the middle class, the upper-middle class, and the rich that it was possible to take a public stand against the government and remain apart from the Communists, the only element of Philippine society that, until then, had had the courage to make such a move.

Demonstrations didn't normally take place in Makati. The town's mayor, Nemesio Yabut, a tough, backroom brawler who had been a longshoreman and a policeman and was worshipfully loyal to Marcos, was shocked. A few days later he organized a demonstration of a couple of thousand high school students and local government workers who were bused in and paid a few pesos apiece. It was a mistake. Hardly had the group, led by the mayor himself, imposingly large for a Filipino at nearly six feet tall and around two hundred pounds, arrived when they came under attack, verbal and otherwise, from thousands of office workers hanging out of their windows and dropping plastic bags filled with rotten tomatoes, oranges, and eggplants. As his rented crowd dissolved, Yabut stood his ground, attempting vainly to deliver a pro-Marcos speech. Then someone threw a soft drink bottle, which clipped the mayor on his balding head, followed by a plastic bag containing urine. Wet and humiliated, Yabut, too, fled.

If a first-time visitor to the Philippines saw only Manila International Airport and Makati, he could be excused for thinking that the country was rich and modern. A new, well-planned town, Makati is home to just about every high-rise building not only in Metro Manila, but in the rest of the Philippines as well. The stock market is there, along with the head offices of most of the major corporations. The concrete-and-glass towers, while a little shoddy on close inspection, form mini Manhattan-style canyons along the two main boulevards, Paseo de Roxas and Ayala Avenue. Mingling with the office towers are five-star hotels and exclusive condominium apartment buildings. Appended to the central business area are exclusive residential colonies for the very rich. The people who built Makati, who owned its buildings and companies, its hotels and condominiums, who worked there by day and retired to their nearby mansions by night, got where they were by going along with Marcos and keeping their political complaints to themselves.

So, for their employees to be out in the streets, demanding that the president step down, accusing him and his regime of complicity in the Aquino assassination, was stunning. Moreover, the office personnel weren't there behind their bosses' backs. Not only did they have their employers' approval, some of the bosses were standing at their open office windows, hurling shredded Yellow Pages and joining in the shouting. But few were ready yet to come down from their towers and march alongside their workers.

Any such inclination was blunted a few days later, on Sunday, September 25, when Marcos appeared live at noon on nationwide television. He was livid, outraged by the indignity spilled on his mayor. But his deeper concern sprang from the significance of the middle class and wealthy of Makati involving themselves in political protest. Marcos went on the offensive, his first real steely-eyed, fist-clenching tirade since the assassination. He issued a frightening threat to all businessmen that they would be hunted down, taken to court, and force used if required. Further, he singled out organizations newly identified with the effort to remove him from office. These included the Ayala Foundation, set up by the multimillionaire family of the same name, which had been instrumental in building Makati; the Bank of the Philippine Islands, owned by the Ayala and Zobel families; Solid Bank, owned by the Olondriz and Madrigal families; Development Bank of the Philippines, a government-run institution; and Security Bank, run by Marcos's son, Ferdinand, Jr. The inclusion of Development Bank and Security Bank in the list was significant because, despite their government links, their employees were participating in the opposition demonstration.

"Some businessmen feel they can find sanctuary in the tall buildings of Makati," Marcos said. "Let me tell you we are now in the process of identifying those who attacked Mayor Yabut with a bottle . . . and urine. . . . I understand some executives in coat and tie were engaged in that demonstration. If they think they've gotten away with it, they have two other guesses. We have pictures and videotapes that clearly show their faces . . . whether they're members of Ayala Foundation or Security Bank. . . . We'll look for these men. . . . Men will be assigned to track you down. . . . We'll meet you in court. . . . You resist the force of the law, you will meet force, legally applied by the government. . . . I'm not threatening or intimidating. . . . Do not test the force and strength of the government.''

It was a virtuoso Marcos performance. Whether the authorities had pictures and tapes never became clear. No one was taken to court. The threat was expected to be sufficient, and in many cases it was. Businessmen who had been speaking openly reacted by taking their complaints underground. Certainly, the rules had changed. Even in the darkest days of martial law, men of Aquino's class and background rarely were killed. As in Aquino's own case, they might be sentenced to death, locked up, and the key thrown away. But not executed. No longer able to rely on that assurance, and now that the president had threatened to hunt down particular individuals, more than a few members of the upper classes allowed their passions to fade.

Others, though, insisted that Marcos was acting out of desperation and that his threats lacked muscle. "That speech lifted my spirits enormously because it made clear that Marcos is the one with the greatest problem—no credibility," claimed Jaime V. Ongpin, president of Benguet Corporation, a successful gold- and copper-mining firm. "He's lost his cool. He's gone completely off his rocker or else he doesn't realize the extent of his credibility problem. Every time he opens his mouth he makes it worse. When you examine his threats, what can he do? Unless he's got a photo of someone throwing a grenade, what can he get you for? I sat with four of my friends this morning, all of them senior executives, and they were rolling with laughter. It's a threat that he can't make good on. People aren't stupid enough to believe it. It's all bluster.''

Ongpin may have believed his own words or he may have just been trying to lift his morale. In either case, he was not yet marching in the streets or, for that matter, tossing shredded paper out his window. But, he said, his wife and two teenaged sons had taken part in the Makati demonstration and had met a lot of people they knew. The same thing was spontaneously happening in a number of middle-class and wealthy households around Manila. Women and children with time to spare decided that they ought to join in. Walking in a demonstration in Makati, where they shopped, went to the movies, and met friends for lunch or coffee, seemed secure enough. Eventually, the notion of putting women and children in the front ranks of protest marches took hold and became a regular tactic. Unlike police in the United States, who didn't differentiate between the sexes when they were breaking up antiwar protests during the Vietnam era, Filipino policemen were loathe to interfere with women. To do so would have subjected their macho self-esteem to derision. Finally, when enough women and children had marched for long enough, their executive husbands and fathers joined them.

However, like big businessmen anywhere, those in the Philippines were subject to pressures not just from the government but from their partners in other countries, their boards of directors, their shareholders, and, ultimately, the tyranny of the bottom line. For many of them, the decision to move into the streets would be made only when business had grown so bad that they realized Marcos no longer represented stability, but deterioration.

The rich and middle classes were inhibited, too, by the prospect of violence. The skirmish that had taken place outside Malacañang on August 31, the night of Aquino's funeral, had been relatively calm. Three weeks later, on Wednesday night, September 21, a full-scale riot erupted. It would be the first and the bloodiest of many, and it revealed that the moderates could exercise little control. Violence became a tool employed by those Doy Laurel termed "hotheads of every stripe" and was adopted by the government, the Communists, the poor who may have been apolitical but were simply bitter, and just plain thugs. And the bloodshed frightened the fledgling middle-class marchers back into their shells.

The occasion was the eleventh anniversary of the imposition of martial law, which the Marcos regime had ironically declared a national holiday—Thanksgiving Day. Anti-Marcos forces had gone into the streets to protest on other Thanksgiving Days, but this time, the absurdity of giving thanks to the regime was heightened by the coincidence that it was taking place exactly one month after Aquino had been assassinated.

The day began calmly; at noon Masses in churches throughout the city, priests sent their parishioners into the streets with prayers for "a successful but peaceful demonstration." The people made their way to Liwasang Bonifacio, a tree-framed square fronting the city's main post office, an imposing Greek Revival structure that frequently served as a backdrop for mass meetings.

A crowd of perhaps 300,000 listened to predictable speeches from Cory Aquino, Diosdado Macapagal, José Diokno, and Salvador Laurel. Cory expressed gratitude for "showing us so overwhelmingly that we are not alone," Macapagal described the day as one of "great darkness, sorrow, and fear," Diokno demanded the closure of the U.S. military bases, and Laurel, his fists clenched overhead, roared, "Justice, justice, justice!" Most people in the crowd, although attentive, were enjoying themselves, buying cold drinks and chilled pineapple slices from the vendors who are a feature of every public event in the Philippines.

Chatting among themselves, many in the crowd acknowledged that they had never participated in a demonstration before. A gray-haired woman wearing a faded, floral housedress and gold wire-rim glasses told a young man standing next to her that she believed Marcos would resign. "He's got to understand that the people are against him," she said. "If I were in his place, I'd resign." The young man, his neat, plaid shirt hanging outside his trousers, said he would like to agree with her, "but, personally, I doubt that he'll step down. He has all the guns and the power." Everyone seemed to have an opinion, and spoke it.

At 4:30 P.M., when the permit for the demonstration expired, the oratory stopped. The finale was the burning of stacks of government-controlled newspapers. Then people began heading home. Most, anyway.

Perhaps 15,000, mainly young men, split off and, as darkness descended, began moving slowly toward Mendiola Bridge. Waiting for them were a thousand men, half in the tan uniforms of the Metropolitan Police and half in the olive drab of the Philippine Constabulary, a force that grew from the Philippine Scouts, founded by the U.S. Army during the colonial period. The PC, as they were known, were under the command of Lieutenant General Fidel ("Eddie") V. Ramos, a graduate of the U.S. Military Academy at West Point, a thoroughly professional soldier, and a favorite of American officers in the U.S. mission.

The security forces were lined up abreast, holding tall riot shields on the ground in front of them, with heavy wooden truncheons slung from their belts. But their holsters were empty, and only a small number of officers carried either sidearms or M-16 rifles. A police sergeant, with the name J. A. Atienza on the breast of his uniform, explained, "We've been warned by our superiors that we will be suspended ten days without pay if we carry guns." Behind the men, two buses had been drawn up, nose-to-nose, to help cut off access to the bridge. As the crowd approached, many of the young men were shouting, "Peace! Peace!" and jabbing the air with fingers formed into Vs. They got to within twenty yards of the security lines when, from the middle of the crowd, a torrent of stones and broken bricks was unleashed. What had been a crowd instantly became a mob. The uniformed men heaved their shields over their heads, looking like a formation of medieval soldiers warding off arrows loosed from high on a castle wall. They did not counterattack despite repeated barrages.

It quickly became evident that opposing forces were at odds within the mob. As some were hurling missiles, others were waving their hands frantically and shouting, "No one will throw rocks, do not throw anything!" But the power was with the more violent. Suddenly, a shout went up, "Burn the buses!"

At once, flaming bottles of gasoline—Molotov cocktails—were hurled at the buses and at a yellow construction crane that was parked near the bridge. At the same time, explosions began to reverberate from crude but deadly homemade grenades called pillboxes—bottles and cans filled with gunpowder, broken glass, nails, and pebbles. Two men in sweaty undershirts were running toward the crowd pushing wheelbarrows filled with rocks when one suddenly fell to his knees and then collapsed on his side, his chest bloody, apparently shot. An amplified voice shouted from the midst of the crowd, "Be careful— someone has a gun. Be careful—there are infiltrators among us."

Chaos reigned amid screaming, cries for help, explosions, gunshots, and flames. Simultaneously, pistol and rifle fire erupted, and the security forces thundered out from behind the blazing buses. The mob broke and ran back down the avenue, the uniformed troops in full chase, augmented by five hundred or so marines in camouflage fatigues. Anyone caught was beaten savagely with truncheons. Two policemen grabbed a long-haired teenager next to a fast-food stand called the Jollibee Yumburger and beat him over the head with their clubs until blood streamed down his face and chest and he stopped screaming. They dumped him there and trotted away, looking for another target. Some in the mob fled into the dormitories flanking the street and pelted the security men with rocks. Others diverted the authorities by toppling sidewalk kiosks and setting them afire, along with stacks of old tires. Within half an hour there were scores of fires throughout the university neighborhood, spewing thick, acrid smoke into the steamy air.

Eleven people, one of them a marine corporal, were killed, and about 150 were seriously injured.

As had been obvious during the rioting, various forces were exploiting heightened tensions for their own ends. While most police and military troops followed orders and did not carry arms, some did. Similarly, some marchers had handguns, which they used not only on the security forces but on some of the tamer members of the mob. Whether the agents provocateurs were government plants or Communists remained a mystery.

The next day was one of licking wounds and blaming others.

Marcos went on television and accused "the opposition," though he didn't name names. "Do not force my hand. Do not compel me to move into extremes you already know of. If necessary, I will do so." He left his warning vague, but it sounded to a lot of Filipinos very much like a threat to reimpose the same type of martial law strictures he'd applied in 1972.

Lorenzo Tañada charged that the responsibility for the violence "rests solely on the government," that the security forces had used not just truncheons but rifles and pistols "against unarmed citizens." Flushed and shaking his fist, though unable to hear reporters' questions, Tañada said his opposition group "condemns in the strongest possible terms this ruthless assault by the government."

Cardinal Sin, delivering a tough speech written for him by Felix Bautista, accused the Marcos regime of "adherence to practices that bring back memories of Dr. Goebbels in Nazi Germany." Extravagant though this charge was, Sin was closer in other respects to reality than either the president or Tañada. He clearly charged the regime with provocation, but he acknowledged that the mob responded with "a naked display of public indignation against anything and everything remotely connected with government."

Protest demonstrations continued for two more days in various parts of the city, including one in Makati, but the steam had gone out of them. Marcos and Ver ordered police to resume carrying their weapons, and they were quick to rely on tear gas in prodigious quantities. A march on the U.S. embassy by about a thousand students from Far Eastern University was halted abruptly by police lobbing canisters of gas and swinging their truncheons. The students were carrying posters denouncing the "Marcos-Reagan Dictatorship" and demanding that President Reagan not visit Manila, as he was scheduled to do as part of a trip that would take him to Japan and South Korea in November.

Views among U.S. officials working behind the concrete lattice of the embassy were mixed on whether Reagan should visit the Philippines. Certainly Marcos would exploit the visit as a U.S. seal of approval for his regime. The more popular line of thinking among American diplomats in Manila was that while the Aquino assassination had done a great deal of damage to Marcos's credibility, he was still very much America's man. If he were further weakened or somehow forced from office, the greatest beneficiaries would be the Communists. There was no middle ground—it was either Marcos or the Communists. Reagan himself shared this view and was inclined to follow the advice from this camp, which was that he come.

In Washington, however, a White House official said that the killings and injuries at Mendiola Bridge could make it "very difficult" for the president to proceed to Manila. Nancy Reagan was reported as "very concerned" about her husband's safety. But Assistant Secretary of State for Human Rights and Humanitarian Affairs Elliot Abrams said that the State Department was recommending that Reagan not cancel the trip. Indeed, said Abrams, the human rights picture in the Philippines had actually grown a bit brighter since the Aquino killing, though he didn't say that the former was a direct result of the latter.

The visit meant a great deal to the Marcoses. They had entertained then Governor of California Reagan and his wife in 1969. In December 1980, Imelda Marcos had been accorded a rare, preinaugural meeting with the president-elect, and the Marcoses had made a state visit to Washington soon afterward. Marcos liked to boast about his direct channel of communication to the American president and that he and Ron, as well as Imelda and Nancy, were personal friends. The White House quietly dismissed the notion of a close relationship. Marcos knew that the great majority of Filipinos were strongly pro-American and that TV and press coverage of himself and Reagan shaking hands and toasting each other at Malacañang would boost his stock greatly. He also knew that nothing mattered more to Reagan, as well as to the departments of State and Defense, than the future of Clark Air Base, north of Manila, and Subic Bay Naval Base, on the South China Sea to the east. With this in mind, and because his health was somewhat improved, he launched himself into a media blitz intended to put his case before the American people. After being unavailable to foreign newsmen for a month, Marcos suddenly was accepting requests for interviews. He was on CBS for an early morning appearance with Diane Sawyer and on ABC for a late night chat with Ted Koppel. A stream of newsmen and TV cameras began flowing in and out of the Malacañang guest house.

With two other correspondents, I was shown into the main reception hall of the guest house, a huge, bright room, one wall made entirely of glass two stories high, looking across immaculate lawns to the white palace itself. Gold-framed chairs had been arranged in a row facing one of the carved-and-gilded leather-topped desks at which Marcos always sat. A matching chair with a red-velvet cushion and back, really a throne by its scale and ornate design, was placed behind the desk, and behind that, on a blue-velvet drape, hung a large red, white, blue, and gold presidential seal. The presidential desk was placed on a platform raised about a foot above the floor. A camera from the government-run TV station, Channel 4, was in place to record the interview. Carefully selected portions would be shown on the evening news.

The president entered the room from behind a row of potted palms wearing a cream-color *barong tagalog,* the see-through shirt that men use as formal wear in the Philippines. His was buttoned to the throat, and a white T-shirt showed through it. He walked slowly and unsteadily, with obvious determination. His right arm hung at his side, and he did not offer to shake hands with us. He had some difficulty stepping onto the platform and lowered himself carefully onto his seat. Looking at him, I was shocked by how severely he'd deteriorated.

I had last interviewed Marcos in 1977, when he was at the height of his powers, politically, mentally, and physically. Though fifty-nine years old, he appeared then to be a good ten years younger. His short, about five feet six inches, frame was wiry and muscular, his black hair thick and glossy, slicked into a high forties-style pompadour, his eyes piercing above prominent cheekbones, his brown skin taut. I recall that he wanted to talk about land reform, a pressing issue in the Philippines as in most of the former colonial world. His voice deep and strong, without a glimpse at a piece of paper—there was none on his desk—he reeled off figures, dates, statistics, accomplishments. For all I knew, he could have been making them up as he went along. But he was convincing and charming.

That interview had taken place two years after the U.S. client regime in South Vietnam had fallen to the Communist North. The domino theory was still alive in the minds of many Americans, as well as among the pro-American governments of Southeast Asia. If they could hold the line against the Communist cancer in Vietnam, Cambodia, and Laos, perhaps the dread realization of the theory could be averted. To do that, America needed leaders like Marcos in the region. Here was a man who was seen by many of his own people, as well as by Americans and other Westerners, as a pillar of hope and promise, a man who held the future of his country and its people in his hands, in his agile mind, in his great heart. In addition to being a friend of America and an enemy of the Communists, he was a war hero—the most decorated Filipino soldier to have fought the Japanese alongside the Americans—the husband of a striking beauty, the father of three bright, young children.

Of course, some people had suffered under the martial law Marcos had imposed to save his political future. He had broken up many of the vast holdings of the great old Filipino families, those he called "oligarchs," and hundreds of his political enemies, Ninoy Aquino among them, were still in jail. There was no freedom of expression; newspapers were a mockery of the freewheeling—some would say irresponsible—Philippine press of a few years earlier. But, if their lives had not yet been improved by Marcos's grand plans for land reform and industrialization, rural electrification, free education, improved roads, and dozens of other programs advertised as Southeast Asia's answer to the New Deal, most Filipinos were at least no worse off than they'd been before martial law.

More importantly, perhaps, martial law was good for business. During its nine years, U.S. commercial investment in the Philippines had multiplied nine times. Presidential decrees, by which Marcos imposed legislation, were a boon to Americans who needed special arrangements or favors in order to smooth out their operations or assure their profit margins. And what was good for U.S. business was good for Marcos. The president and his wife, who had gone easy on graft during his two elected terms, cast caution to the winds once they had the protection of martial law. With American money pouring in from private companies and a consortium of private banks, as well as funds from the World Bank and its loan window, the International Monetary Fund, the president beefed up his arrangements for kickbacks and skimming. By the time he fled, he had amassed a personal fortune of billions of dollars; lumped together with the money sucked out of the Philippines by his cronies and relatives, it may have equaled the national debt—some $26 billion.

But neither Americans nor Filipinos knew how deep the drain ran. Of course, the American diplomats and politicians who spent fabulous evenings at Malacañang parties and aboard the enormous, white presidential yacht, the R.P.S. *Ang Pangulo* ("The President"), winked at each other occasionally. Of course, they knew that the president couldn't be expected to get by on his token salary of some $5,000 a year, that he had to have a few numbered accounts in Swiss banks, probably some real-estate holdings abroad, and a portfolio of choice corporate investments. And anyone could see that the beautiful First Lady wore magnificent necklaces and earrings, that her clothing was designed for her by some of Europe's greatest couturiers. But, what the United States cared most about was that Ferdinand Marcos placed the power of his office behind Clark Air Base and the naval facility at Subic Bay, the largest overseas U.S. military installations in the world. The future of these bases, and of the Philippines, seemed secure under Marcos.

The man being interviewed in 1983 seemed little more than a faded shadow of the Marcos of six years earlier. This was not just a man who had aged from fifty-nine to sixty-five. This was a very sick man attempting to hide his sickness. His old-fashioned pompadour was thin and dyed, his scalp, too, colored black, giving him the look of a has-been tango dancer. His quarter-moon-shaped eyes, an inheritance from his mother, who was part Chinese, were bleary, and he dabbed at them frequently with a wad of tissue clenched in his left hand. Small, purple triangles were deeply sunken at their outer corners. His speech was slurred and slow and his voice raspy. Several times he lost his train of thought, grasping for words as an aide sprang to his assistance.

But he was still fighting. And he still knew that the way to get a rise out of Americans was to wave the twin issues of the bases and the Communists in front of them. Thus, he warned that if President Reagan were to cancel the Philippine leg of his Asian tour, it could severely weaken Marcos's relentless struggle to keep the bases safe for the United States. "It is something unthinkable to us, that President Reagan might not come," he said. "We have never thought of it. The economic repercussions could be serious. It might rock the boat on the withdrawal of investments and even loans. It would be devastating to the point where it might be taken as an intention to support the Communist role and the Communist conspiracy. I'm sure all of this will be taken into account by President Reagan. It's unthinkable." But, clearly, he had thought a great deal about it and wasn't sure what he could do, beyond raising the two bugbears, to keep Reagan from altering his itinerary. "I would have to go all the way back to square one, as it were, in the fight for the continuance of the military facilities."

By "square one" Marcos meant pre–World War II days, when nationalist Filipino leaders fought against retaining the U.S. military presence that would remain after the colonial administrative apparatus was dismantled. They lost, and the United States had had use of the facilities ever since the war ended. In fact, at the time of the Aquino killing, Reagan had signed a letter of intention under which the United States would pay the Philippines $900 million to extend the agreement for another five years.

The second part of his message to the American people was that he was alive and well and calling the shots, despite those nagging rumors that he was sick and possibly dying. One of those concerned about these rumors, he said, was Ambassador Armacost. "The American ambassador has seen me twice," he said. "He wanted to see if I was really running the government or not, if I was healthy. I told him I can't play tennis with him now, but give me a week or two and I'll meet you on the golf course. . . . All this talk about kidney transplant, dialysis, it's ridiculous." What was troubling him was one of his old war wounds. "Pieces of shrapnel, steel fragments, became imbedded in the abdominal wall and in back. It caused an infection, and it coincided with severe allergy, like hay fever. There was no operation. They took out the infection, that's about all.'' He obviously felt the need to keep up a front, to posture on his corner of the world stage. That was his way, and he would stick to it even after he fled to Hawaii.

He was inflexible. Once he took a position, he would refuse to budge. Until the assassination, he'd pretty much been able to use muscle to assure that things worked out as he wanted them to. But the murder, coming when he was sick and not in control, changed the pattern permanently. For the next two years, there would be extended periods when it looked as though he might win again, but there were signs all along the way that the game was coming to an end.

There could be no question of implicating him in the killing, he said during the interview: ''The opposition knows this is not the way I handle political problems. Aquino was legally dead, he had been sentenced to die. But when he got sick we sent him to the United States and saved his life. We've been very generous to him. We tried to save his life by refusing to give him a passport and so forth. Our agents confirmed that there were people out to kill him. Our conscience is clear.''

He had appointed a commission and ordered it to conduct ''a fair, dispassionate investigation'' of the assassination. Asked when the commission would make its report, he replied, ''I don't know. I don't want the impression that I'm running things.''

From the moment that Aquino had been gunned down, Marcos, aware that he was suspect, had immediately turned to his favorite bogey, the Communists, as a counteroffensive. On the day of the assassination, the president was too ill to appear on television. According to the best information available at the time, which was confirmed subsequently, he was suffering from a chronic disease, systemic lupus erythematosus, and had undergone a kidney transplant shortly before. A second transplant would be performed in 1984. During the periods of surgery and recuperation, government-run television had shown old clips of him without saying when they had been filmed. A statement in his name was issued on the day of the assassination. It said, in part, that ''It's now futile to recall the antecedents to this dastardly act when the government practically humbled itself to prevent his return during this period, when according to intelligence reports, the danger against the life of Ninoy Aquino was highest and un-abated. . . . But, apparently on the advice of some of his more influential persons and on his own judgment, he decided to disregard the confirmed reports of the serious conspiracy against his life. It is with a feeling of deep and profound frustration therefore that we now see the complete uselessness of our efforts to protect him. The protection of a public official's life against a determined killer who is ready to die in the attempt at assassination will always be one of the most difficult, if not impossible, tasks of security men all over the world."

The next night, Monday, Marcos, making a supreme effort, appeared before a hastily summoned televised news conference at the palace. "I am a little angered by what is happening because, as I said, no matter what explanation we make now, there will always be some kind of shadow over the entire government, and this was never, never our purpose," he said. "We had hoped that the matter could be handled with a little more finesse."

Then, speaking of the problems the authorities were having in identifying the man who was shot to death seconds after Aquino was killed, the president said, "It is not easy to identify a professional killer like him. The indications are that he belonged to the subversive group. One of the theories is to the effect that . . . the killing might have received the blessings of the NPA [New People's Army] or the Communist hierarchy, because they would shoot two birds with one stone. They would eliminate Aquino, who was responsible for some of the liquidations, according to them, of some of their men . . . at the same time they would embarrass the government and place it in an awkward position, which they have. . . . The other theory, it is just a plain Communist rub-out job. . . . Ninoy Aquino was shot by a civilian with one single shot, with a .357 magnum at close quarters, and this idea of the security men having shot him, which was started by some of these correspondents allegedly from witnesses, is probably planted deliberately in order to malign the good name and reputation of the Filipino people, especially of its leaders and the government itself."

Thus, even before ballistics tests were conducted and before the alleged gunman was identified, Marcos was creating the impression that Aquino had been killed by the Communists. He never abandoned this thesis.

It was obvious to everyone watching TV that day that he was very ill. His speech was badly slurred, his left arm was propped on the desk before him, his right hung limply at his side. His appearance would mark the beginning of an intensive Marcos health-watch by Filipinos, foreign governments, and journalists. Observers would comment on his up days and his down days, when his mind seemed clear and sharp and when he seemed to be sedated, when scabs or bandages on the backs of his hands betrayed intravenous needle punctures.

During my interview with him, the president continued to dismiss reports that the assassination had caused a change in relations between the United States and the Philippines. "That conclusion is based on a presumption that the government had anything to do with the assassination," he said. "The evidence, as far as I know, shows that it was a Communist conspiracy—not to say that I've made up my mind about it. I would like to have the investigation free, unimpeded, dispassionate, scholarly, so that we can find out the truth."

This search for the truth, he explained, was why he was now speaking to foreign correspondents. The press had been spreading rumors and distorting facts. For example, although one or two million people had turned out for Aquino's funeral procession, a government survey showed that most went because of "curiosity or sympathy," not to express their dissatisfaction with the government. In fact, the president said, a survey taken before the assassination showed 87 percent "acceptability" of the government, while the latest survey, conducted a week after the funeral, showed that "acceptability" had risen to 89 percent.

Whether such surveys were taken was in itself questionable; even if they were, there was little chance to know whether they were honest. But here was the president of the Philippines telling the world that his popularity had risen 2 percent as a direct result of the Aquino assassination. The "increased acceptability" was reported on Philippine TV news that night and carried by the next morning's newspapers. While many of the more sophisticated viewers and readers laughed or shook their heads, and even some of the less skeptical were able to filter out much of the deliberate misinformation they received each day, constant repetition had its effect. Furthermore, much of the misinformation was meant for the short term, and intended to be forgotten.

An example was Imelda Marcos's announcement that she was

retiring from politics. While many of Marcos's political enemies were willing to give him the benefit of any doubt linking him to the assassination, there was a widespread feeling that his wife, in conjunction with General Ver, had planned the killing. This was partly the result of Mrs. Marcos's "dragon lady" image, particularly among middle-class and wealthy Filipinos, and partly because the killing had been so clumsy that it didn't seem to carry the president's imprimatur. "He's not that stupid" was a common observation. "She's the one."

4

*T*HE JOYS OF POWER

Not that Imelda was stupid. To the contrary, she was impressively cunning. She had come from a background of genteel poverty and, using her great beauty to its fullest advantage, had drawn Congressman Ferdinand E. Marcos into a whirlwind, eleven-day courtship and marriage during the Easter season of 1954. Moving easily into the political milieu, she soon discarded her cloak of demure shyness and developed a reputation for avarice and love of power that ultimately earned her the distrust of the old, moneyed families. They snickered at what they considered her tastelessness, as she spent a fortune redecorating Malacañang Palace in her and the president's images—commissioning nude portraits and plastic, imitation stained-glass doors of the two of them as Adam and Eve, and ordering historical paintings cut in half so they would fit into new rooms. She had become a "dragon lady," a familiar character at the side of powerful rulers throughout Asia. In recent years, equally well cast have been Jiang Qing, Mao Tse-tung's brutal third wife; Madame Ngo Dinh Nhu, the manipulative sister-in-law of South Vietnam's bachelor Prime Minister Ngo Dinh Diem; and, in Indonesia, President Suharto's wife, Madame Tien, whose reputation for demanding a cut of business deals earned her the sobriquet "Madame Tien Percent."

To Ferdinand Marcos, only power mattered. He became a believer in the mystical energizing forces of the pyramid and had the entire ceiling and floor of his bedroom made over into a repetitive pyramid design. His wife, however, was driven by other demons. While he thought himself increasingly secure in power, she never overcame the feeling that she was still a poor girl, that someday the incredible dream in which she was First Lady, with more clothing and food and money than she ever could have imagined, would suddenly disappear. In her insecurity she, too, turned to occult practices. She installed near the foot of her bed a circular black-marble table inlaid with a five-pointed star, the letter Z, and her name, which was said to help its owner predict the future and consult the spirits. Through her good friend Saudi Arabian billionaire Adnan Khashoggi, she became a follower of a jet-set Hindu seer, Shri Chandra Swamiji Maharaj. So devoted did she become to Swamiji that when the president seemed to be near death around the time of the Aquino killing, Imelda dispatched daughter Imee to New Delhi to invoke his avowedly supernatural powers. And she courted the rich and the famous from around the world, even if some of them were no longer as rich or as famous as they had once been. She gave magnificent parties and flew out guests such as Hollywood actor George Hamilton, pianist Van Cliburn, and Cristina Ford, divorced wife of automaker Henry Ford II. She traveled around the world to visit friends and to shop, endlessly shop, spending millions in a day, for clothing, jewels, antiques, and works of art, many of which turned out to be bad copies. Members of her inner circle, whom she frequently took with her on trips, applauded as she provided them with the comforts of her chartered airliner, the best hotels, sumptuous meals and parties, even generous daily allowances. But Manila's best families never were won over, and that bothered her always.

Imelda didn't live for just the social whirl, though. Early on, she learned from her husband the joys of wielding power and, with him behind her, elbowed her way into the male-dominated world of Philippine politics to build her own power base. In 1975, her husband appointed her governor of Metro Manila, which gave her day-to-day influence over the lives of the 8 million residents of the capital region. In 1978, the same year she defeated Ninoy Aquino, who was campaigning from his prison cell, in an election for the National Assembly, Marcos made her minister of human settlements, giving her control of billions of dollars intended to improve the living conditions of the impoverished. Her manipulation of the vast sums available to her became legendary. In 1981, when Pope John Paul II visited the Philippines, she constructed an entire false-front neighborhood, no more than a Hollywood stage set, in the capital's worst slum, Tondo, where the pontiff stood and addressed the masses.

In the aftermath of the assassination, however, Marcos determined that he could take the heat off himself by creating the impression that his wife was going to step aside. She would appear to be a sacrificial lamb, thereby lessening the shouting in the streets, particularly in the streets of Makati. Such an impression might also help offset the widely held belief that the Marcoses were building a dynasty: Marcos was sick, there was no vice president, there was no mechanism for succession, his wife was powerful, and their children were well on their way to political careers. The Reagan administration was leaning on him to alter the dynastic image and to create machinery for an orderly succession. So, while Marcos was telling the world that President Reagan's visit was vital to the future of the U.S. bases, his wife went on stage and announced that she was retiring from politics.

On September 19, over lunch with a group of correspondents at her favorite hostelry, the Manila Hotel, she said that she knew about the "accusations and suspicions" linking her with the Aquino killing, and she wanted to clear the air. First, she repeated her husband's account of how he and she did everything in their power to persuade Aquino to remain in the United States for his own sake. Then, in a tricky transfer of guilt, she said it wasn't the First Lady or the president who was being accused of murder, it was the entire population of the country. "The stigma is now over fifty-two million beautiful human beings. Now fifty-two million beautiful human beings are being accused of being criminals." The burden now shifted, she said she had made up her mind to change careers. "I've had it with politics," she said in the accented American-style slang that so many Americans find endearing about Filipino English. "My decision to retire from politics is definite and irrevocable." Indeed, she said, she would have made her move "the other day," but "the blind, the mute, the jeepney drivers, and other beautiful, poor people protested too much. My problem is my sensitivity and my Girl Scout mentality." But now she was ready to forsake her constituents and make her break.

That established, she went on to sketch her plan for her future, a rambling, hazy, half-formed notion of working with the little people. "If I'm going to be suspect I'd better get out and be in the private sector for small- and medium-size enterprises, to bring about economic prosperity. I hope to go to the rural areas and set up linkages, processing centers, financing, and technology relevant to people in the rural areas; set up markets here and abroad for small-scale industry and aquamarine. I'm raring to go, to roll my sleeves up and get to work where the real ball game is.''

For sheer audaciousness, Mrs. Marcos's performance beat her husband's hands down. Just looking at this fifty-four-year-old woman, her black ''mourning'' dress now discarded in favor of brilliant red, cut straight to minimize the excess weight she'd accumulated in recent years, a blue-and-white silk scarf tied with affected casualness to hide her double chin, her fingernails exquisitely lacquered in red to match her dress, each nail accented by twin white crescents, her every hair in place, was dizzying; but the image of her rolling up her sleeves and getting down to work in ''small-scale industry and aquamarine'' was ridiculous. Her luncheon companions looked at one another in embarrassment, eyes rolling, or stared at their plates. Asked later what he thought about Mrs. Marcos's announced retirement, Salvador Laurel said, ''Nobody believes it. They'd rather judge her by what she does than what she says.''

What the Marcoses were doing, or trying to do, was to put the Aquino assassination behind them as quickly as possible and get back to business as usual. When he had to, the president threatened and shook his fist; at other times he mollified and made token allowances. Neither tactic was effective in convincing Filipinos to forget the killing. At the same time, the population had grown so used to Marcos as president, to his seemingly incomparable shrewdness and use of power, that no one really expected him to change. But outrage over the assassination had triggered deeper revulsion and anger than anything that had happened in recent memory. For as long as these emotions could be sustained, protest achieved more than anyone had a right to expect.

An early example of what Marcos was willing to offer, and what the people were unwilling to accept, was the Fernando commission. The president had appointed this body, headed by Supreme Court Chief Justice Enrique Fernando, on August 24, just three days after the airport killing. The appointment was made in response to instantaneous urging by the Reagan administration that the assassination be investigated and that the inquiry be quick, thorough, and honest. The message from the White House was that if Marcos was able to create the impression that he had gotten to the bottom of the Aquino killing and then followed that up with National Assembly elections, the elections would be perceived as fair, and Marcos could count on victory. Marcos's reaction was to tap the sixty-eight-year-old Fernando. The appointment was typical. Fernando had a reputation as a decent person, but hardly an independent one. He was frequently seen at public functions holding a parasol for the First Lady. The four other members of his commission were retired members of the Supreme Court. Once word got out that Fernando was in charge, several more independent-minded candidates declined to join the commission. One of these was Cardinal Sin.

The cardinal was as cagey a politician in his own right as Marcos. With a wide, toothy smile all but permanently carved into his broad face, he was able to slip from silly little jokes to sober political assessments without losing a beat. Draped in his white cassock, he would stand at the threshold of his official residence and say, "Welcome to the house of Sin," playing on his delightfully inappropriate name, which was of Chinese origin. Then, he would immediately launch into serious commentary on affairs of the day. The president had telephoned and asked him to join the Fernando commission, but he dodged the request. "I asked him, 'Why chase me? I'm a churchman, not a lawyer. I'm not prepared to investigate people. As a priest, I'm trained to forgive.' " What was evident, though, was that Sin didn't want to be associated with a body whose findings might be suspect. He managed to evade the president's appeal.

Fernando was a dour man of rigid habits. He rarely smiled. Every day, he wore the same outfit, a white linen suit, white shirt, and thin, black tie. Every day, precisely at 12:30, he would enter the coffee shop of the Manila Hotel, his pace careful and measured, his arms hardly swinging, and would be shown to the same table. He was a tall, angular man, with steel-gray hair cut close at the back and sides, his face narrow and pinched, his glasses steel-rimmed. His commission almost immediately became the subject of denigratory posters and taunting chants. Sitting at his table six days after he'd been appointed, he brought up his role as the lone dissenter in several Supreme Court cases to show that the criticism was unfounded. But he conceded that he was not prepared to carry on with the commission if he was not trusted by the public. He acknowledged, too, that the cardinal's refusal to join had hurt. "I'm sorry he declined. I would like to have him with us. If suspicion against me persists, if I can't be of help, why should I stay? One reason I'm there is the Supreme Court has credibility."

Fernando said the commission would not subpoena the Aquino family or the Marcoses. "It is not in our tradition," he said. He anticipated that the investigation would be completed and a report issued by November. In fact, the Fernando commission was finished even sooner. It met first on September 7 and halted its investigation on September 12 before resigning on October 11.

Even if the members of the Fernando commission had been above reproach, the Marcos machinery was operating at full speed to frustrate a legitimate probe. For example, Major General Prospero Olivas, whom Ver appointed to lead the police investigation of the assassination, went on television the evening of the assassination and displayed a .357 magnum Smith & Wesson revolver that he said was the murder weapon. Five days later, Olivas brought the weapon to a news conference. It still had not been submitted to police forensic experts. As he spoke to newsmen, the beefy Olivas, sweating profusely in his tight-fitting tan uniform, a leather Sam Browne belt stretched across his chest, turned the gun over and over in his hands. If there ever had been any fingerprints on it, other than his own, they certainly were gone now.

Then there was the mysterious matter of the embroidered briefs. Two days elapsed after the assassination before the police announced their first lead: the name Rolly, presumably a nickname, was found to be stitched into the undershorts on the body of the alleged assassin. Two more weeks passed during which the entire police and intelligence network of the Philippines evidently was unable to learn the full name of the man in the embroidered underpants, whose body had been allowed to lie on the tarmac for five hours after the assassination, thereby delaying an autopsy. When Rolly was found to be Rolando Galman, a small-time thug, the discovery was made not by the police or the military or intelligence authorities, but by a Philippine newspaper reporter.

In reality, the Fernando commission faced a much bigger job than just solving a murder; it had to reconstruct the shattered remnants of public confidence in the Marcos government, at home and abroad.

Filipinos were long accustomed to little people, the nameless and the faceless, being killed by police or soldiers. The authorities termed such killings, with unintentionally bitter irony, "salvagings." These crimes were seldom solved. But Aquino had a name, a face, a reputation, he came from an influential family, he had money and power. His friends and family would not simply squat on their haunches and weep softly. The Fernando commission would have to come up with answers to satisfy both these people and the Reagan administration.

The commission was not up to its task, and its resignation was a blow for Marcos. But worse was coming. Michael Deaver, President Reagan's emissary, arrived quietly in Manila and advised Marcos that Reagan would be cutting the Philippines out of his Asian trip in November. As a sop, Reagan also eliminated Thailand and Indonesia and limited his visits to Japan and South Korea. Deaver offered Marcos a menu of excuses: there was a particularly demanding legislative calendar coming up early in November; travel to five Asian countries in fifteen days would be too strenuous; Nancy Reagan was worried about her husband's well-being. But what lay behind the cancellation was the White House's fear that Reagan would look bad on television in the United States in the likely event that Filipinos took to the streets to protest his visit as a sign of support for Marcos.

Furthermore, the United States had worked hard to impress Marcos with the need for a thorough probe of the killing. At least as important as having the investigation *be* honest was that it be *perceived* as honest by the public, in the Philippines as well as in the United States. Appointing a man whose reputation was in doubt from the start was a sign to Washington that Marcos was not serious, that he believed he could get away with a charade of an investigation. By canceling his visit with a flimsy excuse, Reagan wasn't pulling the rug out from under Marcos, he was merely stressing how important a legitimate investigation was. The move was effective. For one thing, Reagan gained a few public relations points in Manila, at least among the Makati marching set, some of whom carried a banner in their next demonstration proclaiming, THANK YOU MR. REAGAN FOR SUPPORTING DEMOCRACY.

More importantly, Marcos quickly appointed a new commission, one that eventually would surprise even its creator. At first, though, it looked little better than a replay of its predecessor. The new panel was headed by retired Appeals Court Justice Corazon Juliano-Agrava, a woman whose reputation for judicial independence was just a shade brighter than Fernando's. Many Filipinos shrugged their shoulders in resignation. Marcos controlled the courts and the judges; how could anyone expect justice?

The Philippine judiciary had been thoroughly corrupted by martial law. Marcos's pride in his ability as a lawyer (his bar examination score was the highest in Philippine history) left him with a predilection for couching even his more draconian moves in legalism. In some Third World countries, a dictator wouldn't bother going through the motions of revising the constitution or seeking legal justification. The fact that Marcos did so reflected not just his own thinking but the legalistic nature of the society. The country's legal system had been blended from an American passion for litigiousness, Spanish- and Church-inspired dogmatism, and Malay-style tribal rule to produce a melange that confused foreigners but met Filipino expectations.

Like Marcos, just about everyone in and around Philippine politics is an attorney, and the contraction 'Torney is an even more respected title than Doctor.

Marcos filled the Supreme Court bench with lawyers he could easily control, though one or two free thinkers were kept on for the sake of appearances. Lesser benches, too, were filled by attorneys beholden to the president. Thus, as the assassination investigation and subsequent trial grew excruciatingly protracted, Agrava and the courts became regular targets for protest.

Another frequent target was the local press. Filipinos had long since become embittered that another democratic institution about which their former American masters had preached had become a mockery. The press was even more obviously a tool of the Marcos regime than was the judiciary. In the years before martial law, Philippine newspapers were among the most outspoken in Asia, ranking alongside those of India with their liberal British traditions. But, unlike that of India, much of the Philippine press was free to the point of irresponsibility. It was a mixed bag. Many papers drew their inspiration from the worst American tabloid journalism; others were highly responsible. Some Filipino journalists were world class; others were simply careless or vindictive and ruined reputations and lives with slanderous articles. Martial law eliminated the diversity by forcing editors to self-censor their papers, and during the next nine years Marcos learned how much easier it was to run a government without carping and criticism from reporters and columnists. He also learned that he didn't want to see his old foes regain voices they'd raised against him in the days of freedom.

Many of the papers, as well as radio and television stations, had been controlled by the families that Marcos called the oligarchs. The most powerful had been the Lopez family, whose main source of wealth had been the giant Manila Electric Company, MERALCO, the country's main public utility. The Lopezes had owned the largest radio and television networks in the Philippines, Alto Broadcasting Systems and Chronicle Broadcasting Network, as well as a major daily newspaper, *The Manila Chronicle*. While the communications media had been profitable operations, they also had provided a voice for the family's own political and financial interests. Marcos ousted the Lopezes not only from MERALCO but from the broadcasting stations and the *Chronicle*, and arrested family heir Eugenio Lopez, Jr., who, like Aquino, would remain in jail for many years. The president placed his golfing partner, Roberto S. Benedicto, in charge of the former Lopez empire. This takeover at the outset of martial law established what became known generically as the "crony press."

With the president's men in charge, the news outlets became uniformly subservient to Marcos and the First Family. Although never quite so obsequious as the press in Iran under Shah Mohammad Reza Pahlavi, where editors were instructed to feature His Imperial Majesty's name prominently on the front page of every issue, it was a rare day in the Philippines when most papers didn't have a major headline featuring "FM" (for Ferdinand Marcos) or "FL" (for First Lady) or both.

When Marcos lifted martial law in 1981, with promises of more press freedom, a number of journalists with a longing for the old days scraped together some money from friends and family and began publishing a series of skimpy tabloids intended to give readers a variety of viewpoints. But failure was preordained. One example was a paper called *We Forum*, put out by José Burgos. In December 1982, after it had published an article questioning Marcos's heroic World War II record, the government closed it down, seized the printing press, arrested Burgos and nine of his staff members, and jailed them for a week. They were charged with subversion, but their trial was never concluded.

During the martial law years, as well as afterward, the crony press was not, technically speaking, censored by the government. But it didn't take too many calls from the Office of Media Affairs, which was run directly from Malacañang Palace by Information Minister Gregorio Cendaña, before an editor learned how to sanitize his own editorial product.

So when Aquino was killed in August 1983, the press was no freer than it had been during the nine years of martial law. Publications uniformly and solemnly adopted the president's assertion that the Communists were responsible for the assassination. When American and other foreign correspondents began reporting that many Filipinos were skeptical, they and their publications were taken to task by loyal columnists in Manila. But, in part because so many Filipinos travel to the United States and have friends and relatives living there, what was being printed in America quickly made its way back to the Philippines. And, in a time when many middle-class Filipinos owned video-cassette recorders, tapes from American TV networks were soon being circulated. It wasn't long before demonstrators were burning heaps of newspapers in the streets and demanding honest journalism.

A group of prominent businessmen, many of whom were the same executives who were marching through the streets of Makati, or at least smiling benevolently on their employees who were out there marching, called a meeting with a number of editors and publishers to "dialogue" about the problem. (In Philippine English, *dialogue* is a verb more often than a noun.) The meeting was organized by the Makati Business Club, the core of the increasingly vocal, noncrony business community. The club was founded on October 1, 1981, by Enrique Zobel, a relative of the Ayala family. One of the wealthiest bankers in the world, the fifty-six-year-old Zobel was as shrewd politically as he was financially. He perceived that, in the postassassination atmosphere, Marcos would be susceptible to greater pressure from businessmen at home and abroad than at any other time. Zobel and most other business leaders harbored no illusions; they did not expect Marcos to resign, no matter how many tons of shredded yellow paper were dropped from offices or how many students were clubbed into submission. They believed, though, that they now had an opportunity to squeeze the president for changes in the economic, political, and social spheres in return for their cooperation. One concession they wanted was a press that would carry their voices.

That the businessmen chose the press as one of their early means for achieving their goals revealed a great deal about the nature of the Philippines. Compared with other Southeast Asian nations at similar stages in economic development, the Philippines had the highest standard of literacy in the region, 82 percent. And with English as the widely used second language, Filipino readers could readily be reached by a broad range of American, British, and regional magazines, and by daily newspapers, including the *International Herald Tribune* and *The Asian Wall Street Journal*. As a result, large numbers of Filipinos were sophisticated about world events and about foreign perceptions of their own circumstances. But only a relative handful of readers could afford to buy these imported publications, and the Makati Business Club recognized the need to open up the columns of the local papers.

The discussion on the press, held over a luncheon at Makati's Intercontinental Hotel on September 27, five weeks after Aquino's death, was attended by three hundred businessmen. It marked the first time that many of them had publicly taken an anti-Marcos stand, and they were ill at ease. Several corporate public relations officers circulated among foreign newsmen, jokingly but nervously asking them to go easy on their bosses during the question-and-answer period. Jaime Ongpin, the mining executive whose profile was rapidly rising, addressed the group. He had been in the United States when Aquino was assassinated and said he was shocked to realize that he had a more accurate understanding of developments than his friends and family back in Manila. "They had no real idea what was going on because their information was all coming from limited official sources," he said. "I was far better informed through American television and newspapers and ended up telling people back here what was going on in their own city." He also pointed out that many of the people he talked to over the telephone were utterly confused because, in the absence of honest journalism, they were susceptible to wild rumors.

"I've now concluded that except for a couple of smaller papers, the local media have failed miserably," Ongpin said. "The local media have forfeited what little credibility they formerly enjoyed. Unless their credibility is somehow restored, the local media will lose their reason for existence and will destroy themselves. This crisis in media should concern every Filipino.''

Ongpin then asked a series of tough, mainly rhetorical, questions:

''Who is responsible?

''Is it the president, who created a climate of fear and subservience with martial law in 1972 and transferred ownership of the press to his friends and relatives?

''Is it the Office of Media Affairs, which gives 'guidelines' to the press?

''Is it the publishers, who are afraid of what may happen if they cross those guidelines?

''Is it the advertisers, the editors, the writers, or is it the viewing and reading public—you and I included—who are afraid to take effective action?

''We have to admit that we are all responsible for letting the local media deteriorate to the shameful and miserable condition in which they find themselves.''

By the standards of the time, Ongpin's speech was a powerful attack on a number of sacred cows, and his colleagues responded with an outburst of cheers and applause.

The villain of the luncheon was the publisher of the leading crony newspaper, *Bulletin Today,* General Hans Menzi. A Filipino citizen of Swiss origin, Menzi was seventy-three years old and looked like the retired army general that he was. With a reputation among the businessmen for taking orders directly from the presidential palace, he knew he was in enemy territory. But he made as good a defense for a controlled press as was possible under the circumstances: ''Whatever I say I'm castigated. Whatever anyone from the press says here today may fall on deaf ears.''

Indicating that it was better to publish than to perish, he maintained that those papers permitted to operate under martial law had to abide by very tight controls. Government licensing on a monthly basis gave the regime the ability to shut down a paper on a whim. Menzi was chosen by Marcos to head a self-regulatory body called the Press Council and was issued a brief list of don'ts: ''Don't conduct trials by publicity; don't criticize the First Family on personal matters; don't print anything inimical to the security of the nation.''

The regulations seemed to be intentionally vague, thus putting additional self-constraint on publishers. "When I asked what 'inimical to the security of the nation' constituted, I wasn't told," Menzi said. "Under those circumstances, it's mighty hard to publish a newspaper."

The businessmen had been cool but polite to that point. But then Menzi went on to claim that his paper's policy was to "print both sides" of all issues and, as for the assassination in particular, "we have printed both sides of the game and let the public decide; we stay away from gossip and rumors; it may mean a drab paper." This was too much for the hostile audience, and many in the large dining room began jeering. Menzi flushed but forged on angrily: "Don't judge me by the standards of people who don't care for the truth and for the country. You want both sides, help us." He was booed even more roundly, rare behavior by Filipinos.

In fact, Menzi was not being entirely facetious when he said that the crony papers were presenting both sides of the assassination. The first faint signs of change were beginning to creep onto the pages of local papers. A few days earlier, for example, the *Bulletin Today* had carried a front-page account of JAJA's claim that the government had provoked the Mendiola Bridge riots that cost eleven lives. The article was brief and appeared under a small, single-column headline. An article about Marcos blaming the opposition for the same rioting ran beneath a banner headline across the full width of the top of the paper and was accompanied by four other, supporting front-page articles. The coverage was hardly balanced, but the single item reflecting an opposing viewpoint was a step forward and represented a government concession.

Other steps were being taken at the same time. *We Forum* publisher Burgos, even though he was supposed to be under house arrest, was at the luncheon in his role as publisher of a new, outspoken paper, this one called *Ang Pahayagang Malaya,* which means "The Free Newspaper." *Malaya* was the most respected of the new crop of sensational, antiregime tabloids that were being hawked by tattered newsboys edging their way between tightly packed lanes of traffic. The skimpy sheets were enlivened by bold headlines in red or green that usually were more suggestive than definitive, for example: ARMY TO BLAME FOR AQUINO SLAY?

Throughout the dialogue, Zobel, who sat at the center of an elevated table reserved for guests of honor, had remained silent. His colleagues and local journalists in the audience were anxious to hear from the flamboyant figure whose family had been in the Philippines for a hundred and fifty years. Burly, with blue eyes and wavy auburn hair, with German-Jewish ancestors who had emigrated to Spain centuries earlier and converted to Catholicism, Zobel was a reserve fighter pilot and an outstanding polo player whose teammates included the billionaire Sultan of Brunei and one of Marcos's sons-in-law, Gregorio Araneta. A long-standing friend of Ninoy Aquino's, he was godfather to one of the Aquino children and had told intimates that he was shattered by the assassination. His pronouncements carried weight. "When they killed Ninoy, they threw away the rule book," he had said.

Now Zobel was in an uncomfortable position. He'd been stung just a few days earlier by published reports of his leading the big demonstration in Makati. Parading through the streets was not his style, and a lot of people in his elite circle were surprised by the news. The reports were incorrect; the marcher had been the wife of his cousin, Jaime Zobel de Ayala, with whom he was on bad terms. But Enrique got the credit, or blame. A few days later, Marcos told foreign newsmen that "my friend Enrique Zobel telephoned and assured me that he did not participate in the Makati demonstration." Suddenly, the banker had found himself in a damned-if-you-do, damned-if-you-don't situation and had evidently decided to keep his mouth shut. But when a foreign newsman, ignoring the appeals of Zobel's public relations aide, asked him to speak and the audience cheered, he was on the spot. Rising, he warmed up for a few moments and then let loose a characteristic blast. "You've heard a lot of truth here today," he said, "you've heard a lot of bullshit. . . . We don't believe the local newspapers, and we'd like the president to know this. . . . The Philippine media are scared of telling the truth, or they've been bribed. We have no respect for the Philippine media."

With heavyweights like Zobel and Ongpin taking an aggressive stance for a free press, the Makati Business Club luncheon was the opening round in what was to become a running battle. In 1984, Ongpin and some of his business associates, together with several Jesuit priests, launched a Church-backed magazine called *Veritas,* Latin for "truth," to reinforce the views of an existing radio station of the same name. The *Veritas* print-and-broadcast combine would become a vital instrument to the Church, the opposition political camp, and to reformist military officers as their struggle with Marcos intensified. The slick weekly magazine was polished and contained contributions from some of the more respected minds in and out of the religious community. Because it was Church-supported, *Veritas* enjoyed more authority and freedom from harassment than other opposition publications. Nevertheless, at around the same time, several laymen screwed up their courage and managed to introduce a measure of differing opinion that Filipinos had long done without. Two of the more successful new publications were *Business Day*, a low-key, business-oriented paper akin to *The Wall Street Journal*, which worked balanced reporting and opinion on a variety of subjects into its gray pages, and, oddly enough, a lighthearted society weekly named *Mr. and Ms.*, which over time developed a social conscience.

5

THE HOUSE OF SIN

Marcos had learned well the lesson that the shah had missed in his final years on the Peacock Throne—that a dictator is at his weakest when he starts making concessions. All over Asia, autocrats had been taught for centuries of the danger faced by any who rode the back of the tiger to power and then attempted to dismount. Marcos knew that once the throngs in the streets and the ambitious but squabbling political opposition sniffed the first signs of weakness, they would be at his throat.

But, for now, at the outset of 1984, the judiciary and most of the press remained under the president's thumb, and the armed forces and the police were loyal to him alone. Marcos appeared to believe that he could keep the lid on the caldron that had been seething since the assassination.

There was the Church, though.

The Philippines is the only Christian nation in Asia. Although it has a significant Muslim minority in the south, growing numbers of adherents to Protestant evangelical sects, and two homegrown churches, the Aglipayan and the Iglesia ni Cristo, it is overwhelmingly a Roman Catholic country. About 85 percent of all Filipinos (the rapidly growing population stood at 55 million around the time of the assassination) are Catholics. And Filipino Catholics are among the world's most fervent adherents to the faith. Annual reenactments of the crucifixion, in which huge crowds solemnly observe young men voluntarily being nailed to a cross for a few moments, are just one of the more graphic examples of the depth of religious devotion. By sheer numbers, then, and by commitment, the Church can speak for, and to, almost all Filipinos.

The Catholic religion, which was brought to the Philippines in the sixteenth century by Spanish friars and imposed by them over the indigenous animistic faiths, is the main reason for the largely erroneous notion that the Philippines has much in common with the onetime Spanish colonies of Latin America. Even though the Spanish language has long since faded into disuse, newcomers to the Philippines inevitably cite similarities to countries like Nicaragua and El Salvador. Yet the Philippines is intrinsically and inseparably Asian, as much so as Thailand or China.

Politically, the Catholic Church in the Philippines was years behind the volatile churches of Latin America. It had its radical heroes, though. Beginning in the 1970s, a handful of young priests had taken off their cassocks and gone into the mountains with the Communist guerrillas of the New People's Army. One of these, Conrado Balweg, developed a reputation as a kind of Robin Hood. He was admired by poor Filipinos throughout the archipelago and hunted, unsuccessfully, by the military. A few other young clerics traveled to Central America and stayed there for years, studying liberation theology at work in the field but never succeeding in transferring it to their homeland. A relative handful of nuns also espoused leftist views and, as is not uncommon among large Filipino families where brothers and sisters often take widely divergent paths, one of the most outspoken was Sister Christine Tan, a sister of Bienvenido Tan, a wealthy businessman and a powerful attorney who was appointed a counsel to the Agrava panel investigating the Aquino assassination.

But the great majority of Filipino clergy were deeply conservative. True, many chafed at the abuses of the Marcos regime and its military personnel, but few were willing or thought it advisable to follow the route of their revolutionary counterparts in Latin America.

Probably in no hierarchy in the world is the pattern of behavior for underlings more clearly established at the top than in the Catholic Church. And perhaps in no other country is the direction more closely obeyed by those at the lower levels than in the Philippines. As a result, some of the more daring priests working in the Philippines tend to be foreigners, particularly Americans, Irishmen, and Australians, or Filipinos who have been educated abroad.

Six years before the Aquino killing, while martial law was still very much in force, President Jimmy Carter was bringing pressure to bear on U.S. allies who were notorious human rights abusers. One of these was Ferdinand Marcos. Bishop Francisco Claver, a Filipino Jesuit who was ordained in Baltimore and held a doctorate in anthropology from the University of Colorado, told me at that time that he regretted that an American president had to take the initiative in what was so obviously a Philippine domestic concern. The struggle for human rights advances should be led by the Church, Claver said.

The nominal head of the Church in the Philippines was Cardinal Sin, who was appointed archbishop of Manila in 1974. At that time, he was a regular visitor to Malacañang Palace, celebrating Mass there and attending parties with the Marcoses and their friends. The thought of involving himself with a man like Claver, who though innately conservative seemed a firebrand by comparison with himself, would never have crossed Sin's mind.

Marcos had warned young priests that if they continued to encourage the Communist rebels, he would not hesitate to "utilize force and violence to stop illegal force and violence utilized against the state." Claver said that those priests who joined the rebels did so out of "frustration" and that he sometimes felt that "violence was the only alternative" to counter the excesses of martial law.

By 1983, the numbers of outspoken Church dissidents had increased, but they were still a distinct minority. Cardinal Sin remained conservative, but the temper of his flock was changing. In a country where half the population was in its teens or younger, the cardinal was finding himself out of step with an impatient generation. Sin was also beginning to realize that his efforts at influencing Marcos to institute change by working from within the regime were proving dismally unsuccessful. Gradually, he came to understand that a Church that was going to be an instrument for reform would have to join the people, and that meant going into the streets.

Soon after the assassination, Sin began speaking about the "Parliament of the Streets." The phrase grew out of student and leftist protest demonstrations that began during the period of martial law and, over an extended period of time, took on middle-class respectability. The Philippine parliament, the *Batasang Pambansa* in Tagalog, was housed in a sprawling complex of cream-colored buildings set on beautifully cared-for rolling lawns in the far reaches of Quezon City. Built in 1978, the main session hall was huge, an imitation of the United Nations General Assembly hall, its expansive floor thickly carpeted in deep blue, its walls paneled with oiled nara wood, a Philippine mahogany. Salvador Laurel, an assemblyman at the time that the building was inaugurated, recalled thinking that it was ostentatious. Moreover, Laurel said, for some reason the legislature was swarming with flies. "I think they had to hire a professional exterminator to rid the place of flies, but during our first days there we didn't dare open our mouths."

Even after the flies were eliminated, opening one's mouth in parliament seldom amounted to much more than a physical exercise. From Malacañang, Marcos was able to observe the assembly sessions over closed-circuit television, and his party, the New Society Movement, held an uncontestable majority. So, people looking for a voice in government formed their own "Parliament of the Streets."

This "parliament" was the continual round of demonstrating and speech-making that went on, almost exclusively, in Manila. While there were occasional mass rallies in provincial cities and towns, including one in the market town of Escalante, on the island of Negros, that resulted in the massacre of twenty-seven demonstrators and caused a brief nationwide flurry of outrage, the action that mattered took place in the capital. This is common in virtually all developing nations, where the centers of government, finance, and social innovation are one and the same. Mendiola Bridge, the spacious Liwasang Bonifacio in front of the main post office, the bayfront Luneta park, and scores of gritty roads became regular forums for "parliament" sessions. But because the participants came from such diverse backgrounds and had diverse complaints, the "Parliament of the Streets" all too frequently deteriorated into disjointed shouting matches, and often no more than a few thousand people turned out, many of them simply idle curiosity seekers.

A key problem was the growing contest for control of the crowds between what had become known as the "Yellows," the predominantly middle-class Aquino supporters who were identified by their yellow

T-shirts, dresses, or headbands, and the "Reds," the Communist or Communist-front organization members. As became evident early on, the Communists were highly organized and disciplined. The "Yellows," who in every sense were moderates, quickly realized that they faced the very real danger of being taken over by the far left. Yet they didn't want to alienate the Communists or lose their organizational talents. Fortunately for the "Yellows," the "Reds" understood that their time had not come, that if they were to take control of the "Parliament of the Streets" they would lose the all-important middle class. The result was an uneasy standoff.

Among the regulars in the streets was Elmer Mercado. A talented speaker, Mercado came from the same mold that formed "student leaders" throughout Asia. In his mid-twenties, he no longer was a student at all but the chairman of an underground organization called the League of Filipino Students which, he said, had 10,500 members. Because he was wanted by the police, he would appear briefly in public, speak, and then slip away. His principal role was organizing university students as an antigovernment force. In a conversation that took place on the broad steps of the main post office during a discouragingly small demonstration in October 1984, Mercado said a major problem in keeping the "parliament" focused was that different classes of Filipinos had differing goals. "The professionals, the Makati crowd, the middle class, for them it's enough to determine who killed Ninoy and ascribe guilt. But ordinary people, students and workers, they won't be satisfied with that alone. For them, for us, there can be nothing less than the removal of the regime. You've got to understand that people are dissatisfied with their lives because their economic situation is so bad and they put all the blame on the Marcos regime. That means there's a basic difference between the great numbers of ordinary Filipinos and the middle and upper classes. It's going to take a great deal of organizational work to come to grips with these differing concerns. For now, all we can do is continue the protests while continuing to try organizing at the grass roots."

This was where Cardinal Sin came in. Although he once described himself as "not the marching kind" and, indeed, he never ventured into the streets at the head of a demonstration, his comments from the pulpit had enormous impact. The problem was that Sin vacillated. On one Sunday his homily at Mass might incorporate a direct and scathing attack on President Marcos, blaming him for corrupting the government and instilling a climate of fear in the country. The next week he was fully capable of calling for "peace and reconciliation" with the regime. On Marcos's birthday, September 11, 1985, he stood alongside the president at the Luneta and embraced him warmly, after which the two released doves of peace into the sky. The cardinal received a lot of criticism for that act, the most commonly heard being that he was "a slippery customer." But he merely shrugged off his detractors, insisting that Marcos was "one of my flock." More often than not, though, Sin left the interpretation of his words and actions up to the individual.

He preferred to describe his artful dodging in, of all things, automotive terms. "If a car has nothing but brakes it will never move forward," he once said. "The brakes are the conservatives in the Church. But, if a car has nothing but an accelerator, it will crash. The accelerator is the radicals among us. For a car to function properly, there has to be a judicious combination of brakes and accelerator. That's me. When necessary, I am an accelerator and people accuse me of being a radical. When the situation calls for it, I am the brakes . . . because I have to make sure these people don't lead us down the road to destruction."

Some insightful anti-Marcos figures said Sin probably was the most crucial player in the struggle between the regime and its opponents, including the Communists. "The cardinal is the key to everything," said Napolean Rama of JAJA, one of the stronger Aquino advocacy groups. "He's the only man in the country whom Marcos fears, the only man he'll listen to because he carries the full weight of the Roman Catholic Church."

Sin also was subject to criticism because of his supposed political ambitions—to become president of the Philippines as well as the first Asian pope—ambitions he denied absolutely and repeatedly. He tended to portray his role in the Philippines as that of an honest broker, or sometimes as a bridge, seeking to span the rift between the regime and the people.

Like Mrs. Marcos, Sin freely tossed around the terms *love* and *beautiful* in conversation. (She named the city buses Love Buses and had big pink Valentine hearts painted on their sides, a mockery of the rattletrap vehicles and the broken roads they plied.) But the prelate and the First Lady had little else in common. In fact, their mutual distaste was well known in Manila's loftier social circles. Through her close friend Bienvenido Tantoco, Philippine ambassador to the Vatican, she tried several times to have Sin transferred out of the capital. Her efforts came to nothing, in part because of Sin's close relationship with Pope John Paul II. Friends of hers said she passed snide remarks about him, more spiteful than her husband's occasional grumbling references to "meddling friars." Sin, in turn, once told an interviewer that he would listen to Imelda when she came to him, "because she is the First Lady," but otherwise he didn't take her seriously. He recalled a visit from her on Christmas Eve of 1985: "She was the one talking and I was the one listening. She talked for two hours. She was talking about problems, about Philippine insurgency, the usual explanation she gives when she is talking to people. And I just listened to her. . . . And she is crying . . . she was actually shedding tears. . . . But when she was talking, I did not contradict her. I did not say a word. Why should I? I just listened. So, how could she be angry with me? I did not argue. I didn't do anything."

Sin's recollection of Mrs. Marcos's worrying aloud to him about the Communist insurgency certainly rang true. She was using a ploy both she and her husband frequently resorted to, and who better to use it with at a time of crisis than the most important Catholic priest in the country? Sin clearly was uncomfortable in discussing and dealing with communism in the Philippines. It was on this issue, more than any other, that he was at odds with the liberation theologians of Latin America and, more to the point, with the young priests and nuns of his own parishes. He would, when pressed, offer clerical banalities like, "We can hate the sin but love the sinner, we can hate communism but love the Communist." But his heart wasn't in it. In some of the dirt-poor *barrios,* priests who, with their parishioners, faced hunger, disease, and the brutality of army troops turned to the guerrillas and thus were labeled Communists. Sin lived in the luxury of Villa San Miguel, tucked behind high, whitewashed concrete walls in the suburb of Mandaluyong, with a swimming pool in the basement and beautiful gardens in which to stroll.

Furthermore, he made no bones about his feelings for the United States, where two of his sisters lived. "I love that country" he told an American journalist. "I am very biased." His bias extended even to a tolerance for U.S. interference in Philippine domestic affairs. "I think it is normal for America to interfere in our politics," he said. "It is loaning money to us because we are very poor, and it is normal when you are loaning money to put down conditions." Before he could be questioned too closely, though, he slipped into one of his escape-route jokes: "Of course, there are some abuses. Money is a necessary evil, and even though it is the excrement of the devil, it is a good fertilizer."

Sin's well-known pro-American attitude was, of course, anathema to the Communists as well as to non-Communist nationalists. It was, however, realistic. The Philippines needed the United States, economically, militarily, and psychologically, and if an accurate survey could have been conducted throughout the archipelago, it probably would have shown that the majority of people were willing to accept U.S. interference. Even though Japan had replaced the United States as the Philippines' leading economic aid donor, U.S.-backed multilateral aid was more significant. Just as importantly, Japan took many of its foreign affairs cues from the United States. As to military ties, the Philippines not only received some $500 million in American arms assistance but was under the so-called U.S. defense umbrella in the Pacific. Conversely, the United States needed the Philippines, in part because it needed all the Southeast Asian friends it could get in the post-Vietnam era and, more specifically, because it needed the military bases.

But these were practical ties—aid, money, bases. Of greater significance in the relationship between the two countries was the psychological and emotional bond between Filipinos and Americans. A direct outgrowth of the colonial era and the comradeship of the war in the Pacific, this intangible tie was far more important to Filipinos, to whom Mother America always loomed large whether they loved her or hated her, than to Americans, for whom the Philippines was rarely more than a fleeting curiosity. Marcos continually played on his personal war record and his friendship with various American officers for political advantage. More than forty years after the war ended, General MacArthur remained a national hero in the Philippines. When a rumor began circulating in the fall of 1983 that his aged widow, Jean, was planning a sentimental journey to Manila, it became front-page news. (She didn't make the trip.) A kind of time warp blurred popular images of Americans in the Philippines, from the obvious wartime origins of the jeepney, to the common reference to things "Stateside," to the way that every American male was hailed on the street by hawkers, beggars, prostitutes, and just friendly kids—"Hey, Joe!"

Thus, millions of Filipinos shared Cardinal Sin's personal bias for America. Despite mass poverty and the abuses of the Marcos regime, the great majority of people were deeply religious and committed to attaining or maintaining middle-class values. They wanted improvements but were unwilling to throw out the baby with the bath water.

There was the Communist Party, though.

6

THE REDS

Communism had no right to succeed in the Philippines. The country was rich in natural resources, its people were individualistic, God-fearing, and instinctively capitalistic, and they were powerfully motivated to participate in a democratic government. The potential for the Philippines to become a chapter in the Asian economic success story that included Japan, South Korea, Taiwan, and Singapore was real, and this potential, combined with the power of the Catholic Church and the popularity of the United States, should have made the Marcos regime impregnable to communism. Yet the barometers of the U.S. and Philippine intelligence agencies showed plainly that, in the five to six years immediately preceding the Aquino assassination, Communist strength had risen in direct proportion to the spread of corruption from Malacañang Palace and was continuing to grow during the chaotic aftermath of the shooting.

Marcos and his cronies had been draining billions of dollars out of the country since the early 1970s. The economy was in a tailspin that could take years or even decades to reverse. Senior military officers, emulating their civilian bosses in Manila, helped themselves to funds intended for troops in the field. Ordinary soldiers, deprived of arms, ammunition, rations, and clothing, turned from defenders of the poor to vultures, raping, murdering, and stealing food, cash, and whatever else they could snatch from peasant villages.

The poor, with nowhere else to go, turned to the Communist Party of the Philippines and its armed wing, the New People's Army. The Communists, adroit at making the most of this kind of opportunity, assumed the roles that should have been filled by the armed forces, local government, and civilian welfare workers—providing villagers with defense, help with harvests, and rudimentary health care. Even village priests could see that the NPA were not devils. NPA soon became shorthand for "Nice People Around."

By the late 1970s, however, the Communists had become at least as oppressive as the armed forces had been, taxing villagers, conducting kangaroo courts, and summarily executing supposed enemies. Although martial law was in effect, the Philippine army was unable, or unwilling, to confront them. Marcos limited the battle to anti-Communist propaganda and ineffectual policing, responding to the symptoms while ignoring the disease.

During World War II, Southeast Asian Communists had vigorously fought the Japanese, cooperating in varying degrees with the Western Allies, but with peace these forces were lost to pro-Western governments. For instance, in the Philippines, the predecessors of the NPA called themselves the Anti-Japanese People's Army when they were formed in 1942. Better known by their Tagalog abbreviation, *Hukbalahap,* or Huks, they made a significant contribution to the victory over the Japanese. But internal dissension weakened the Huks, and the returning U.S. Army wiped out their remnants.

In 1969, the Communist Party of the Philippines reformed itself and called its reconstituted guerrilla force the New People's Army. According to Bernabe Buscayno, who later became the NPA's commander in chief, its armed strength consisted of thirty-five men.

By mid 1976, "Commander Dante," which was Buscayno's *nom de guerre,* claimed that the NPA had 3,000 men under arms, although U.S. military specialists placed the figure closer to 2,000. By mid 1984, though, the NPA and U.S. Senate staff analysts Carl W. Ford and Frederick Z. Brown concurred that the NPA had 12,500 members. Still, this figure didn't begin to compare with the 200,000-man Armed Forces of the Philippines. But its area of operation had spread from the mountainous regions of central Luzon island to far-flung areas of the country where, only a few years earlier, it hadn't even existed.

Both the Marcos and Reagan administrations claimed they were seeing red everywhere. Whether the two governments were intentionally overemphasizing the Communist menace is questionable. Certainly this tactic would have been useful for Marcos. As for Reagan, he showed until the very last moments of the Marcos regime that he preferred doing business with the devil he knew. Nevertheless, it was easy to see that each year the Communists were becoming far more active. In 1985, Philippine Constabulary chief Lieutenant General Fidel Ramos stated that fifteen people were being killed daily as a result of "NPA-related violence." The number included guerrillas, soldiers, and innocent bystanders caught in the cross fire. More to the point, Ramos said, the NPA was initiating 70 percent of the incidents. The Communists could launch attacks almost at will, and their hit-and-run tactics were frightening and effective.

Armed and political activity on this scale was a far cry from a decade earlier when "Commander Dante" was captured with his pregnant wife and tried along with fifty-five other Communists. U.S. influence was then at its peak in the Philippines. U.S. industry was investing heavily, and products by Ford, Chrysler, General Motors, Coca-Cola, Pepsi-Cola, Procter & Gamble, Colgate-Palmolive, Goodyear, Goodrich, Firestone, IBM, Xerox, Shakey's, A&W, and MacDonald's were visible everywhere and selling fast. The middle class was on the move, and fabulous shopping centers that wouldn't have been out of place in any comfortable American suburb were opening at Green Hills and Harrison's Plaza in Manila.

Even if he had not become a Communist and gone into the mountains and changed his name to "Commander Dante," Bernabe Buscayno would almost certainly never have had the opportunity to go shopping at Harrison's Plaza or to lunch on pizza at Shakey's. He was the son of a plantation overseer, one of eighteen children, a peasant boy whose formal education ended after his second year of high school. His background made him a rarity in the party and in the NPA, where leaders tended to be middle-class university graduates. His authentic peasant credentials were flaunted by the Communists to recruit well-meaning university students and recent graduates. That the universities would be spawning grounds for Communist leaders was neither surprising nor peculiar to the Philippines.

At the time of his trial, Buscayno was thirty-three years old, his boyish looks accented by a Beatles-style bob. He would serve nine years, his young son living with him in the prison, before being released in a general amnesty, looking older but as confident as ever. "I studied Marx on my own and learned how to analyze the Philippines situation through his writings," he said. "I'm absolutely convinced that my views are correct." Those views were doctrinaire Marxism. Buscayno believed that the Philippine Communists must concentrate their organizational efforts on the landless peasants and the poor urban workers, thereby gradually building popular reaction against Marcos. "Martial law is hindering us, no doubt, but political repression will eventually work like a dam, building up water until it bursts through." He felt that the powerful U.S. military and economic presences would hasten the process. "As long as the United States maintains military bases in our country over which the Filipino people have no authority and as long as American and other multinational corporations control our economy, we cannot consider ourselves independent."

Clergymen who worked among the poorest people confirmed that the Communists were limiting most of their armed activity to self-defense while they emphasized what Buscayno called "mobilizing and educating" the most susceptible parts of the population. "We don't make any effort to hold or control any areas because this would lead to decisive engagements and we would lose," he said. "In the present conditions here, we have no intention of launching a war." A priest who worked among a minority tribal group in northern Luzon told me that his parishioners had been "bitterly offended by the army's insensitivity and arrogance, while the guerrillas have proven themselves to be of the people and frequently provide practical assistance in their everyday lives."

The regime stifled public debate on social grievances, angering a people who by nature are gregarious and love nothing better than to gossip and argue. Occasionally, though, the pattern would be broken. In mid September 1977, for instance, an exceptional series of articles by Lucino M. Rebamonton appeared in the Manila *Evening Post,* documenting government abuses on the eastern island of Samar. One of the articles referred to a "vexing and potentially explosive battle for the hearts and minds of the masses" that was being waged on the island between the Communists and the government. The writer left no doubt that the authorities were at fault, citing "indifference of local government officials, bureaucratic abuses, unemployment, massive poverty, rampant criminality, lack of health service facilities and a pervasive sense of neglect."

By 1984, when U.S. Senate analysts Ford and Brown wrote their report, conditions had not changed—the insurgency had simply spread to more islands. Indeed, their report could have been taken for an installment in the *Evening Post* series: "There is widespread resentment of corruption, cronyism and economic inequality. . . . Most disturbing is the fact that the insurgency—the rationale for imposing martial law fourteen years ago—is stronger today than ever before."

By the middle of 1985, with the economy deep in trouble, with workers losing jobs, employers closing plants, creditors demanding repayment, and the poorest of the poor starving, big businessmen felt it was time to talk to the Communists.

In October, a representative group from the Makati Business Club met secretly with members of the National Democratic Front, an umbrella organization that covered the CPP and the NPA. Afterward, several of the executives acknowledged sheepishly that they were "positively impressed" by what they'd heard. "Businessmen are becoming more open to the economic appeals of the Communists," said Jesus P. Estanislao, a highly regarded economist who worked with the Center for Research and Communications, a well-funded think tank backed by both the Church and big business. "The Communists have done their work well. I notice a significant increase in sympathy among members of the business community and the professionals. There's no doubt that the businessmen are allowing themselves to be deceived. But this shows how desperate they are."

This desperation was felt even more keenly by less affluent Filipinos whose fears and concerns provided the Communists with a splendid whetstone against which to hone their weapons. Two weeks after the businessmen met with the NDF, some five hundred middle-class people attended a symposium organized by a panel of pro-Communist clergymen and academics at a Church-run center in Manila. The overwhelming worry of the audience was that religion would be crushed if the Communists took power. When a priest who had spent fifteen years in Central America assured them that this would not happen, they applauded enthusiastically. No one addressed the question of Communist brutality. Living in Southeast Asia as they were, these white-collar Filipinos seemed oddly insensitive to the stories pouring out of Indochina of wholesale torture and murder.

Through well-conceived military actions and clever, low-key public relations work, such as the Makati meeting and the symposium, the

CPP-NPA were laying the groundwork for widespread acceptance of their active participation in what they envisaged as a "united front" government. The incessant guerrilla fighting and the street demonstrations were the showpieces; the real goal was a political solution.

The Communist movement in the Philippines essentially was "homegrown," with no supply of arms or funds from abroad. Operatives claimed that they had made a single purchase of "several hundred" Soviet-made AK-47 rifles from the Palestine Liberation Organization in 1982. The agents who handled the deal had been caught, and twenty-eight were arrested. Since then, the Communists had relied entirely on a program of *agaw armas,* or "grabbing arms," from the government forces. Ironically, they had found the Soviet weapons to be more reliable than the American-made M-16s with which the armed forces were supplied. But because the M-16s were more readily available, they were painstakingly converting the AK-47s to accept M-16 ammunition, much of which they bought from underpaid soldiers.

During an interview in Manila in October 1985, a central committee member said that over recent years the party had been making what he termed "great efforts" to gain international support from other Communist countries—which he declined to identify—but the offers they'd received had had strings attached. "Under the circumstances, after all our sacrifices, we're not interested in letting the lion out only to let the tiger in," the official concluded. He referred to his own life as an illustration of sacrifices Filipino Communists were making. Only weeks before, he and his wife, both in their early thirties, had left "the hills," a term used to cover all guerrilla locations, after fighting with the NPA since 1979. Now they were assigned to the capital, to coordinate party activities with student and labor organizations and special-interest groups. "We have been fortunate in being allowed to serve together," he said, "but we have had to forgo the pleasure of having a family. This is not at all unusual, I assure you. Many make these and much greater sacrifices, including the sacrifice of their lives, every day."

Despite the pinch-penny level of their operations, at the end of 1985 the guerrillas intended within the next three to five years to invade certain smaller towns and hold them for a few days at a time. Such shows of force would demonstrate to the government that they and the Communists were at a point of "strategic stalemate." At the same time, the CPP expected to be able to stage frequent industrial strikes and civil uprisings in Manila and other major cities, at least temporarily paralyzing the nation's industrial base and political machinery. With a "strategic stalemate" achieved, the party then planned to force its way into a coalition "united front" government with moderate anti-Marcos parties.

Developments beyond that point could not yet be perceived. In all likelihood, whoever replaced Marcos would be only incrementally more acceptable to the Communists, nearly as much a creature of the United States as his predecessor was. So, in one form or another, the struggle would continue long after Marcos's departure.

What was evident was that the Communists dreaded the possibility, remote though it seemed at the time, that Marcos might be replaced by a genuinely popular president. They recognized that a large proportion of their members, particularly the young foot soldiers of the NPA and the unemployed men who could be scraped together on short notice to throw stones during demonstrations, were not committed Communists. People like these might desert if a popular leader was found and more jobs and better living conditions became available. A man identified only as "Carlos," the chief organizer for the National Democratic Front in the Visayans, a group of islands between Luzon to the north and Mindanao to the south, acknowledged in an interview in mid 1985 that "right now, our revolution is at the nationalist level, it's not necessarily communism." Thus, the Communists felt it crucial to keep alive the notion that whoever succeeded Marcos would be a dictator under whom the poor would continue to suffer.

There is no question that the Aquino killing gave the Communist Party of the Philippines a great boost. One of the first top-level American officials to realize how dramatically antigovernment sentiment had risen was Admiral William J. Crowe, Jr. Crowe, who visited the Philippines in March 1984 as commander of U.S. military forces in the Pacific, was not a typical military officer. In addition to being a graduate of the U.S. Naval Academy at Annapolis, he held a master's degree in personnel administration from Stanford University and a doctorate in politics from Princeton University. Although his trip was intended to be a fairly routine investigation of alleged instability in the Philippines, he was shocked by what he saw and heard. Upon his return to Washington, he submitted a most unroutine report that supported studies conducted by the Central Intelligence Agency and the U.S. embassy: The NPA was stronger and more of a threat than Marcos recognized. If the Marcos regime fell, which was a distinct possibility, the United States might very well be forced to abandon the Clark and Subic bases.

Crowe's assessment probably was alarmist in that virtually every non-Communist potential successor to Marcos favored retaining the bases agreement, and top officials of the CPP-NPA acknowledged that they were at least fifteen years from *possibly* having the armed strength to topple the government militarily. But Crowe's warning intensified the U.S. demands on Marcos for reforms. When Assistant Secretary of Defense Richard L. Armitage received Crowe's report, he passed it on to Defense Secretary Caspar W. Weinberger, who decided to have Crowe personally brief President Reagan. According to an official who was familiar with the briefing, which took place at the White House on April 23, 1984, Crowe, in analyzing the military situation throughout the Pacific, emphasized the rapidly expanding Soviet presence centered at the strategic Camranh Bay base in Vietnam. He told the president that the cornerstone of American strategy was the Philippines, with its two virtually irreplaceable bases. That same year, Congress approved a new $900 million agreement to take effect in 1985 that would extend American control of Clark and Subic through 1990. Of equal importance, the admiral told the president, was the United States' long history of genuinely warm relations with the Philippines, the sort of relationship that money alone couldn't buy. Crowe then told Reagan that these vital interests were threatened by the corrupt and repressive Marcos regime, by the political cronyism that not only had bled the economy but infected the Armed Forces of the Philippines, and by the growing power of the CPP-NPA.

The president was so impressed by Crowe's assessment that, according to the official who knew what transpired, he turned to Weinberger after the admiral left and said, "If we ever need a new chairman [of the Joint Chiefs of Staff], this is the guy." Just over a year later, Crowe was installed as chairman.

By early 1985, an inter-agency task force organized by the National Security Council, with the backing of Armitage, had drafted a secret study called "U.S. Policy Towards the Philippines." The study, which had taken about a year to complete, described the Marcos regime as a "kleptocracy" and the president as an inveterate liar who would promise anything but deliver nothing. The middle-level officials who wrote the report believed that the only way to bring about change in the country would be to "mousetrap" Marcos—to force him to reform the military, free the press, dismantle crony-controlled enterprises—and thus to weaken his position for the presidential elections that were scheduled for 1987. Knowing that Reagan would resist anything he viewed as a deliberate attempt to undercut Marcos, Armitage sold the recommendations to the president on the basis that Marcos "is part of the problem, but he is part of the solution, too."

Thus, over the long run, the bureaucracy would force Reagan's hand. But the change in his position on the Philippines would evolve slowly, making repeated turns on itself, and at the moment the president was far from being ready to help any of Marcos's opponents.

Meanwhile, the action in Manila had shifted to the political arena.

7

A STURDY ALLY

The parliamentary elections that had drawn Ninoy Aquino back home were set for May 14, 1984. At stake were 183 of the 200 seats in the National Assembly. Under the constitution, Marcos would directly appoint the remaining seventeen. The president's KBL party controlled more than 90 percent of the seats in the outgoing assembly, and as election day approached few anticipated a significant shift. The opposition parties were, as usual, in disarray. And, as usual, the cards were stacked against the president's opponents. For example, UNIDO, the largest and best-organized opposition group, was fielding 180 candidates. But only eighty-four of them would be permitted to place their party's inspectors in voting precincts to try to monitor the notoriously corrupt vote-casting and -counting systems.

The official explanation for limiting the number of UNIDO inspectors given by the Marcos-controlled Commission on Elections, or COMELEC, was worthy of a master rule-maker. UNIDO was entitled to "dominant" opposition party status in only seven of the country's thirteen administrative regions, and only the "dominant" opposition party was permitted to field its own inspectors. All others would be subject to the government-controlled inspectors. Such was a typical example of how the Marcos regime did its business. In another regime, the strongman would simply stuff the ballot boxes and be done with it. But here was Marcos again wreathing himself in an aura of propriety through maddeningly legalistic rules.

Ernesto Maceda, Aquino's lawyer in New York when he was trying to get a new passport for his return home, was now acting as UNIDO's campaign manager in the Manila metropolitan area and in central Luzon. Entering a contest against Marcos without one's own inspectors, he said, was akin to being "Don Quixote against the windmill."

But UNIDO and the rest of the splintered opposition groups were jousting with one another as well. Francisco Tatad, Marcos's onetime information minister who later broke with the president, was refused permission to run as a UNIDO candidate from Quezon City. So he formed his own four-man Social Democratic Party ticket.

In Quezon City and Makati, three UNIDO candidates quit the race for various reasons. One dropout, Domingo Jhocson, Jr., said that he didn't feel right about challenging a candidate personally selected by "my *compadre,* the mayor." Mayor Yabut, it developed, was a longtime friend and business partner of Jhocson's.

The anti-Marcos forces couldn't even agree about whether to go through with the elections. Ninoy Aquino's younger brother, Butz, was agitating for a boycott, leading mass demonstrations against the elections, insisting they couldn't possibly be even "fairly clean." Aquino maintained that at least half of the country's 25 million registered voters would boycott the elections "because they don't believe in the process of elections under a dictatorship." He also predicted that because "Marcos and the U.S. would like this exercise to boost the credibility of his government . . . he will allow anywhere from one fourth to one third of the opposition candidates to win." These guesses would turn out to be respectively off, and on, the mark.

Aquino was backed in his boycott drive by a mixed bag from the near and far left. Those who knew the limits of his political expertise questioned who was pulling the strings, Aquino or the leftists. Aquino realized the risks, he said, but thought he could control his allies. "We're trying to use each other, of course, I know that," he said in an interview. "But if I didn't think I could win them over I wouldn't be doing this." Aquino would have done well to have taken a lesson from former Cambodian head of state Prince Norodom Sihanouk, who once predicted that the Khmer Rouge would use him for as long as he was of value to them and then would spit him out "like a cherry pit." Aquino was a wishful thinker; Sihanouk had it right.

While Aquino tried to whip up boycott fervor, Laurel and his large, powerful family were betting that many Filipinos were angry enough about the assassination and bitter enough about their empty pockets that they would vote against Marcos, if not for UNIDO. Furthermore, the Laurels had their eye on the brass ring: If the opposition in general, and UNIDO in particular, could establish a visible presence in the new assembly, Doy would be in a strong position to emerge as the principal challenger to Marcos in the forthcoming presidential elections. Laurel, therefore, did not run for an assembly seat but began the longer-term task of building a national constituency by stumping the country on behalf of the organization's candidates. He was able to enlist the active support of Corazon Aquino and other members of her husband's family who decided that boycotting was a bad idea.

Well before the elections, opposition candidates got a good taste of what they would be up against on May 14. During four days of voter registration at the end of March and the beginning of April, an estimated 2 million fraudulent names were added to the voter lists. Primarily, these were the so-called flying voters, poor people who were paid a few pesos apiece by the KBL to register, and later vote, in several polling stations. At the same time, 3 million potential voters decided to avoid the procedure, possibly because they had been swayed by the boycott idea.

Their abstention was a great disappointment to many, including José Concepcion, Jr., a prominent businessman who, six months earlier, had created and become chairman of a volunteer group known as the National Citizens Movement for Free Elections, or NAMFREL. It was intended to counterbalance COMELEC, the government's election body. NAMFREL and COMELEC would become household words throughout the Philippines by the time the elections were over.

Concepcion, along with his new organization, would be a major force in familiarizing Filipinos and the world with just how corrupt the country's electoral system was. Dissatisfied though he was, he didn't simply go away and sulk. A large, fleshy man, who wore thick, black-rimmed glasses and never seemed to be without a soggy cigar unraveling in his mouth, he waded into the shabby COMELEC headquarters in Intramuros, Manila's ancient walled city, and did battle with chairman Vicente Santiago, Marcos's appointee there. And he twisted arms among businessmen, extracting favors that would prove critical in the National Assembly polls and even more so in the coming presidential elections. His catchy slogan for NAMFREL captured the imagination of millions of Filipinos: "Better to light a candle than curse the darkness."

With perseverence, Concepcion was able to wring from Santiago a new regulation requiring all voters to have their fingers stained purple with indelible ink, thereby making it difficult to cast more than one ballot. It seemed like a good idea. Concepcion was pleased. Laurel said the stain would help opposition candidates. UNIDO tested the ink and found it could not be removed. But either the formula was changed later or the "flying voters" were better at making things disappear, for on election day they found that a little alcohol or turpentine, or even spit, rubbed on a finger got rid of the ink.

And yet, despite intimidation and violence, some 90 percent of the country's 25 million registered voters cast ballots when the time came. Cory Aquino had stumped hard for the opposition coalition, comprising UNIDO and her late husband's organization, the Pilipino Democratic Party-Laban, or PDP-Laban, and she'd been effective. Her one basic speech, reciting the story of events leading up to Ninoy's assassination, seldom failed to draw tears from her listeners. Although neither she nor they realized it at the time, her exposure during the campaign was to alter her image from that of simply the grieving widow to a political figure. In part because of Cory's active participation, voters cast many more of their ballots for opposition candidates, or against KBL candidates, than either side had guessed. A final count didn't emerge until mid June, a full month later, probably because COMELEC, under Marcos's direction, was fine-tuning the numbers and because NAMFREL was monitoring them closely.

Ultimately, fifty-nine opposition candidates won seats, tripling their strength. The president's party dropped from 90 percent control of the house to 70 percent. And the ruling party suffered its severest loss where it hurt most, in the greater-Manila area.

Because of its population of 8 million and, more importantly, its high visibility as the center of national and political life, Metro Manila was highly prized by both the government and the opposition. On top of all that, the governor of Metro Manila was Imelda Marcos. Thus, when the sophisticated voters of the capital gave the KBL only six of Metro Manila's twenty-one seats, the country read it as a clear rejection of the First Family.

For the moment, though, the president responded to the elections in two different ways. Seeking to calm jittery foreign lenders, he said that "only a strong and stable government could have conducted such a divisive political campaign. These election results also indicate there is no attempt on the part of government to cheat or change the results." He also let it be known that he had ordered an "intensive analysis" to determine whether Filipinos had voted against his party because of any particular government policies or whether they were repudiating "any individual person in the political leadership, like the president and the First Lady. If they did, we must know, and why."

Here was Marcos at his best again, asking his people if possibly the well-meaning president and his lady had let them down. Just in case, he said, we're going to look into the matter. And to help create the proper atmosphere, Imelda Marcos once again exited suddenly from the political stage, avoiding public appearances for about a month.

Marcos, in fact, considerably increased his standing with the Reagan administration. Reflecting judgments at the State Department, the U.S. embassy interpreted the election results positively, saying that the balloting had been conducted fairly and cleanly and that the vote and the emergence of bolder alternative newspapers showed that Marcos was beginning to heed Reagan's calls for reforms. Some American analysts continued to cling to those slender reeds for another year. But the more astute among them recognized that Marcos had no intention of instituting genuine reforms.

Seldom has a modern national leader been more Machiavellian than Ferdinand Marcos. Certainly, he was, as Butz Aquino guessed, fully capable of organizing the cheating to such a fine degree that the opposition would gain a stronger presence in the National Assembly while Marcos would gain a cleaner image in Washington. After all, he would firmly control the assembly. If he had given his nod, there would have been no holding back the savagery against possible opposition voters and no stinting on fraudulent counting. But it is also conceivable that Marcos simply misread the tea leaves, not recognizing how badly tarnished his image was, and that the outcome surprised him as much as it did the opposition.

In either case, credit had to go to Concepcion and NAMFREL, which mustered an astonishing 450,000 volunteers to watch the polls. Because of its support by the Church, NAMFREL attracted thousands of ordinary citizens who might not otherwise have risked clashing with the KBL-hired toughs and "flying voters." And because Concepcion was president of the $86 million Republic Flour Mills Corporation, he was able to attract high-level support, ranging from society women who did volunteer duty to companies that loaned computers. The technology enabled NAMFREL to conduct its own rapid tallying and announce trends long before COMELEC could come up with approved figures.

What Marcos probably did not perceive at the time was the invigorating effect that the elections were to have on the opposition. Even though he still controlled the National Assembly, his opponents had tasted victory, however limited. They began to use their newfound strength against the KBL more than against one another. Although individuals within the disparate opposition would continue to squabble, the huge turnout at the polls put an end to the groups that had fought for a boycott. Acknowledging that Filipinos would vote no matter how skeptical they were about an honest election, Butz Aquino and his more moderate backers joined the mainstream opposition.

Nonetheless, Marcos remained in control, aided by some of his most draconian powers from martial law. Under article six of the constitution, he still ruled by decree, and since he'd never reestablished the right of habeas corpus he could continue to arrest and hold his enemies for as long as he pleased without bringing charges against them.

Thus, from Washington, the moderate opposition didn't look viable. Just five months after the election, Reagan told the world that the only alternative to Marcos was the Communists. On October 21, he was asked in a debate with Walter Mondale in Kansas City, "What should you do and what can you do to prevent the Philippines from becoming another Nicaragua?" Reagan compared the Philippines to Iran before the fall of the shah. The parallels—particularly between the Communist Party of the Philippines and the Islamic fanatics who overthrew the shah—were largely spurious, but the analogy appealed to Reagan and other conservatives who saw the shah and Marcos as America's friends and ignored their domestic standings. "The shah had done our bidding and carried our load in the Middle East for quite some time," he said, "and I did think that it was a blot on our record that we let him down. Have things gotten better? The shah, whatever he might have done, was building low-cost housing and taking land away from the mullahs and distributing it to the peasants so they could be landowners, things of that kind. But, we turned it over to a maniacal fanatic who has slaughtered thousands and thousands of people, calling it 'executions.' ''

Continuing the comparison, Reagan went on, ''I know there are things there in the Philippines that do not look good to us from the standpoint right now of democratic rights, but what is the alternative? It is a large Communist movement to take over the Philippines. They have been our friends since their inception as a nation, and I think that we've had enough of [a] record of letting, under the guise of a revolution, someone that we thought was a little more right[ist] than we would be, letting that person go and then winding up with totalitarianism, pure and simple, as the alternative. I think that we're better off, for example, with the Philippines, of trying to retain their friendship and help them right the wrongs we see rather than throwing them to the wolves, and facing a Communist power in the Pacific.''

Asked if the U.S. military bases would be threatened by Marcos's removal from power, Reagan reiterated that, since Marcos would be replaced only by the Communists, his departure would certainly work against U.S. strategic interests.

The president's remarks were exploited by Marcos in the crony press. The moderate opposition felt stunned and betrayed. Here was irrefutable proof that the president of the United States was still standing solidly behind the regime just a few months after they had won a significant victory at the polls. The Reagan administration realized that the president had blundered and immediately issued a clarification, claiming that ''there is certainly recognition on everybody's part that there are other forces working for democratic change in the Philippines.'' State Department spokesman John Hughes said, ''I think what the president was saying was that the Philippines has been a sturdy ally of the United States and his policy is to try to work with President Marcos's government for the kind of change and reform that we would like to see.'' Continuing to defend the president, Hughes added that ''there is a very vigorous Communist insurgency in the Philippines and, if one were to look for a nondemocratic change in government, it would come likely from that particular source. And, clearly, that would not be something that the United States would find satisfactory.''

But the damage had already been done. Reagan's comments had been boiled down to their essence—Marcos or the Communists—and the moderates felt that they could not look to the United States for support. This reaction seemed to be of little consequence to the White House, though, and the administration, buoyed by the relatively honest National Assembly elections, pressed Marcos for another sign of reform. However, this request was too big for him to swallow. The Americans were asking him to retire twenty-seven "over-staying" generals, starting with his chief of staff, General Fabian Ver. Marcos needed these men and had kept them on past retirement age because of their deep personal loyalty to him. While the military establishment had taken a beating as a result of the Aquino assassination and the ongoing Agrava board hearings, it was Ver who had been stained the most. The White House reasoned that if he were replaced, the rest of the military could be more easily cleaned up. Ver's graceful retirement, followed, perhaps, by an appointment to a diplomatic post, would presumably be acceptable to both Filipinos and the United States.

What the administration was looking for, in a broader sense, was the "professionalization" of the Philippine military, replacing the top officers who'd been promoted solely on the basis of their loyalty to Marcos with field-tested professionals. Naturally, a substantial number of aging colonels and even some generals supported such a change. Their careers were playing out with little or no hope for promotion. Chief among them was Lieutenant General Fidel Ramos, who, as number two in the armed forces, had been passed over in favor of Ver for the top position. Ramos, more than anyone, wanted to see the institution of "professionalization."

Ramos was as professional as any officer in the Philippines. Not only was he a West Point graduate, but he had had combat experience in Korea and had commanded the Philippine forces that served briefly, though for the most part without distinction, in Vietnam. He also was genuinely respected by the majority of the younger officers and men. At fifty-six, he still looked the part of a soldier, lean and fit, though he saw no contradiction in lighting up a cigar at the end of a jog. He maintained his paratrooper's qualification with regular jumps, often into jungle outposts, carrying down little gifts, such as a case of beer, for his men. In addition his family had a record of public service.

Ramos and Ver both were cousins of Marcos's. But Ver's connections ran deeper. He and Marcos came from the same hometown, Sarrat, in Ilocos Norte province, and as Ilocanos, they were bound by tribal as well as familial ties. While Ver's blind devotion to Marcos, which he unflinchingly acknowledged, was the frequent topic of gossip and jibes, their "blood debt" ran both ways. Ver owed everything he was to Marcos, and Marcos relied entirely on Ver for his personal security. So intertwined were the lives of the two men that it would be almost impossible to say whether Ver's loyalty was payment for Marcos's favors or Marcos's payoffs to Ver were in return for his loyalty. Whichever the case, while Ramos was serving in Vietnam, Ver was serving at Marcos's side. He began as the then senator's chauffeur and graduated to the post of his adviser on military affairs. His advancement was not meteoric, though, and for years he was frozen in rank as a captain while Ramos rose to the prestigious title of chief of the tradition-steeped Philippine Constabulary, to which he'd been appointed after his Vietnam assignment. In this role he was charged with domestic security for the whole country. But Ramos's star began to fade when Marcos imposed martial law in 1972.

One of the president's first moves then was to vastly expand the military, from 58,000 men to over 200,000, and completely reorganize its structure. He placed Ramos and his Philippine Constabulary under the control of the Armed Forces of the Philippines; and from that point on, Marcos and the military were inseparably bound together. As long as the military remained loyal to him, he would remain in power. To ensure that loyalty, he rewarded the right people. The military budget was raised from $82 million to nearly $1 billion. The United States helped with annual military aid of about $85 million. Much of the money was misused, ending up in the pockets of selected officers and not in the field. Suddenly, officers who had been scraping by on military salaries were granted timber concessions and construction contracts, as well as carte blanche to conduct a variety of smuggling operations and control of the black market in dollars.

General Ver, the most loyal of the loyal, collected his due. He rose rapidly in rank and responsibility, taking charge of the country's key intelligence organization, the National Intelligence and Security Authority, or NISA, and the Presidential Security Command, a 6,000-man army within the army, which was charged with protecting the First Family. In time, the relationship extended to the next generation.

As First Family children Imee and Bong Bong (Imelda, Jr., and Ferdinand, Jr.) moved into politically powerful positions, she as a National Assembly member from Ilocos Norte, he as governor of the province, so did the children of the Ver family move into key military positions. The general's three sons, Irwin, a full colonel, Rexor, a lieutenant colonel, and Wyrlo, a major, took charge of the Presidential Security Command.

An even greater source of Ver's power was his domination of the country's intelligence network. The information he gathered on the president's enemies and friends was of inestimable value to Marcos. At the same time, he became privy to the Marcoses' most sensitive secrets.

In 1981, the president, ignoring the rule of seniority, made what would prove to be a fateful mistake. He pinned a fourth general's star on Ver's thick shoulders and appointed him chief of staff, with Ramos as his deputy. Ver was the only former enlisted man, the only nongraduate of the Philippine Military Academy or a Western equivalent, ever to be appointed chief. Working closely together, he and Marcos broke the military out of its American-style, apolitical mold and recast it as an extension of the presidency. From then on, generals were appointed or kept on past retirement age on the basis of their preparedness to swear fealty to Marcos rather than to the country.

Martial law had not displeased Ramos, any more than it did his military colleagues or the United States government; he believed it was required to reestablish the rule of law. But being passed over by the president in Ver's favor diminished his self-esteem. Furthermore, he began to grow concerned about the bigger picture, about the country deteriorating into a classic banana republic, with *el presidente* and *el generale* in lockstep, mocking all that he cherished about the flag and the constitution. Rather than turning on his commander in chief, which would have been out of character for him, he retreated into himself, becoming a wooden soldier who saluted on cue, obeyed orders automatically, and answered questions with prepared responses. And he kept his own counsel. Close friends knew he was chafing, giving rise to rumors that he had attempted to retire and that Marcos had refused his requests. But his wife, Amelita, whom Ramos and their friends called Ming, insisted that he would never tolerate a bad word about the president. "At home no one could say anything against Marcos, never!" she told an interviewer.

Other military men were quietly stewing, too. Their dissatisfaction originated with personal gripes, principally poor salaries and lagging promotions. With time, though, they grew agitated about the increasingly dismal image of the armed forces among the people of the Philippines. The problem had already become apparent in rural areas before the Aquino assassination. Country people saw the military as persecutors, not protectors. After the assassination, this view spread to the cities, particularly Manila, where armed troops were being sent into the streets alongside the police to quell anti-Marcos demonstrations. Although the mobs frequently provoked the troops, public sympathy inevitably turned against the military. It didn't matter if a student or a street urchin cast the first stone, an alternative newspaper could always manage to photograph a policeman swinging a truncheon or a soldier squeezing off a round at unarmed civilians.

Of much greater impact than these street clashes or even pillage and plunder in the countryside was the perception of the armed forces as being *Marcos's* army. He had imposed martial law, he had increased their strength five times, he had made their generals rich, he had ordered them to club and kill innocent people.

Had he ordered them to kill Aquino, too?

Ultimately, more than any other issue, the association between the military and the assassination came to nag at some younger officers, and it provided them with the vehicle they needed to popularize their grievances. Early in 1983, several months before Aquino was killed, five young graduates of the prestigious Philippine Military Academy brought together by Colonel Gregorio B. Honasan, a member of Defense Minister Juan Ponce Enrile's staff, had begun meeting occasionally in Manila to discuss their ethical—and personal—complaints. They agreed that the military needed to be reformed. After the assassination, this little corps of dissatisfied officers expanded quickly to about forty, who would remain the leaders. By the time the Agrava panel dispersed at the end of 1984, the organization had attracted 1,500 fellow officers, mainly captains, majors, and colonels.

A group this size was more than adequate to do a great deal of damage to the entire military structure, and to its political master. A coup d'etat was easily within reach. In other Southeast Asian nations, Thailand, for example, such a coup would have been quickly carried out. But, this being the Philippines, the frustrated officers felt the need for more talk, not just among themselves but with their seniors and with the public. And, of course, they would need a name and an acronym. At first they called themselves We Belong. That was soon changed to the cumbersome but all-encompassing REFORM Armed Forces of the Philippines Movement. The REFORM stood for Restore Ethics, Fair-mindedness, Order, Righteousness, and Morale, later boiled down to RAM, for Reform the Armed Forces Movement.

The young RAM officers didn't have to look very far to find a sympathetic father figure, two in fact. Ramos would be their first man, Enrile would follow, then almost immediately become dominant. Enrile, by far the more cunning of the two, would see in RAM an instrument for furthering his own ambitions. Ramos's mind didn't work that way. He was still faithful to Marcos, his commander in chief, and he was still a good soldier, second in command to Ver. His future, and much more, would depend on how Ver fared before the Agrava Fact-Finding Board.

8

*T*HE DEAN AND ROSIE SHOW

I'm not asking you necessarily, Lord, to tell us who pulled the trigger, or who was behind who pulled the trigger. But please, please lead us to a conclusion that will bring peace and harmony among my Filipino brothers and sisters. Please guide us to a finding which will bring peace and harmony and happiness.

—Bedtime prayer of Justice Corazon Juliano-Agrava

Through the Marcos years, as the president filled the courts with compliant judges, as his opponents were arrested and held without trial, as those cases that went to trial were blatantly prejudged, Filipinos had come to regard the scales of justice as hopelessly lopsided.

When Marcos appointed a second investigative board under Justice Corazon Juliano-Agrava to replace the panel headed by Chief Justice Enrique Fernando, which had so quickly fizzled for want of credibility, few expected a finding that would be much at variance with the government's position—that Rolando Galman, a Communist hit man, had killed Benigno Aquino and, in turn, had been killed by security forces. A handful of junior soldiers in the security detail might be sacrificed for appearance's sake, but there was no reason to expect the truth.

The presidential decree of October 14, 1983, forming the Fact-Finding Board, or the Agrava board, as it became commonly known over the endless cups of bitter barako coffee that fuel gossip sessions in Manila, was sanctimonious. It ordered a thorough probe of the assassination, a "national tragedy and national shame," and stated that no one could refuse to appear before the board because his testimony might afterward prove self-incriminating. "But," it went on in language that seemed intentionally unclear, "his testimony or any evidence produced by him shall not be used against him in connection with any transaction, matter or thing concerning which he is compelled, after having invoked his privilege against self-incrimination, to testify or produce evidence.'' Later, a Supreme Court interpretation of this passage, finding that some Agrava board testimony could not be used, would play a crucial and destructive role in the Aquino assassination trial.

The board gathered its evidence with agonizing slowness, frequently appearing to be fumbling in the dark. In fact, though, the panel proceeded with predetermined direction, but given who the members were, it was understandable that they would proceed cautiously. All five came from the upper tiers of society, and they had more to lose than most Filipinos. If they determined that the assassination was a military plot, involving the president's favorite general, or the president himself, they would put their positions, even their lives, at the mercy of armed men with sworn loyalty to Ver and Marcos. If they found that a Communist hit man had actually shot Aquino, they certainly would be attacked by an infuriated public. They were in a no-win situation, but if they had any preconceptions at all, they were inclined toward maintaining the status quo.

Justice Agrava, the chairman, who was sixty-eight and had spent much of her career on the bench dealing with juvenile delinquents, unabashedly admired Ferdinand Marcos and his wife. As she acknowledged in the bedtime prayer she recited to the gallery at a hearing one day, she was more concerned with coming to a popular conclusion than with getting to the bottom of the assassination. She wore frilly outfits that, combined with a girlish demeanor and a high-pitched voice, created a less-than-serious appearance.

Luciano E. Salazar, sixty-five, was a partner in one of the country's foremost law firms and had direct links to the president. His wife was a member of the Blue Ladies, a group of about 130 women organized by Imelda Marcos in 1965 to help in her husband's election campaign. The women, in their matching blue, brass-buttoned dresses, canvassed votes in Manila's exclusive neighborhoods and elite clubs. Many later accompanied Mrs. Marcos on her international shopping jaunts.

Ernesto F. Herrera had spent his entire career in organized labor, rising through the ranks to become counsel to the 1.2 million-member Trade Union Congress of the Philippines. At forty-two, he was the youngest board member. But he was not the rabble-rousing union organizer that his background might have suggested. The TUC was wholly a pro-Marcos organization.

Amado C. Dizon, seventy-five, was the eldest member of the board and its most enigmatic. His colleagues never quite fathomed him and were unable to anticipate which way he was leaning as the hearings progressed. An expert in jurisprudence and education, he drafted the country's Education Act of 1982. He was a UNESCO delegate and a former Fulbright Scholar.

Dante G. Santos was an engineer by education, a self-made millionaire who was president of the Philippines Appliance Corporation and the Philippines Chamber of Commerce and Industry. He was fifty-nine years old, sometimes gruff, and he proved to be an aggressive and occasionally profane questioner. The cluster of Agrava board groupies that evolved during the eight months of hearings came to think of Santos as being skeptical of government witnesses, though he developed a reputation for being frequently absent, too.

But the most influential and effective individual associated with the Agrava board was not an appointed member but its chief legal counsel, Andres R. Narvasa. Narvasa hadn't wanted the job. He was fifty-nine and powerful in appearance with broad, heavy shoulders and a large head accentuated by a precisely maintained gray crewcut. For seven years he'd been dean of law at the 360-year-old University of Santo Tomas. He had then opened a small private practice, holding office in cramped, rather down-at-the-heels quarters above a tailor shop in Quezon City. The slow pace suited him. He enjoyed leaving work early most afternoons for a game of tennis and spending evenings at home with his wife, Janina. He wasn't looking for challenge.

The presidential decree forming the board specified the requirements of the legal counsel, stating that he "must have all the qualifications of a Justice of the Supreme Court." The board members would have had little difficulty in finding an ambitious, aggressive attorney to serve as their counsel, one who would have jumped at the chance to be in the spotlight. Instead, they chose a man who wanted to be left alone, attracted by his blunt frankness and his very lack of ambition. On October 28, the board hired Narvasa. Much later, after the eight months of hearings had been completed and the four additional months needed to hammer out a conclusion had passed, Narvasa explained his reason for accepting the assignment. If he hadn't already proven himself a true folk hero, it would have sounded like the stagiest kind of posturing. "Somebody had to do the job," he said.

Although his nickname to friends and family was Andy, Narvasa became known to hearing habitués as the Dean, for his former law school position, and sometimes as the Gray Dean, because of the color of his crewcut. Justice Agrava's nickname, like Corazon Aquino's, was Cory. But a member of Narvasa's legal staff, Bienvenido A. Tan, recalled that years earlier she'd been known as Rosie, and he resurrected it. Newspapers and TV were amused to call the hearings "The Dean and Rosie Show."

Not many Filipinos found the Agrava board entertaining, though, particularly not in the early months of its operation, when it was perceived to be a Marcos smokescreen. The entire Aquino family, to the fury of all board members, declined to cooperate. On one occasion, Butz Aquino appeared before the panel but refused to answer questions and wouldn't even sit down. Because the board had been appointed by Marcos, the assumption was universal that at least some of its members were beholden to the president. There was a rumor that Agrava was financially indebted to Marcos because of a real-estate loan. Santos, because of his huge appliance manufacturing business and its reliance on U.S. connections, was considered vulnerable to presidential pressure. Salazar was tainted by his wife's status as a Blue Lady. Herrera's Trade Union Congress stood with the regime. Dizon was an unknown quantity.

Furthermore, the Agrava board was modeled on the Warren Commission, which had investigated the assassination of President John F. Kennedy. Since the Warren Commission had blamed Lee Harvey Oswald alone and had not attributed the killing to a widely suspected broader conspiracy, those who believed that the Aquino assassination had been plotted by top-level government and military figures found the precedent discouraging.

Under Narvasa's guidance, the board members decided to start at the outer edges of evidence and move slowly to the center in order to establish the one crucial point upon which their conclusion would rest: where Aquino was at the instant the bullet entered the base of his skull. If he had reached the tarmac, Galman could have done the shooting. But if he was still on the stairway, there would have been no way for a gunman on the ground to have fired a round into the back of his head; only one of the soldiers following him down could have placed such a shot. And, if that were the case, concluding that the military had plotted the assassination would seem inescapable.

Following a logical and chronological course, they began on November 3, 1983, with a visit to a morgue, where, screaming hysterically, Saturnina Galman identified the bullet-riddled cadaver of her son, Rolando. Six days later, the board's regular sessions began, in a capacious, second-story auditorium of the bustling Social Security System building in Quezon City. These sessions, 125 in all, ran through July 6, 1984. During that time, board members made brief trips to Tokyo and Los Angeles to interview people who had been at Manila International Airport on the day of the assassination, but most witnesses came to the auditorium to testify.

With few exceptions, the hearings were public. There always were reporters, photographers, TV crews, and at least a few interested bystanders present in the auditorium's gallery. On several occasions, when big names such as Imelda Marcos or General Ver appeared, loudspeakers were set up outside so the overflow crowds could hear. The numbers of devoted fans grew. From newspapers and TV, Filipinos became familiar not only with Rosie and the Gray Dean but with other members of the panel's legal staff, such as pugnacious former police chief Francisco Villa and smooth-talking Bienvenido Tan. Depending on their biases, the audience booed at Rodolfo Jimenez, the aggressive and tenacious lawyer for the Aviation Security Command, or AVSECOM, which had performed so abysmally at the airport, or laughed at the animated antics of the Galman family's lawyer, Lupino Lazaro, who wore lavender-tinted glasses with shirts and ties to match. And the fans came to be intimately familiar with the two central characters in the drama, both of them dead, who, more often than not, were identified not as Aquino and Galman, but as "the man in white" and "the man in blue."

The hearings were, for the most part, slow going and tedious. Some witnesses led the proceedings up blind alleys; others were militantly uncooperative, refusing to acknowledge the most obvious facts. There were times of raging tempers and absurdity but also moments of insight and discovery. Throughout, though, there was no real breakthrough, no gasp-producing moment when everyone realized that the depth of truth had been plumbed. There was no one witness who came forward with an uncontestable key to the mystery of who killed Benigno Aquino. There were just countless bits and pieces, testimony and documents, photographs and videotapes, metal fragments and chemical tests, all of which had to be sifted and painstakingly pieced together. The mosaic formed by the board at the end of a year was incomplete and imperfect, but it was far better than any Filipino had the right to expect.

While the panel members were agonizing over their puzzle, residents of Manila and other major cities were venting their frustrations in the streets, battling against police truncheons, water cannon, and tear-gas grenades, demanding that Marcos resign but knowing that he wouldn't. "It's true that Marcos does not intend to step down," conceded Butz Aquino, who week after week led antigovernment demonstrations. "But that just means it will take us longer." The president, sick as he was, kept up a machismo front, winning grudging admiration from his enemies. His office was "God-given," he said. "You stay there until you have done your job. Otherwise, you are a complete coward."

In Washington, the Reagan administration stood uneasily behind Marcos, waiting and watching, along with Filipinos, for the Agrava board to reach judgment.

Of the 195 witnesses to appear before the panel, the great majority had little of value to offer. And those who knew the most about what had happened at Manila International Airport on Sunday, August 21, 1983, and during the time leading up to the assassination tended to be the least cooperative. This was particularly true of military personnel. But despite the blocking efforts of officers and enlisted men, board members succeeded in finding many missing pieces of the assassination mosaic. One of the earliest and most important was "the man in blue."

Until his body fell near Aquino's on the tarmac, Rolando Galman was a nobody among 50 million or more poor Filipino nobodies. He had never finished elementary school, and he had scraped through life. For thirty-three years, he'd gotten into trouble and wheedled his way out. He once told a friend that he'd killed two men who'd murdered his father. In 1982 he'd been put in jail, charged with robbery and assault, and kept for a year. He was eminently expendable, a perfect candidate for a set-up.

The name stitched in his undershorts was Rolly, but most people who knew him called him Lando. He and a woman named Lina Lazaro lived together with their eleven-year-old son, Reynaldo, and her sixteen-year-old daughter, Roberta Masibay, on five acres in Bulacan province, north of Manila, where they planted rice and raised pigs. They also owned a cycle ricksha in which Lando and some of the other family members would pedal passengers along the rural roads to earn a few extra pesos. But Lando liked a good time, too. He could put away a lot of bottles of San Miguel beer, as his spreading belly showed, and he regularly stopped in at the Del Monte Super & Disco Club, near Quezon City, where he enjoyed the attention of a twenty-eight-year-old woman named Ana Oliva, who was a "hospitality girl" there along with her sister, Catherine.

For a man who lived a marginal life, a man the military said was a gun-for-hire who sold his services to the Communist New People's Army, Galman had a rather unusual friend, a well-connected Philippine air force lieutenant colonel named Arturo Custodio. It was Custodio who got Galman out of jail in 1983, and they had been seen together several times in public, eating and drinking. The Galman children told the Agrava board members that Colonel Custodio and three other men picked up Galman at home on August 17, 1983, four days before both he and Aquino were killed. What then happened to Galman was pieced together from testimony by Ana and Catherine Oliva's mother, Ester Oliva, and some of the young women who worked at the Del Monte.

Accompanied by soldiers in civilian clothes, Galman apparently picked up Ana at the club, and they were taken first to a "safe house" in Bataan, site of the infamous World War II death march, in which they stayed for two nights, and then to a seedy motel, the Carlton, two miles from Manila International Airport. They spent the night of August 19 there and made love while the soldiers accompanying them remained in the room, according the couple the scant courtesy of turning their backs. The next day, Ana told the soldiers that she had to attend to her four children but that she'd return to the Carlton that night. They let her go. She went home and stayed there, saying nothing about the previous three nights. But on the twenty-first, when she saw Lando's dead body on TV, she burst out, "He's my customer!" and told her family what had happened. On the night of September 4, Ana and her sister, Catherine, were picked up at the Del Monte by two men. The men had guns stuck into the waistbands of their trousers and were driving a Toyota equipped with a telephone and a walkie-talkie. Ana and Catherine were never seen again.

The Galman children had testified that one of the three men who came to their home with Colonel Custodio on August 17 to take their father away was called Boy and that he had a large brown birthmark on his right arm. They also said that on January 29, 1984—a little more than a week before Lina Lazaro was to testify before the board—Boy returned to the house and forced Lina and a neighbor, Rogelio Taruc, to leave with him. Neither was ever seen again.

Colonel Custodio had appeared before the board on November 9, 1983, the first day of formal hearings, and was not forthcoming. He was brought back on March 12, 1984, to respond to the Galman childrens' testimony, which seemed to indicate that he'd turned their father over to other military men who set him up as what family attorney Lupino Lazaro called the "fall guy."

This time, Custodio acknowledged that he had known Galman and that in February 1983 he and his lawyer, José Espiño, had gotten him released from jail. The last time he'd seen the alleged assassin, Custodio testified, was one evening in the last week of July 1983 when he found Galman waiting for him at his home, looking gloomy, "as if worried," and they'd sat together until about 11:30, drinking beer. But Custodio insisted that he had not gone to the Galman house on August 17, that he had not taken him anywhere, and that he'd been at his own home that day.

At that, Bienvenido Tan, who acted as go-between for the public and the board, raised a slip of paper he'd received from Reynaldo Galman, the chubby youngster who was sitting in the gallery with his grandmother, his aunt, and his sister. " 'Why do you refuse to admit you fetched my father on August seventeenth?' " Tan read. Custodio answered calmly, "How can I admit something that isn't true?"

The testimony of Custodio's attorney, José Espiño, turned out to be unsupportive of the military's claims that Galman was the killer. Espiño said that on August 22 or 23, one or two days after the assassination, he and Custodio had been talking about the airport killings. Galman had not yet been identified and therefore, Espiño said, neither he nor Custodio knew that he was the "man in blue." But Custodio told him his AVSECOM friends believed that the man in blue had not killed Aquino; he couldn't have, because he was already dead himself. Agrava asked Espiño if he had any ideas about who might have killed Aquino. "As far as I can remember, Your Honor, I think what Colonel

President Ferdinand E. Marcos was at the height of his powers, politically, mentally, and physically, when the author interviewed him in 1977 at his office in Malacañang Palace. Marcos was fifty-nine but looked much younger.

First Lady Imelda Marcos and California Governor Ronald Reagan dance at Malacañang Palace in 1969 to celebrate the opening of the Cultural Center of the Philippines. The occasion also marked the beginning of a friendship between the Marcoses and the Reagans.

Andy Hernandez

Roger Margallo

A somber Cory and Ninoy Aquino during his court-martial trial on charges of subversion, murder, and illegal possession of weapons. The trial lasted five years, and on November 25, 1977, Ninoy was sentenced to death by firing squad. The Aquinos appealed, and he remained imprisoned until Marcos allowed him to go to the United States in 1980 for heart surgery.

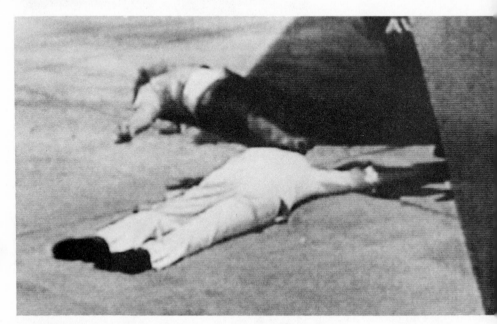

The body of Ninoy Aquino, "the man in white," lies on the tarmac of Manila International Airport on August 21, 1983. Minutes after he returned to his homeland, he was shot to death with a single bullet to the back of his head, allegedly fired by "the man in blue," Rolando Galman, whose body lies nearby.

Aquino's funeral procession clogged the streets of Manila ten days after his murder. A trailer truck was used instead of a hearse so people could see the coffin. The giant turnout was the beginning of three years of demonstrations against the Marcos regime.

Within hours of the Aquino funeral, demonstrators massed at Mendiola Bridge, an entry point to Malacañang Palace, which over time came to symbolize the barriers between the Marcos regime and the public. Mendiola became the site of repeated clashes between government troops and anti-Marcos demonstrators.

During a hearing of the Fact-Finding Board, Justic[e] Corazon (''Rosie'') Agrav[a] studies a key witness, Sergeant Filomeno Miran[da,] one of the two security guards who followed Nin[o] Aquino down the stairs fr[om] the plane.

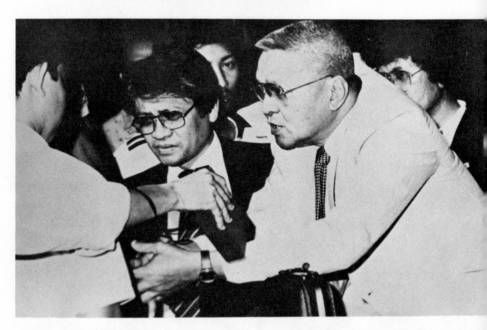

Crew-cut ''Gray Dean'' Andres Narvasa, counsel for the Fact-Finding Board, and pugnacious military counsel Rudolfo Jimenez are interviewed during a break in the hearings. Narvasa drafted the board's findings, which found twenty-five military men, including Chief of Staff General Fabian C. Ver, and a lone civilian ''indictable for the premeditated killing of Aquino.''

At a stop on the campaign trail, Cory Aquino and Doy Laurel give the thumbs-down sign before the massive, sculpted concrete Marcos Monument, set into a hillside overlooking the Marcos Golf and Country Club, off the Marcos Highway, north of Manila.

The accused stand for their arraignment in the Aquino assassination trial. The first four in this row are Major General Prospero Olivas; Hermilo Gosuico, the only civilian; General Fabian C. Ver; Colonel Arturo Custodio. Reversing the Fact-Finding Board, the court acquitted all twenty-six accused.

Aquino and Laurel flash the "L" sign for *laban*, or "fight," during a January 1986 horn-honking procession in the sugar-producing province of Negros Occidental, one of their numerous stops during the intensive nationwide campaign.

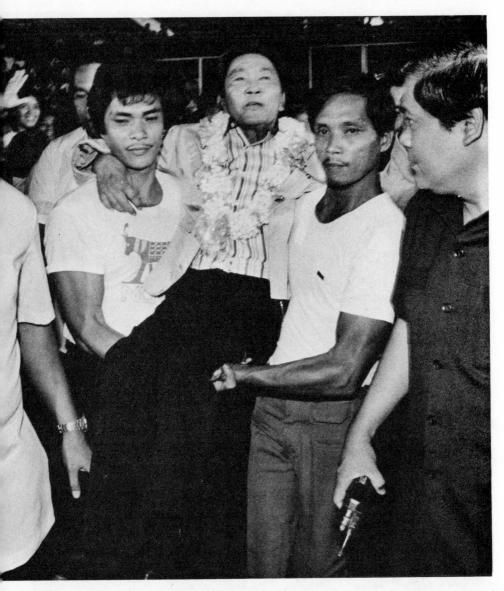

Marcos's frail health prevented him from campaigning vigorously. When he entered the Manila Hotel to formally accept his party's nomination, he was carried by aides. This scene recurred often. The presidential office gave various excuses for his inability to keep speaking engagements.

Immaculately coiffed and manicured, Imelda Marcos serenades crowds while her husband looks on. Vigorous campaigners, the First Lady and vice-presidential candidate Arturo Tolentino frequently stepped in for the ailing Marcos.

Aquino supporters protect a truckload of ballot boxes in Manila after the close of polling on February 7, 1986. Despite such efforts by nuns, teachers, students, and others, fraud of all kinds was rampant.

Philip C. Habib, President Reagan's troubleshooter, and white-haired Ambassador Stephen Bosworth call on Cardinal Jaime Sin during the turbulence following the fraudulent election. Habib's departure from Manila for Washington hours before the military rebellion raised widespread speculation of U.S. backing for the plan to topple Marcos.

Cigar in hand, Lieutenant General Fidel V. Ramos and Defense Minister Juan Ponce Enrile announce on February 22, 1986, that they are breaking with Marcos because he stole the election and was about to arrest them. They neglected to mention that they had been plotting a coup d'etat that may have included Marcos's murder.

Bullit Marquez

Mustachioed Colonel Gregorio Honasan, right, one of the key coup plotters, leads Enrile from Defense Ministry headquarters at Camp Aguinaldo to nearby Camp Crame to combine forces with General Ramos. Many of the weapons carried were bought by Enrile as part of a secret deal with a shadowy British organization.

Hundreds of thousands of people flocked to Epifanio de los Santos Avenue, known as Edsa, a broad boulevard separating camps Aguinaldo and Crame. Collectively, the crowds became known as people power, and they played a fundamental role in forcing back tanks and armed troops ordered by Marcos and Ver to crush the rebels.

Marines disembarking from tanks after being stopped by huge people power
crowds find it difficult to retain their military composure when handed blossoms.

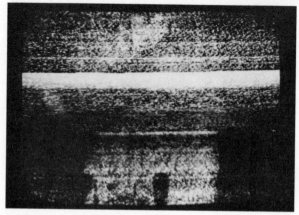

In the midst of a live news conference, Marcos fades out as rebel troops capture the government-owned Channel Four. The loss of the TV station cost the president dearly, giving the impression to millions of Filipinos that the rebels were in control.

President Marcos gives a final, teary speech to supporters from the balcony of Malacañang Palace following his inauguration; his wife and family look on. Hours later, at 9:05 P.M., Tuesday, February 25, 1986, the Marcoses fled aboard U.S. military helicopters, stunning the handful of faithful who remained inside the palace grounds.

Youngsters who scaled the palace walls two hours after Marcos's flight joyously flash the "L" sign as they pose on the presidential dais. Malacañang was the paramount symbol of the dictatorship, and they were now at its very epicenter.

President Corazon Aquino and her family in March 1986. On the sofa with her are grandson Justin Benigno Cruz ("Jiggy") and daughter Maria Elena Cruz ("Ballsy"). From left to right are daughter Victoria Elisa ("Viel"), son Benigno III ("Noynoy"), daughter Maria Aurora Abelleda ("Pinky"), sons-in-law Manuel Abelleda and Eldon Cruz, and seated on the floor, daughter Kristine Bernadette ("Kris").

The new president poses in the Malacañang guest house, where she established her office. Aquino declined to work in the palace, which was turned into a museum, its central attraction being Imelda Marcos's enormous collection of shoes and dresses. Aquino eliminated the eagle that Marcos had placed on the presidential seal and restored the original mythical sea lion.

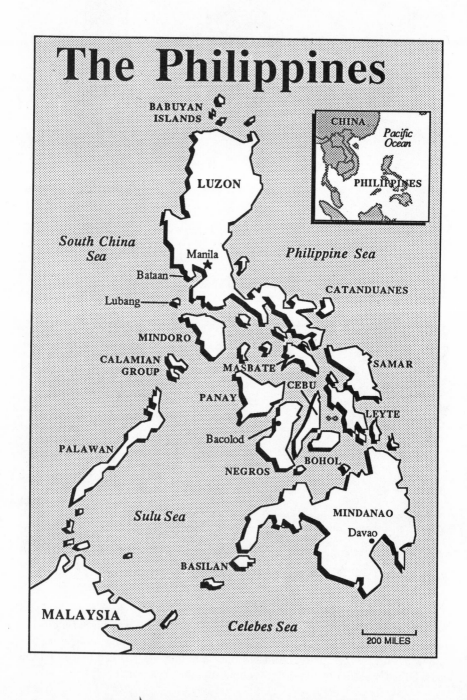

The Philippines

BABUYAN
ISLANDS

CHINA

*Pacific
Ocean*

PHILIPPINES

LUZON

*South China
Sea*

Manila

Philippine Sea

Bataan

CATANDUANES

Lubang

MINDORO

CALAMIAN
GROUP

MASBATE

SAMAR

PANAY

CEBU

LEYTE

Bacolod

PALAWAN

BOHOL

NEGROS

MINDANAO

Davao

Sulu Sea

BASILAN

MALAYSIA

Celebes Sea

200 MILES

Custodio told me was that it may have been the military escort who shot the late senator,'' he said.

Another Custodio associate to appear was Hermilo Gosuico, forty years old, who made a comfortable living as a heavy-equipment contractor to the Armed Forces of the Philippines and other government agencies. Gosuico had the common Filipino nickname of Boy. That much he confirmed during his testimony, but very little else. Dean Narvasa's deputy counsel, Francisco Villa, asked Gosuico if he had known the late Rolando Galman and if he knew Galman's common-law wife, Lina Lazaro, his neighbor, Rogelio Taruc, his "girlfriend," Ana Oliva, and Ana's sister, Catherine—all of whom were missing. "Nobody," answered Gosuico. "I don't know him. I don't know anything."

When Villa recalled that Galman's stepdaughter, Roberta, had testified that Colonel Custodio and three other men, one of them called Boy, had come to their home and taken Galman away, Gosuico replied that that must have been another Boy because he had been in Isabela province that day, inspecting a National Irrigation Administration project. Besides, he didn't even know a Colonel Custodio. Villa asked to see his right arm. Slowly, reluctantly, Gosuico pulled up the right sleeve of his *barong tagalog* to reveal a large brown birthmark.

The next morning, when they brought Gosuico back, he said that he did not want to submit to a lie-detector test. Justice Agrava responded, with gloomy resignation, "Well, so that's it. The witness's reluctance disqualifies him from undergoing the test."

The standard for obfuscation from a military witness was set by the commander of the Aviation Security Command, Brigadier General Luther Custodio, who was not related to Lieutenant Colonel Arturo Custodio. The general had been placed in overall charge of the arrangements for Aquino's return by General Ver. He appeared in the Social Security System auditorium on November 21, 1983, with a slick and largely uninformative presentation, a slide show that covered security preparations at the airport. Pictures of documents marked "secret" flashed on and off the screen, and the show ended courteously with a final slide marked "thank you" in Tagalog. Custodio wore a white *barong tagalog* and, on his left wrist, a heavy gold ID bracelet. On his chin and right cheek were two moles, with long, gray hairs carefully maintained in the fashion of Asia, where many men believe that hairy moles denote virility.

General Custodio's testimony gave the impression that he and the other officers who planned the security arrangements were either well-meaning incompetents or clumsy assassins. He confirmed that closed-circuit cameras mounted on the exterior of the airport terminal monitored the arrival of flight CAL 811 with Aquino aboard, as they do of all flights, but that no videotapes had been made because this was done only in the event of a hijacking. Some of the board members remained unconvinced and felt that tapes, which would have provided unimpeded views of the shooting of Aquino and Galman, had been hidden or destroyed. Board members also were skeptical when General Custodio acknowledged that he had not stationed paramedics at the plane's docking area, even though this was standard procedure in any high-risk situation.

It got worse.

There was a medical clinic inside Manila International Airport, and Custodio himself noted that it was located "right in front of Gate Eight," where CAL 811 had docked. Yet the blood-soaked Aquino was not taken into this convenient facility. Instead, the blue AVSE-COM van carrying the body drove out of the airport, bypassed still another medical facility, at adjacent Villamor Air Base, and went across town to Fort Bonifacio General Hospital. Narvasa questioned Custodio, wanting to know if "it did not occur to you that the wound might be critical and therefore [Aquino] needed medical attention as quickly as possible?"

"What occurred to me, sir," the general answered, "was to bring him immediately to the hospital."

The military's star witness was, of course, General Fabian C. Ver, chief of staff, Armed Forces of the Philippines, the most senior officer in the country, an intimate associate of President Marcos's, and in the minds of many Filipinos the key suspect in the Aquino assassination. Ver came before the board three times, always courteous, always courtly, giving the impression of an officer and a gentleman who wanted only to serve his country. His initial appearance, on Friday, April 6, 1984, was a major event, and the auditorium was packed minutes after guards unlocked the doors at 8:00 A.M. Facing the board members was a new desk and a leather-covered executive chair, replacing the simpler furnishings that had served lesser witnesses. The general wore civilian dress, a soft white *barong tagalog* draped over beige trousers. He slipped on his half-glasses and read an opening statement in which he said he welcomed the opportunity to help the board "in its quest for truth and justice."

Until Ver's appearance, the board had focused on the events surrounding the shooting at the airport. Now, questions were directed more toward the matter of a conspiracy. Sometime in February 1983, Ver testified, he began hearing "scuttlebutt" and receiving "reports about a plot to assassinate Senator Aquino." Board member Ernesto Herrera referred to earlier testimony by Aquino's political associate Salvador Laurel, who had recalled Ninoy's telling him about a warning from Imelda Marcos in New York two months before he was killed: "You'd better not come home because some of our boys will kill you, feeling that it would make us happy. But we will not order it." Herrera asked Ver if he'd ever heard of a plot "that might have been planned by friends of the First Lady and the president, but who could not be controlled by them." No, said Ver.

On the other hand, the general affirmed, the "scuttlebutt" and "reports" indicated a plot to murder Aquino in such a way as to implicate the government. In that case, Narvasa wanted to know, had Ver immediately begun monitoring Aquino's movements? "We did not monitor," replied the officer who was head of the country's armed forces and of its intelligence network.

The significance of this disclaimer was that Ver wanted the board to believe the authorities had no foreknowledge of Aquino's plans beyond learning at the last moment on which day he'd be returning. This would support the fundamental contention that the military was not involved in a conspiracy and would lend credence to the allegation that the killing was a Communist plot. Thus, Ver testified, in July, five months after he'd heard the initial "scuttlebutt," he launched something he called Project Four Flowers, which was intended to "look into all these reports, collate them, evaluate them, and recommend proper action." Unfortunately, the chief of staff said, while he was able to discern the shadowy outlines of a Communist plot in the works, he did not learn of the hit man Galman until after the tragic shooting of former Senator Aquino.

The board shifted its focus back to Aquino's reception at the airport.

Ver said that he had ordered AVSECOM commander Custodio to draw up a security plan based on two options for handling Aquino: "First, to return him to his country of origin in the same aircraft he came in, should he arrive without travel papers, or, to return him to his former detention cell at the Military Security Command in Fort Bonifacio, should he come with travel papers." Ver claimed that even though the government had the legal right to arrest Aquino and to carry out the death sentence reaffirmed against him in 1982, it really wanted him to stay away, at least until authorities could "identify and neutralize the plot against him." That was why so many top government representatives, including the First Lady, had tried to talk him out of returning. "It was only in the morning of August 21, when we already [had] reliable information that he was coming, that we decided to effect the warrant of arrest," Ver said. "We could no longer dissuade him from coming."

Custodio submitted the security plan to Ver on August 20, one day before Aquino's expected arrival, having given it the code name *Oplan Balikbayan,* or "Operations Plan Homecomer." This name was cruelly ironic. A *balikbayan* is a Filipino who's gone off to seek his fortune, perhaps in the United States or an oil-rich Middle Eastern land, and comes home loaded with electronic marvels, fancy clothes, and other acquisitions to prove his success and make life more pleasant for his family. Such homecomers can count on being met at Manila International Airport by dozens of jubilant relatives, happy to have him back and equally happy to examine his treasures. Aquino's homecoming was to be a different matter, controlled by exactly 1,199 soldiers. Ver told the board that he approved *Oplan Balikbayan* the day he received it, having determined that it was comprehensive and tactically adequate "if properly implemented."

On the Sunday when *Oplan Balikbayan* was underway, Ver testified, he was in his office at Malacañang. At 1:30 P.M. he received a telephone call from one of his officers at the airport, Colonel Romeo Ochoco, who said that Aquino had arrived. "He reported to me that somebody was shot," Ver said. "And so I told him, 'Who was shot?' He did not know. So I said, 'You better go back and investigate and report back to me.' " Half an hour later, General Custodio telephoned and "informed me that Senator Aquino had arrived but that he was shot and that he was brought to Fort Bonifacio Army General Hospital but unfortunately he died on arrival."

Justice Agrava asked, "Did he tell you who shot him?"

"He did not, Your Honor," Ver answered.

Ver continued his testimony in a second appearance, on April 10. By this time, people were beginning to wonder whether the armed forces, if they were implicated, would accept the board's findings or whether there might be some kind of military rebellion. When another of Narvasa's deputies, attorney Mario Ongkiko, asked this question, Ver responded with a ringing promise of support for the investigation: "Inasmuch as the honorable board is a creation of the president, Your Honors, and we are acting only in accordance with the desire of the president to uncover and tell the world all about this plot and about this assassination, we will abide by whatever the honorable board finds, if we have to prosecute our own people, if the findings or evidence support so!"

This earned him a round of applause from the gallery and from the board members.

When Ver came back for a third and final time, on April 23, he brought with him a four-page report prepared by the chief of the Criminal Investigation Service, Colonel Hermogenes Peralta, supporting the contention that Aquino could not have been shot by one of the military men coming down the stairs behind him. According to the report, the autopsy results indicated that the assassination weapon had been pointing upward. It also noted that there were no blood stains on the metal stairway.

The second-most senior officer to testify before the Agrava board was Major General Prospero Olivas, the military's own chief investigator in the Aquino assassination. He ranked just behind Deputy Chief of Staff Fidel Ramos in the chain of command and was also a highly qualified attorney. Yet, even though he'd been stationed in the sweeping, circular driveway in front of the airport when the killing took place, he told the board that he had heard no shooting, had noticed no commotion, and was completely unaware of anything untoward. The first he knew was about forty-five minutes later, when Ver telephoned and ordered him to investigate.

One of Olivas's first actions was to go on television and announce that an unidentified man had shot Aquino and was himself then shot by security forces. Olivas displayed the .357 magnum Smith & Wesson revolver that he said was the assassination weapon and at a news conference five days later handled the weapon again. Olivas told the board that he had not had the weapon tested for fingerprints because prints could not be detected on the rough surface of the handle and that it was important to show the gun immediately to the "curious and concerned public."

Under questioning, Olivas told the board that although thirty-three AVSECOM men had been tested for nitrate traces on their hands to determine if they had fired guns, Sergeant Filomeno Miranda, who descended the stairs directly behind Aquino, had not been tested. The slipup had been discovered too late, he said. Not that it mattered much; with the military investigating itself, explanations were plentiful. For example, nitrate specks found on the hands of Constable First Class Rogelio Moreno, who had descended the stairs alongside Miranda, were the result of target practice the day before the assassination. The nitrate specks found on Galman's hands, however, proved that he was the assassin.

Olivas put on a slide show of ballistics tests that he said proved that the .357 magnum Smith & Wesson was the murder weapon. He also showed a slide of the metal stairway, pointing out that it was blood-free and noting that "this is in color, so it would be readily discernible if there was blood." While Olivas was a fund of detailed technical knowledge, he proved ill-informed when the board got down to basics. Bienvenido Tan had a simple question from a citizen in the gallery: "General, can you explain how Galman entered into a secure area?"

"It is something which I cannot really explain with accuracy, Your Honor," he answered. "I can only speculate . . . Galman had some disguise of some sort."

The military's chief investigator also seemed to impose unusual self-limitations on his orders. Tan asked what he had done to locate Galman's missing common-law wife, Lina, his friend, Ana, and her sister, Catherine. Had he, for example, questioned Hermilo "Boy" Gosuico, the man with the large birthmark on his arm?

"No, Your Honor."

"Is it not a fact, General, that you were requested by the board to look for Lina Lazaro and the Oliva sisters?"

"Yes, Your Honor, look for Lina Lazaro. But it has been interpreted as looking and, you know, not to investigate."

The enlisted men who came before the board were no more cooperative than their officers, and they were uniformly unshakable in claiming that they'd seen the man in blue shoot the man in white.

Sergeant Rolando de Guzman testified that he'd been sitting inside the AVSECOM van and was peering through a narrow opening between its two rear doors when he witnessed Galman shoot Aquino. The senator and his escorts had been walking across the tarmac to the van, de Guzman said, when a man in blue appeared behind Sergeant Arnulfo de Mesa, pointed a gun at Aquino's head, and fired. De Mesa swung his right hand up with great force, deflecting the gunman's arm and causing him to whirl so that he was standing with his back to de Guzman, who immediately opened fire, pumping seven rounds into him before his body hit the tarmac, he said.

De Mesa corroborated the story except for saying that after he'd swung his arm up, he swung it back down, clipping the gunman behind the head and knocking him face down to the tarmac, where he was when de Guzman opened fire from the van.

General Olivas also presented a civilian eyewitness whose testimony supported the man-in-blue scenario but, again, with differences. He was Augusto Floresca, an executive in a paint company that was part of the vast industrial empire owned by Eduardo Cojuangco, Jr., the most powerful and most influential of all Marcos's so-called cronies. Cojunagco, coincidentally, was the cousin of Corazon Aquino, whose maiden name was Cojuangco; their two branches of the family had feuded for years. Floresca said that he was standing at a window inside the airport terminal and saw the party reach the rear of the AVSECOM van when the doors swung open, evidently startling Aquino, who appeared to resist entering the vehicle. Suddenly, Floresca said, a man in blue "jumped and pointed a gun at close range at the head of Aquino and the first shot was heard."

Sergeant Miranda and Constable First Class Moreno had come down the metal stairs immediately behind Aquino, whose arms were being grasped by the two soldiers flanking him, Sergeant Claro Lat and Sergeant de Mesa. If the shooting had occurred on the stairway, no one would have been in a more advantageous position to put a round from a handgun into the back of Aquino's head than Miranda or Moreno.

Miranda testified that Aquino, Lat, and de Mesa had actually reached the tarmac when he heard the first shot. He looked to his left and saw

Aquino and Lat falling to the ground. Miranda hadn't seen the shot being fired because he was on the last step of the stairway and was looking down, he said.

Board member Dante Santos appeared determined to squeeze Miranda, to try to force an admission or, more likely, to make him appear a fool or a liar. "Did you know Senator Aquino was shot [from behind]?" he asked. "Later, sir, after . . ." Miranda replied. Santos pursued him, mockingly: "So, if there was nobody [else] behind Aquino, and *you* were behind him, *you* were the one who shot him?"

Jimenez, the soldiers' lawyer, sprang to his feet, objecting: "Your Honor, please. It's very easy for us to shoot these questions because we sit in the comfort of our chairs. But, I wonder, if we had been there, how we would have reacted and what things we would be able to recall."

Miranda's fellow soldier, Moreno, told the board that as they came down the stairs, he was one step behind de Mesa. He had scanned the area, looking to the left, right, and rear. There was no conversation on the stairway. He had not heard a voice shout, *"Ako na, ako na, ako na!"* ("I'll do it, I'll do it, I'll do it!"). They got down to the tarmac, he said, and were approaching the blue AVSECOM van into which they were supposed to direct Aquino. Sergeant de Mesa was still holding Aquino's left arm; Lat his right. The shot! Moreno turned toward the noise and saw that a man in blue had inserted himself between de Mesa and Aquino. The man was holding a gun in his right hand and seemed to have lost his balance. He then saw Aquino and Lat fall to the tarmac. Moreno himself ran for cover.

The board wanted to see all this reenacted, and so two staff members and attorney Villa played it out. Justice Agrava wasn't satisfied: "A little sense of drama, please." They did it one more time.

Sergeant Lat, who had picked up one of Aquino's handbags in the plane and then held his right arm, testified that he knew nothing of a threat on Aquino's life. "They only told us to take good care of the senator," he said, speaking Tagalog in a monotone.

A detailed exchange between Lat and attorney Ongkiko over the relative positions on the stairway of Lat and Miranda demonstrated the recurring difficulty the board encountered in determining whether a witness was lying or was simply confused:

"Was Miranda ahead or behind you?"

"I asked him to go on ahead."

"So you told Miranda to go ahead?"

"What I remember is that he seemed ahead even in coming out of the plane."

"This is because you gave Miranda the bag, right?"

"I gave him the bag."

"What did you tell him? Did you say, 'Bring this'?"

"Follow me with the bag."

"Therefore, Miranda followed you."

"Yes, sir."

Fencing with the military became standard procedure for the board. One afternoon in mid January, Justice Agrava had taken all she could from a Criminal Investigation Service captain named Ruben Zacarias, who was exhibiting a distinctly see-no-evil, hear-no-evil, speak-no-evil attitude. Suddenly she pounced on him: "I expect you to be a military man and not be slouching in the chair and looking around!" When the hapless officer tried to interject, Agrava snapped, "Shut up and let me finish!" And she did, accusing him of being prepared "to let the country hang and let the criminals run loose. If this is the kind of officer we have, no wonder we're in a mess."

Despite the obfuscation by the military, some of the most penetrating testimony emerged from civilian airport personnel who were on the tarmac servicing the plane right after it landed. Ramon Balang, a ground engineer, was one of those who summoned his nerve and came forward. He had been filling out a checklist beneath Flight 811 when he heard a shot, he told the members of the panel. He turned toward the sound and saw a man in white falling, blood spurting from his head. And at the same moment he saw a man in blue, standing among men in AVSECOM uniforms. The man in blue was "smiling" at the others, "as if he knew them already. He was partly hidden, but the palms of his hands were open as though he was handing something to them. Then I heard a shot and saw Galman fall down. . . . From what I saw, Galman had no chance to even approach Aquino."

Balang's testimony was most damaging to the military in that he placed Galman in the company of the security men just as the single shot was fired into the back of Aquino's head. This directly contradicted the claim that Galman had suddenly appeared at Aquino's side and pulled the trigger. It also suggested that Galman had been set up; that he was a "fall guy."

Balang claimed that military men had attempted to frighten him out of revealing what he knew. Understanding the seriousness of what he had to say, he first gave his testimony in front of a video camera in the home of his lawyers, Isidro and Sinforosa Hildawa, a husband and wife team, late on the night of December 27, 1983. Also present were the Manila correspondent of NBC-TV, Benedict David, and a priest who was Balang's confessor. The tape was shown to the board privately the next day, and on January 6, 1984, Balang came to the Social Security System auditorium.

Jimenez was all over Balang immediately. A superb trial lawyer, the AVSECOM attorney held Balang with a hard stare. But the twenty-eight-year-old mechanic was not intimidated. Recalling from the video-taped testimony that Balang's first glimpse of Aquino was of him falling, with blood spurting from his head, the lawyer said, "Therefore, you didn't see the man in white shot?"

"Precisely, yes," the young man answered.

Jimenez demanded to know why Balang had given his information in such an unorthodox manner. Balang explained that he'd originally told the Hildawas, who were his father's lawyers, what he'd seen, and they had advised him "to keep quiet and wait for the right time."

Then, on the night of December 27, he found two armed men waiting at his home. One, identified as Edgar Dantes, a captain in the Criminal Investigation Service, ordered him to appear for questioning at CIS headquarters. The other, Sergeant Benjamin Pisa, worked for Colonel Balbino Diego, chief legal officer of the Presidential Security Command and said he'd been given instructions to invite Balang to go to Malacañang Palace to see the president. If Marcos wasn't there, Balang was to fly to meet him in the mountain resort town of Baguio. Balang was so frightened that as soon as the men left he dashed to his priest. The two of them then went to the Hildawas' home, where the tape was made.

Balang's experience with the military men had frightened a colleague of his, Celso Loteriña, who had also been working under the plane, and he went into hiding. The board had been informed that Loteriña had seen the crucial instant that Balang had missed—Aquino actually being shot. But when he was finally coaxed into an appearance on January 19, Loteriña insisted that he had not seen the shooting and, in fact, had not seen a man in white at all. Board member Luciano Salazar showed Loteriña some photographs and asked him how anyone "with normal eyesight" couldn't have seen the man in white lying a few inches from the man in blue. What had happened, Loteriña explained, was that after watching the man in blue being shot by the soldiers he had seen a soldier pointing a rifle at him. Then he fainted.

It later became known that Loteriña had been interrogated by the police on September 1 and six days later had been admitted to the hospital. Balang's lawyer, Isidro Hildawa, wanted to know if the police had beaten him up, which was what Balang had told him. "I can't remember," Loteriña replied.

On February 9, Fred Viesca, a cargo handler who had been working alongside the plane, appeared before the board and told a story similar to Ramon Balang's, but with a new and critical detail. Upon hearing the first shot, Viesca testified, "I glanced quickly to my left and saw a man in white on the stairs falling to the tarmac." Viesca's voice was shaky as he admitted, "I ran away . . . I was scared."

Justice Agrava recognized the importance of this testimony, and she turned on her most soothing, motherly manner to coax the jittery young man to continue. She smiled warmly at Viesca, her voice calm and lulling: "In my view, a young man like you—why, your hair even looks very nice—won't run from a single gunshot without bothering to find out what it's all about. . . . Let's go over it again, all right?"

"Yes, ma'am," Viesca barely whispered.

"Because you know, Fred, why, you even have the same first name as the man I love. Fred. I can already see that you're going to remember what really happened that day. We're coming so near to it. But, because you're younger than I am, your memory should be sharper, and I'm going to help you remember what you saw. Is that all right with you?"

"Yes, ma'am."

His memory sharpened. He recalled seeing the man in white falling from the "middle part of the stairs," roughly five steps above the tarmac on the nineteen-step stairway.

That damning claim brought AVSECOM attorney Jimenez to his feet with a snarl. "Son of a bitch! The witness must be hallucinating." No, replied Viesca, "That's what I really saw, sir, from where I was."

But when Jimenez, waving a metal pointer, sneering, pressing, demanded that he recall precisely where he was standing, what he was doing, and for how long he'd been in that position, Viesca stammered,

"I can't remember, ma'am," as he turned back to Agrava for comfort.

Elfren Ranas, who worked at the airport for a private security firm, the Lanting Security and Watchman Agency, told the board a story much like Fred Viesca's—that Aquino was still on the stairway when he was shot. The first time he came to the auditorium, on March 8, he testified that Aquino had been shot while he was on the fourth step from the bottom. On March 20 he came back and elaborated.

"I would like to tell the board now that the last time I saw the man in white was on the last step of the stairway. The two escorts, as I have observed, felt heavy with the man in the center which is, I noticed, the man in white." Ranas was speaking in English, and he was losing control of his ability with the language. He switched to Tagalog, and the translation of what he said was, "The man in white seemed too heavy for the two escorts who were holding him, and they appeared to let go of him. He fell head-down on to the tarmac." Ranas added that he'd noticed blood on the back of the man's white shirt when the body fell "from the last step."

Jimenez was on his feet again, furious: "You swore to tell the truth, the whole truth, and nothing but the truth the last time! Didn't you do that?"

"I did, sir."

"Therefore, when you didn't tell the whole truth last time, because you were released from the stand after you were asked whether you had anything more to add, and you said no, you said nothing more, you told a lie! Because you added something new, isn't it?"

As the boyish-looking Ranas contemplated this accusation, Justice Agrava, protector of besieged young men, interjected hotly, "Don't answer that question!" She then ordered three board aides to act out the scene that Ranas had described and, over Jimenez's protests, she concluded that, as Ranas had testified the first time around, when Aquino had reached the fourth step from the bottom his head was drooping to the left.

The hearings occasionally took bizarre turns, as when three expert witnesses, physicians, testified together. They were Drs. Constantino Nuñez, Bienvenido Muñoz, and Juanito Billote. They concurred that the bullet had smashed into Aquino's brain, killing him instantly. The brain had been removed during the autopsy and placed in a plastic bag, "and that was the last time we saw it," said Billote.

There were moments of humor, too, much of it unintended, driving Justice Agrava to distraction. When an AVSECOM sergeant named Reynaldo Pelias, who'd blocked newsmen inside the plane from following Aquino down the stairs, insisted that he couldn't identify Aquino in a photograph, Agrava thrust the picture under his nose, raised a fist over her head, and shouted, "If you still can't identify this, I'm really gonna *bop* you!"

There was even a time for singing.

First Lady Imelda Marcos visited the board on her birthday, July 2, 1984, four days before the hearings formally concluded. She was dressed somberly in a black suit with a slate-gray blouse. Her demeanor was composed; her manner serious. Someone had placed a red rose in a vase on the witness desk, and the palace had sent a bouquet of flowers, which Justice Agrava presented to her.

She discussed her meetings with Aquino in the United States. He had told her he wanted to come home because his heart bypass was failing and he didn't have long to live. She tried to discourage him, telling him that the heat and the uncertain air-conditioning would tax his poor health. She confirmed, too, that she passed on the president's warning that Aquino's life was threatened by would-be assassins. She "impressed on Ninoy the seriousness of threats against his life." But she denied that she had said, as Salvador Laurel had testified, "there are some people loyal to us who cannot be controlled."

She said her meetings with Aquino were "cordial and happy . . . Ninoy was very close to us." As a sign of how close they were, she showed the board a tiny crucifix on a gold chain that Aquino had given to her as he was leaving Manila for the United States "as a token of his appreciation."

Yet another token of appreciation was a letter Aquino had written to a surgeon at the Philippine Heart Center, one of her pet projects, where Aquino had been treated before being permitted to leave. Mrs. Marcos read aloud from the letter: "When the ultimate mist of controversy is melted by the rising sun, her works for our people will find final recognition."

Her testimony was stellar. She wept, smiled becomingly, and referred to herself as "a little Girl Scout." Justice Agrava called for a chorus of "Happy Birthday," but only a few sang with gusto, prompting Agrava to call for a repeat. Many in the room were deeply embarrassed, and Agrava was subjected to sniping, her critics taking the little songfest as a sign of her commitment to the Marcoses. Dante Santos, whose performance throughout the hearings indicated that he was not a Marcos supporter, wasn't present that day, but he told a newsman later that he would have sung along. "You can still be objective and civilized," he explained.

The hearings ended on July 6 without a strong indication of what the board members would decide. The military had put together a tightly coordinated case. There had been important testimony, too, showing that the men in uniform had lied. In his final appearance, Dean Narvasa dimmed the lights and displayed an assemblage of 154 slides, every picture he'd been able to get his hands on, which, when arranged in sequence, amounted to a stop-action film of Ninoy Aquino's final moments. The only picture he'd been unable to find would have shown a gunman firing a single shot.

9

*I*T'S VER

The board members went into seclusion. During the eight months of hearings they had amassed 20,377 pages of testimony, 447 audio cassettes, 1,472 photographs, and 1,294 documents. Now, the object was to come up with an honest conclusion that would satisfy all of them, as well as 54 million Filipinos and much of the outside world. The chances seemed slim.

A full year had passed since Aquino had been killed, and the public was anxious to fix the blame. Implicating the military would give Filipinos a sense that justice had been served, something that had been elusive for almost two decades. To the United States, such a finding would indicate that Marcos was actually on the road to reform, as he'd been assuring the embassy on Manila Bay. Filipinos were indulging their passion for rumormongering, and a great sense of anticipation permeated daily conversation in coffee shops, in neighborhoods, in rattling jeepneys, and at diplomatic receptions. The Manila papers were filled with snippets about when the board would issue its report and what it would say, but the writers were guessing. Journalists, local and foreign, were tapping every source available. I was no exception.

The board had been out of the public eye for a month and a half by August 22, when another correspondent and I went to see Narvasa's deputy, Bienvenido Tan. An urbane and highly successful businessman and attorney, Tan had taken considerable abuse from friends and relatives over his role with the board, and he half-jokingly mentioned a sister who had waved a white handkerchief in his face, taunting, "whitewash."

We spent the afternoon in Tan's airy, antique-filled apartment in Makati, talking about where the evidence pointed, how the board members were interpreting it, how much longer they might remain in seclusion, when they'd release their report, and what its implications would be for the country. I was particularly interested in the chemistry among the five.

Tan wasn't about to give away too much. He did acknowledge, though, that the military had done its best to frustrate the board, slightly adjusting its story each time the panel announced new evidence. But he insisted that the members wouldn't succumb to pressure of any kind, not from the military, the president, or the public. "I have no doubt that the decision will be based on the evidence, whichever way it goes," he said. "If it points to Galman, we'll say so, and my wife will throw me out of the house. If it points to a military conspiracy and President Marcos, we'll say that, and you know what that means."

Tan switched on a video-cassette player and showed us a tape that he and the others had watched "hundreds of times." It was a collection of footage shot by ABC-TV, Japan's NHK-TV, and the local, government-owned Channel 4, had cost $100,000 to produce, and was so technologically sophisticated that every second of footage could be frozen to show thirty distinct movements.

As the tape began, Tan, sitting in an armchair with a remote-control device in his lap, recalled that when Senator Robert F. Kennedy had been assassinated in Los Angeles in 1968, security men had immediately caught the gunman, Sirhan Sirhan. "Why didn't they just grab Galman?" he wondered aloud. The tape rolled forward, and Tan commented as the spirit moved him:

"Look, there, almost certainly something is being passed to Moreno. It may be a gun. But we can't prove it or that he was the triggerman.

"That's [Sergeant Prospero] Bona taking a flash picture of Aquino. He denied it before the board. I'm preparing a perjury recommendation.

"See that intelligence sergeant, that [Armando] de la Cruz, look, he's obviously looking straight down the stairway. He denies seeing anything. We're considering filing perjury charges against him, but he's military, so you know what will happen. I don't know how that fellow can sleep at night.

"Look, all those fellows at the tube door, they're all looking down the stairs. They see what's going on. They're not just holding back the crowd of reporters and photographers.

"See that stairway, see how narrow and open it is. Can you imagine Galman hiding behind an open stairway like that and not being seen by at least thirty soldiers?"

The late afternoon sun was dropping quickly behind Makati's high-rise buildings by the time we finished watching and talking, and I felt that, intentionally or otherwise, Tan had indicated, if not the board's decision, at least his own. So I asked him if he had recommended a finding that would implicate the military. He refused to say but acknowledged that he'd already written his own report to the board members, as had some of the other attorneys. Like everyone else connected with the hearings, he was worried and uncertain about how the military—or the public, for that matter—would react to the board's final report, and so he'd made several copies of his own, giving them to people he trusted, to be released if he was harmed.

Insightful as it was, the meeting with Tan convinced me that for an authoritative view, I would have to try one of the five board members. Journalists hadn't had any success with them but, still, it was worth a try. The next morning I telephoned the office of the one I felt would be most forthcoming. Whoever answered the phone said that he wasn't in and gave me another number. The switchboard operator there said, "Philippine Village," and I immediately realized that the board was secluded in this government-owned hotel and gambling casino adjacent to Manila International Airport. My second surprise came when the operator put me through, and the third when the board member suggested dinner that night. We met at a restaurant he recommended, a large, badly lit place, decorated in dark mahogany and deep, red velvet. We were the only customers.

We ordered martinis and steaks and I asked him how things were going at the Philippine Village. He laughed and said, "You're not supposed to know that's where we're closeted. How did you find out?" Not wanting to admit that I'd just been lucky, I laughed, too, and let him go on. I learned that the five board members had been in the hotel the past two weeks, meeting "day and night." They gathered every morning in Justice Agrava's suite, where the air was growing heavy with the rich smells of *adobo* cooking in the tiny kitchen. Agrava, intent on saving public funds, insisted that they not use room service.

She kept up appearances, though, and showed up each morning in a crisply pressed dress, her hair and makeup immaculate, while her male colleagues were beginning to fray, several of them neglecting to shave. All day they sat at a long table, amid heaps of transcripts, photos, and the jumbled physical evidence they'd collected over the months. They spent hours in the dark, viewing and reviewing a copy of the tape Tan had shown. They were pushing for a conclusion by the first week in September, just two weeks away, he said, "that's why we're sleeping and working there." He seemed to have a dose of cabin fever, and I thought that was why he had agreed so readily to see me. We ordered two more martinis, sipped them slowly, and savored the generous steaks. He was relaxing. I hadn't expected to learn very much, but I was wrong.

He started out with a bang: The board had concluded that the military was lying, that Galman had not killed Aquino. To reach this conclusion, board members had considered anyone with motives to kill Aquino—the Communists, former enemies, and presumed allies who had much to gain with him out of the political picture. Each of these they systematically eliminated. Next, they reviewed circumstances at the time when Aquino began agitating to return to Manila: Marcos was terribly sick, and the people close to him sincerely believed that he was going to die. Among those most worried were Imelda Marcos and the president's friend and intimate adviser, Eduardo Cojuangco, Jr. Mrs. Marcos and Cojuangco fretted aloud about the president's fragile health and about the damage Aquino could cause. The two of them mulled their fears with certain military officers, who already shared their belief that the president was at death's door. In the judgment of the board members, "the military" took its cues from Cojuangco and Mrs. Marcos. Not that they made direct requests to have Aquino assassinated, they didn't have to, but rather they let drop circuitous comments, the kinds of hints to which loyal military officers would know instinctively how to respond. The image my dinner partner evoked was positively Shakespearean in scope and aura: the failing king lying near death in the gloomy recesses of the palace; the scheming queen and her adviser, whispering their wishes but meticulously keeping their hands clean; the faithful military retainer, knowing what must be done and doing it to please his monarch.

We glanced across the table at each other, and I said that he seemed to be telling me that they had reached a final decision, that they knew who had ordered Aquino murdered. Was this so, or were they still thinking in broader terms, of "the military"? But he didn't want his narrative to be rushed and ignored my question. Instead, he reflected on Marcos and said he was not linked directly to the plot. The board was inclined to believe that the president had been too ill to know what was being done on his behalf, though doubt lingered in their minds. "We're not talking about what he might have wanted done."

We had stopped eating. He was talking, I was listening and taking notes, occasionally asking for a point to be explained, for elaboration. He was getting very close to answering the central question, but he wasn't quite ready. So he backtracked, reviewing the evidence that had led them to conclude that the president's people, and not the Communists, had done it: "It's all circumstantial, but it's all there; the manner in which the media were confined at the airport; the manner in which the military afterward searched for everyone who'd seen anything and scared the shit out of them. The immediate and unseemly effort to establish the military view as the only credible one was in itself proof that the initial statement, that the Communists had done it, was not true. The first evidence of this was the president accusing the Communists when Galman's identity wasn't even known."

Then he shifted direction and talked about what it had been like, being on the board and being subjected to public scrutiny and abuse, about the effect it had had on their families. "It's been an honest job," he said. "We don't want to embarrass our grandchildren."

Well, I said, that really leaves just one question unanswered. He took a deep breath and exhaled, "It's Ver. Everyone else was responsible to him."

We left the restaurant together a few moments later. I thanked him for his help. Almost as an afterthought he said, "I think you'd better not single me out." I never have.

Believing it unwise to file from Manila, I returned to Tokyo. The story I wrote said that the Agrava board would accuse Ver, Brigadier General Custodio, and the military escorts of plotting and carrying out the Aquino assassination and would recommend that they be tried. It said, too, that the board hadn't been able to single out which of the escorts had been the triggerman. The *San Jose Mercury News* published the article on August 26, 1984, as did other papers in the Knight-

Ridder group. It was picked up the same day by American papers subscribing to the Knight-Ridder News Service and by the wire services, which played it back to Manila.

The government-dominated papers there ignored the story. But it made a huge splash in the alternative papers, particularly *Malaya, Business Day,* and *Mr. and Ms.,* and forced the board to comment. All five members denied speaking to me. Bienvenido Tan speculated that I had put two and two together after speaking to him, and then guessed. These denials were published in the controlled press, where the *San Jose Mercury News* and I were castigated. But the cat was out of the bag, and that, I came to believe, was where my source wanted it. What he hadn't told me at the time was that the four men on the board were running into trouble with Mrs. Agrava and were afraid that, as chairman, she would somehow override their findings. By getting the majority view before the public, my source evidently hoped to avert the widely anticipated whitewash.

My article had said the board would release its report by mid September. It didn't, and as weeks elapsed I began to fear what every journalist dreads, that I'd been used and intentionally misled. But in the suite at Philippine Village, the four men were at Mrs. Agrava's throat, and she at their's. She refused to implicate General Ver. She agreed with them that the military, and not Galman, had assassinated Aquino. She believed, as they did, that Brigadier General Custodio was involved. But he was as high as she was willing to go in the chain of command; she wouldn't cite Major General Olivas.

Marcos had gotten to Agrava. While my board source and attorney Tan had both insisted that no pressure had been applied, on three separate occasions the president had secretly summoned Agrava and Luciano Salazar to the palace. Each time, presidential assistant Manuel Lazaro, Marcos's chief legal adviser, had arranged to pick up Agrava and Salazar at a church and had driven them to Malacañang where they met privately with Marcos in his nara-paneled study. He warned them that if the board implicated Ver and Olivas the armed forces would react violently and the country would be torn apart. The president had convinced Agrava. Salazar, with great courage, rejected the argument and allowed himself to be guided by the evidence.

Agrava's concern was less with determining who had actually done the plotting and the shooting than with finding a solution that would produce "peace and harmony and happiness." She had told friends that she was afraid of violence, and her fears heightened as leaks began to appear in a variety of news outlets, all indicating that the board would accuse the military. One such article in the *San Francisco Examiner* quoted board member Dante Santos, and he subsequently received anonymous death threats. But Santos and the other men held their ground. They implored Agrava. They shouted at her. They pounded the table. She screamed back. She wept. September came and went. Agrava would not budge.

As so often happens in the Philippines, rumors rushed in to fill the vacuum left by absent facts, and most Filipinos decided for themselves that the board was cooking up a witch's brew that would implicate Galman and clear the military. But on October 10, Bruce MacDonell, NBC-TV's general manager for Asia and the Pacific, obtained a copy of Dean Narvasa's final report. This 479-page document was, with a few minor changes of phrasing, the same as what the four men on the board would submit two weeks later as their own report to the president. MacDonell generously shared it with me, and we both released it the next day.

The report blamed a high-level military conspiracy for the Aquino murder and accused General Ver of taking part in "elaborate plans ostensibly geared towards protecting the life of Senator Aquino [that] were in fact designed to camouflage the taking of that life." Recalling that Ver had testified that "we did not monitor" Aquino's movements, particularly the final leg of his trip, from Taipei to Manila, Narvasa wrote: "Ver's testimony was meant to make the board believe that he and the military authorities had made no efforts to trace Aquino's movements and, hence, could not possibly have learned any of the details of his arrival; consequently, the security plans prepared and executed, as well as their underlying assumptions, were genuine and above board." Narvasa accused Ver of being "less than candid" with the board in twenty-one specified instances. The counsel also charged the general with "speciousness" and of being "misleading" during his three-day testimony. Ver's performance, Narvasa wrote, "cannot but engender suspicion of ulterior motives behind it, such as the projection of a guileless, old soldier, instead of the canny and experienced intelligence officer that he actually is."

Narvasa accused Brigadier General Custodio of aiding Ver: "Custodio was in direct contact with General Ver in the conceptualization and finalization of the supposed security arrangements for Senator Aquino. He certainly had a direct line to Ver during the implementation of those plans. . . . His participation in the conspiracy was an essential one, an indispensable one.''

As for Olivas, Narvasa dismissed as mere ''theory'' for which ''there is simply no proof'' his testimony that Galman had been a Communist killer and that the .357 magnum had been the murder weapon.

Narvasa acknowledged that his accusations of a conspiracy were based largely on circumstantial evidence. But the question of who shot Aquino was another matter; he had hard evidence. The single shot had been fired by one of the military escorts, he wrote, either Moreno or Miranda, the two who were immediately behind Aquino coming down the stairway.

This finding was based on dramatic testimony from a surprising witness during one of the panel's closed-door sessions. The witness was Celso Loteriña, the ground engineer who had testified publicly on January 19 that he hadn't seen the ''man in white'' at all because he had fainted in fright and couldn't recall if he'd been beaten up by police during an interrogation. Loteriña had been much more forthcoming in private, not that he was any less nervous. Indeed, Narvasa wrote, Loteriña ''was so frightened that he had to stop a few times in the course of his testimony to retch and regain his composure.'' He told the panel that he had ''heard the sound of running feet on the stairway and when he looked in that direction he saw Aquino and his guards at about the fourth step from the bottom. At that instant, he saw a hand with a gun appear at the rear of Aquino and discharge a shot at him. He could not see the gunman's body, because his view was obstructed by the post and the airbridge.'' Loteriña's testimony was crucial, and the reason he had not given it when he appeared in the Social Security auditorium was that he feared for his life. When he finally revealed what he had seen, the board members questioned him closely and were unanimously convinced that he was telling the truth.

But that wasn't to be the end of the reluctant Loteriña. A day after MacDonell's and my reports appeared, Colonel Balbino Diego, the Presidential Security Command's lawyer, delivered to the board a letter purportedly written by Loteriña. It said that his testimony had been "induced and influenced" by the board in return for a promise that he and his family could emigrate to the United States. Therefore, the letter concluded, "Please consider my statements before you as withdrawn and no effect." The letter had been written in fluent English, but when Loteriña was interviewed on government television that evening, he could barely speak the language. The Agrava panel termed the letter "a desperate attempt by some quarters to discredit the board and its findings."

Loteriña's wasn't the only testimony that, according to Narvasa's report, "clinched" the finding. Eight other airport workers had told the board slightly varying versions of seeing Aquino still on the stairway when he was shot. Several of them, like Loteriña, had been deeply frightened, and one, Olivia Reyes, a twenty-year-old security agency employee, agreed to testify only after being subpoenaed. "She has since disappeared," Narvasa wrote.

As for the testimony by dozens of military officers and men on how Aquino and Galman had been killed, Narvasa termed it "unworthy of belief." There was no substance to claims that Galman had been involved in a Communist plot. To the contrary, the only way for Galman to have gotten onto the tarmac beneath CAL 811 was with the approval of the military men who were there supposedly to provide security for Aquino. Narvasa wrote that there had been ample testimony and other evidence to establish beyond doubt that "Galman was not Aquino's killer, but was himself an unsuspecting victim of a nefarious plot."

On Sunday night, October 21, after Narvasa had submitted his report to the board, he and the five members gave a little farewell party for themselves and their staffs. Agrava and the men embraced, she calling them affectionately, "my diamonds, my machos." Then she turned tearful and said to her colleagues, "If I happen to differ with you at a small point of our conclusions, I still love you and hope you love me."

The next night, Agrava and the four met in a last-ditch attempt to reconcile their differences over Ver. They failed, and the men told Narvasa that they would adopt his report and Agrava would submit her own.

Around noon on Tuesday, Agrava drove to Malacañang Palace and met privately with President Marcos for nearly twenty minutes. At 1:30 P.M., the two of them, he in an embroidered *barong tagalog,* she in an olive green dress, entered the palace's dim ceremonial hall where she officially presented him with three copies of a blue, cardboard-bound, 121-page book. It was entitled "Separate Report of the Chairman." Agrava's report did not vary a great deal from Narvasa's on most of its central points. She, too, cited Loteriña as a key witness to the shooting, along with Balang, Viesca, Ranas, Reyes, and others, because there was no reason to suspect "that any of them had any ulterior motives to tell an untruth." She concluded, as did Narvasa, that the assassination weapon was not a .357 magnum, as the military experts had claimed, but either a .45-caliber or a .38-caliber handgun, both of which were standard military issue. They both based their judgment on expert analysis of the fragmented bullet that had ended Aquino's life. She concurred, too, that Aquino had been killed in a military plot. But she found that plot to have been considerably more limited than did Narvasa. She accused only the six enlisted men who'd been on the stairway—Lat, de Mesa, Miranda, Moreno, Lazaga, and de la Cruz—and the man in charge of the day's security, Brigadier General Custodio.

Agrava didn't charge General Ver in her report, but she didn't ignore him either. In a section of her conclusion entitled "General Ver Was Not a Plotter," she wrote that nothing implicated him: "Parts of his testimony can always be challenged as untrue, howsoever baseless. But a doubt as to his veracity, if any, will not justify a finding that he was among the plotters."

With Channel 4 cameras carrying the presentation live, Marcos accepted Agrava's "Separate Report" with warm thanks. Her results were acceptable; he was prepared to put Custodio and a handful of enlisted men at risk. In a later TV appearance, the president said he would turn over the report to the government's ombudsman, or *Tanodbayan,* who would take the case before a court known as the *Sandiganbayan,* created to try civil servants charged with graft and corruption. It was an odd choice of venues for a murder conspiracy case, except that its findings could not normally be appealed. So, assuming the court delivered the kind of decision Marcos was after, the matter would be permanently closed. For assurance, three days earlier Marcos had appointed three new judges to the *Sandiganbayan,* even though there were already six. Two of the new men, Augusto M. Amores and Bienvenido C. Vera Cruz, would be joining Chief Judge Manuel Pamaran in hearing the case.

A lot of Filipinos went to bed Tuesday night believing that the accusations would go no further than those in Agrava's report. But, Wednesday morning, the four Agrava board members took their own two-volume report along with Narvasa's original to the palace. Marcos ignored them in an anteroom for an hour before admitting them to his study and receiving their massive findings. The president's mood was chilly, the board members' somber. Echoing Narvasa's report, they cited as "indictable for the premeditated killing of Aquino" twenty-six men: General Ver; Major General Olivas; Brigadier General Custodio; six lower-ranking officers, including Colonel Arturo Custodio; the six escorts; ten other enlisted men; and a single civilian, Hermilo Gosuico, the man with the birthmark on his arm.

TV cameras recorded the formal transfer of their report, which Marcos said he would also forward to the ombudsman, but the few seconds carried on Channel 4's regular newscast that night showed only the president glaring at the foursome and telling them bitterly, "I hope you can live with your conscience, with what you have done."

What they had done, in fact, was push the president a long step closer to the brink of political disaster. Short of the military rebellion that ultimately sent him fleeing from the Philippines, the board's majority decision was one of the most crucial elements in ending Marcos's twenty-year presidential career. The board members surprised and inspired many Filipinos. They had acted independently and courageously, directly contradicting Marcos's contention that a Communist hit man had killed Aquino. Instead, they had determined that the killing had been plotted by the president's favorite general and, by extension, maybe even the president himself.

Ver, who like Marcos knew what was coming, immediately submitted his request for a leave of absence until the trial was completed, writing to the president, "I never imagined in my wildest dreams that I would be implicted in the Aquino case, but now the worst has happened." First the news stories and now the majority report, he continued, "like a bolt of lightning from a clear sky have struck me down without any chance of defense. I proclaim my innocence to the whole world." Marcos responded with an encouraging letter: "We are more than ever aware, General, that the circumstances under which the board had chosen to implicate you in its findings are fraught with doubt and great contradictions of opinion and testimony. And we are deeply disturbed that on the basis of so-called evidence, you have been so accused by some members of the board."

The president's letter also told Ver that unlike the Agrava board proceedings, which had amounted to "trial through publicity and innuendo," the impending court trial would "ferret out the truth and arrive at justice." Meanwhile, his place as chief of staff would be filled temporarily by Ver's deputy, Lieutenant General Fidel Ramos. The letter, though addressed to Ver, was meant for public consumption and was immediately released to the local press. The general and the president knew that arrangements were being made in the court to assure an outcome that would please them both.

The Agrava board's decision stunned the armed forces. At the same time, it set in motion changes that were to become more far-reaching than anyone could have foreseen. Although some military men consoled themselves with the reassurance that only a handful of their comrades had been implicated, most conceded that the entire institution must share the blame. This sense of *mea culpa* provided a timely vehicle for the young officers of RAM. These men were not necessarily motivated by the Aquino killing, but believed they could exploit the sense of shared guilt to increase their strength and influence. Many wished to force out some of the "over-staying" senior officers and win promotions that were past due for themselves.

The young men decided to take their grievances to the public, but because most of them were intelligence officers, analysts, and administrators rather than field soldiers, they characteristically proceeded with caution. On February 17, 1985, nearly four months after the board had submitted its findings, they released a mimeographed sheet condemning "the prevailing military culture that has evolved in the 1980s which rewards boot-licking incompetents and banishes independent-minded professionals and achievers. . . . We will no longer tolerate incompetence and indiscipline. We will no longer close our eyes to the graft and corruption happening in our midst." It was unsigned, identifying the writers only as graduates of the Philippine Military Academy.

Weakened by anonymity, the statement appeared to be all bravado and no substance, and it drew little response from the rest of the armed forces. A month later, the same group issued another broadside, this one detailing nine demands for reform. Two in particular rang bells because so many officers were affected. The first called for wiping out the institutionalized system of *bata-bata* and *padrino,* or protégés and benefactors, in promotions and favorable assignments. The second was broader, but beneath its surface more evocative, since it referred to the system of personal loyalty established by Marcos and Ver. It stated: "Loyalty must be directed to the constitution, not to any individual or group of persons."

One week later, on March 21, the reformists took a daring step. Emerging from behind their anonymous statements, some three hundred graduates of the Philippine Military Academy, classes of 1971 through 1984, unfurled a huge banner as they marched past hundreds of fellow alumni and guests in the annual homecoming festivities at Baguio. It read: UNITY THROUGH REFORMS. RESTORE DIGNITY IN THE AFP. This was a major step for the reformists; they had unmasked themselves and openly challenged the military establishment.

President Marcos spoke the next day at the academy's graduation ceremony and did not refer to the incident. But General Ramos did. Looking every inch the soldier as he strode to the lectern in a gleaming white dress uniform, Ramos said the time had come to restore "professionalism instead of personalism." Sounding almost as though he were reading from the group's latest broadside, Ramos said the armed forces must use merit and performance instead of favoritism as the basis for advancement. Peering out across the parade ground at the graduating cadets, starchy in brass-buttoned gray tunics, chests crossed with white webbing, tall black shakos on their heads, he said dramatically: "We now strive for reform."

Now that they had gone public, the young officers, in true Filipino tradition, needed a father figure to provide mature advice and protection. Ramos, as acting chief of staff, looked like their man. It was not to be, but he was ready to listen, and on April 20 he met with forty or so officers in his office. They talked for seven hours, and Ramos came away impressed with their sincerity and with the legitimacy of their complaints. But because of his soldierly mind-set, he told them that his role as acting chief prevented him from delivering significant change. Sensing their disappointment, Ramos passed them on to Defense Minister Juan Ponce Enrile, who, after his own four-hour session, was impressed, too. He and Ramos recommended to Marcos that he meet with the men.

The reformists went to Malacañang Palace on May 31. One of them, navy Captain Rex Robles, said afterward that Marcos "listened, though not too attentively, and then delivered a lecture." He told them that as an old soldier himself he knew that it was traditional for military men to gripe among themselves. One of the younger officers told the commander in chief that this wasn't ordinary griping; that he and some of his colleagues were ashamed to wear their uniforms; they were appalled by the military's reputation as the enemy of the people; they were horrified by the role played by even a relative handful of their colleagues in the Aquino assassination. But, not wanting to alarm Marcos, the young officers also told him that they had no aggressive designs against him and that they looked to him as their inspiration, gratuitously citing a book he'd written, *Toward a Filipino Ideology*, as the touchstone of their movement. The president responded by plucking a copy from the wall of glass-covered shelves in his study, where he kept multiple copies of his books, and signing it for them. But he warned that if they complained too openly they could create an image of weakness within the armed forces, and this could benefit only the Communists. The young men left Malacañang recognizing that they could expect no change from Marcos. Enrile and Ramos concurred.

The relationship that was developing among the reformist officers, Ramos, and, most importantly, the ambitious Enrile was of growing concern to the president. Robles and Colonel Hernani Figueroa, another group member who'd gone public, were both intelligence officers assigned to Enrile, a situation that fostered close personal relationships between the young men and their civilian boss. Robles and Figueroa appeared to be apolitical. But they could be susceptible to the entreaties of a clever politician, and Enrile was nothing if not clever.

The defense minister, who had grown up as a politician at Marcos's knee, perceived chinks in the president's armor caused by the Aquino assassination and was now doing his best to expose them for his own personal gain. At a dinner a few evenings after the Agrava reports were submitted, Enrile spoke about the "danger" of Marcos being succeeded by his wife with the assistance of Ver. The defense chief saw the RAM organization as a wedge to be driven between the president and the armed forces. In this way, he could further his presidential ambitions. Enrile quietly began to provide financial help to the reformists.

None of this got past General Ver. Although officially on leave, he continued to work out of his office at Malacañang, where, as always, he had the president's ear. He passed along reports that Enrile was encouraging RAM and that Ramos was visiting military units around the country, promising genuine reform in the future and delivering whatever improvements he could. Marcos and Ver began sensing the early signs of military unrest, but they took no action. They believed in their own invincibility.

10

*P*OOR COUNTRY

While the military, the judiciary, the president, and others in control of the national destiny were jockeying for position, ordinary Filipinos had their hands full just finding work and feeding themselves. By the fall of 1984, when the Agrava board issued its explosive report, life was tougher for more people than at any time since World War II. Manufacturing and imports were down by 25 percent from 1983; the gross domestic product was down between 6 and 9 percent; inflation, at 62 percent, had never been higher; foreign debt was a completely unmanageable $26.5 billion; and foreign banks were withholding future loans.

The grinding plight of the poor was visible almost anywhere, in the streets of Manila and in the small towns and villages throughout the islands. People who hadn't visited the Philippines in years would arrive and be stunned to find that the clock had turned backward. When much of Southeast Asia was progressing, the one country that had every reason to succeed was looking more and more like a basket case. Entire families were sleeping on broken sidewalks, some with only newspaper to cover themselves; others lay under roofs of flattened cardboard boxes or plastic sheets, hundreds of them within easy view of the U.S. embassy and the plush Manila Hotel. Parents and children begged together in the streets, dodging precariously in and out of the careening traffic for handouts of two or three pesos. Girls and boys as young as nine sold their bodies to Japanese and Arab tourists in the "entertainment" district of Ermita and to American sailors in the Subic Bay base town of Olongapo.

Appalling poverty had always been the curse of Calcutta, Bombay, Dhaka, Karachi, and other cities of the Indian subcontinent; it had been common in Indonesia, although conditions there had improved in the last decade. The Philippines, too, had had its share of poverty, but in a land of natural resources, where a meal could be plucked off a tree, even the poorest scraped by with a semblance of dignity. In the previous ten years, though, the policies of the Marcos regime had negated such built-in advantages.

For the first time, Filipino economists were comparing the nation with destitute countries like Bangladesh. They blamed Marcos: "The main characteristic distinguishing the Marcos years from other periods in our economic history has been the trend towards the concentration of power in the hands of the government, and the use of governmental functions to dispense economic privileges to some small factions in the private sector," a panel of senior economists at the University of the Philippines wrote in a June 1984 report that was highly critical of the regime in general and its economic polices in particular.

The assassination of Aquino was the last straw for many, who felt that with Aquino went hope. Of all the segments of Philippine society, none felt this loss more dramatically than the substantial and growing middle class. Hope had been the driving force of those who had gone to the colleges and trade schools, who held white-collar jobs, who bought the new shampoos and convenience foods, who aspired to the gas stoves, refrigerators, and cars advertised on TV, who put down-payments on little tract houses, who felt life would get better so long as they worked hard and didn't get involved in politics.

Then Aquino was killed, calling the world's attention to the mess in the Philippines. Investors grew fearful, and capital flight rose to unprecedented levels. Because of this, loans dried up, companies closed down, and middle-class people lost their jobs.

If the term *middle class* had been invented to describe anyone in particular, it could have been for Raul and Mary Rose Domingo. He was a mechanical engineering graduate of Manila's Don Bosco College who had worked for Cummins Engine, Inc., an Indiana firm with a branch in Manila; she a free-lance magazine layout designer. When they were dating in the late seventies, they went out almost every night. "That was the life, man," Raul recalled one day as they sat in their tiny room with their two sleeping children, an infant and a toddler. "Restaurants, movies, whatever we wanted." When he felt like a night with the boys, he and Mary Rose's brother, Ramon, would join friends at the cockfights, where betting was driven up by fast-spending government officials, police and military officers, and businessmen from Chinatown. "Sometimes I'd overdo it and lose too much," Raul remembered, a touch of embarrassment entering his voice. Mary Rose, her long black hair tied back from her pale, oval face, poked him gently on his shoulder. "Never mind, Lito," she said, using his nickname, "we had it then."

They were married in 1981, and life stayed sweet. They had what Mary Rose called "a real nice apartment," and they filled it with their luxurious wedding gifts, "every appliance you could think of, a color TV, a portable radio transceiver for Lito." He was making about $300 a month, her income augmented his, and they thought the world was theirs. Indeed, with 80 percent of the metropolitan area's population earning well below $195 a month for a family of five, the young couple had reason to feel pleased with themselves. Their first baby was born in 1982. "We bought the best of everything," Mary Rose said, "imported Pampers, formula, the prettiest baby clothes."

Raul had already seen some signs of trouble at work. As early as 1980, there'd been a retrenchment. But, with his engineering degree, he felt he had nothing to worry about. There was another layoff in 1981, and a third in late 1983. "It was after the Aquino killing," said Raul. "By then, the economic decline was accelerating, and our customers couldn't afford to buy new engines or even to have their old ones rebuilt." In February 1984, Raul was "allowed to resign" and was given some separation pay, most of it going to pay off his car. "Then reality hit me between the eyes, man. For the first time since I'd graduated from college I had no job, I had no source of income. I had a wife, a baby, and another one on the way. I was really worried."

They turned to their parents, but Raul's father, a former colonel in the Philippine Constabulary, lived on his pension and couldn't help much. Mary Rose's father was a physician with a small practice and an old-fashioned house in the Mandaluyong section of Manila. The young couple moved in, paying $20 a month rent for their room. "My parents pay for all the food," she said. "We can hardly afford even a loaf of bread. It costs ten pesos [about fifty cents] now; a year ago it was two pesos." In a country rich in fresh produce, they were no longer able to afford fruit and instead crushed a vitamin C pill in a glass of water.

They had already sold off most of their wedding presents. "My portable transceiver went just the other day," Raul said. He motioned to a blank space on a book shelf. "Hell, I know it was a pure luxury; you couldn't really say I needed it." Mary Rose sold her camera. "It was mostly a hobby for me, but it was important for my work, too," she said. "But, now there's no work, anyway." One thing they didn't sell was Raul's exercise equipment. Her parents had a spare room in the house, and the Domingos decided that they would paint it, put the weights and the rowing machine in, hang a sign outside, and start a "fitness center." The new enterprise had been open for three months, with five part-time employees and twenty-five members. The membership fee, $15, and the monthly charge of $4.50 provided just enough to cover the salaries of the staff, with nothing left over for rent, electricity, or profit.

What had gone wrong? What had caused such ordinary lives to turn upside down? Raul fidgeted, scuffing his rubber sandals on the bare wood floor. Mary Rose looked at him, then at the floor. "I don't think I should say too much," he said finally. "But I put it down to poor management by the government. Our officials look out for their own pocket."

The Domingos and other middle-class families were struggling, but they would probably bounce back. But the very poor, those who had no exercise equipment, whose parents themselves were looking for spare rooms, had no flexibility; they couldn't bounce back to even their normally marginal existence. And no one was poorer than the sugarcane workers of Negros Occidental. They were starving to death.

The province of Negros Occidental is the western half of an island shaped like an old sock in the middle of the archipelago. Its circumstances symbolized all that was wrong with the way Marcos ran the country, and how his agricultural, industrial, and social policies defeated the natural advantages of the Philippines. In 1966, when Marcos came to power, Negros was the most prosperous province in the country, earning 20 percent of the Philippines' foreign exchange income.

By 1985, it was the poorest. In 1966, there were no Communists operating in Negros. By 1985, they were running free, not just in the inhospitable jungles and hills, but on sugar plantations and in cities and towns.

As the Mekong Delta is the "rice bowl" of Vietnam, Negros Occidental is the "sugar bowl" of the Philippines. Unfortunately, though, while human beings can survive and even thrive eating rice, they cannot exist on sugar. And as a source of livelihood for the people of Negros, sugar was no longer viable. It had become a glut on the European and U.S. markets as weight-conscious Westerners turned to artificial sweeteners. World prices bottomed out, and the United States, the largest market for Philippine sugar, cut its quota. These were factors beyond anyone's control. But there were other, far darker reasons for the shattered sugar bowl.

The sugar industry in Negros Occidental was virtually destroyed by corrupt government managers who were under the control of President Marcos and by profligate planters whose carefree spending drained them of the capacity to respond when the boom faded. Some planters conceded that they had failed to make preparations for the day when sugar would no longer make them rich—and they all saw that day coming for years. But many more refused to accept blame, insisting that the fault lay entirely with Marcos and his golf partner, fraternity brother, and appointed sugar baron, Roberto S. Benedicto.

Benedicto's rule over the sugar domain went back to 1972, when Marcos imposed martial law. Benedicto was then the Philippine ambassador to Japan, a mere token of prestige since he spent most of his time in Manila, near his friend and benefactor. Benedicto was the scion of a wealthy Negros sugar family, but he was not admired for business acumen by others of his class, and Marcos made the most of this animosity. He instructed Benedicto to seize the utility and communications empire of the Negros-based Lopez family, one of Marcos's chief antagonists, and then create a government agency that would take control of the sugar industry, which the Lopezes dominated.

Hortensia Starke was a descendant of the Lopezes and had inherited a substantial share of the family's vast fortune. "My grandfather was a sugar baron," she said at her elegant home one evening. "Sugar made our family and some other families fabulously rich." But, rather than plow their money back into the land and help improve the lot of hundreds of thousands of laborers, the Lopezes, like many other Negros landowners, invested in Manila and abroad. The family bought the Manila Electric Company (MERALCO) and the capital's most powerful broadcasting and newspaper group. They also pumped a huge sum into the 1965 presidential campaign of an ambitious young candidate named Ferdinand E. Marcos. The quid pro quo was that a member of the clan, Fernando Lopez, be Marcos's vice-presidential running mate. Marcos didn't like the idea, but he was in no position to turn his back on the funding. Lopez was Marcos's first and last vice president. Seven years later, when Marcos imposed martial law, he eliminated the number-two position and set about biting the hand that had fed him. The president had determined that the only way to control such independent powers as the sugar barons was to break them, and Benedicto was the tool he used.

The president delighted in squeezing the Lopezes and their ilk, and few were more bitter than Hortensia Starke. Although still wealthy by any measurement, she'd witnessed a precipitous decline in living standards in Negros and resented it deeply. "Negros was once the richest province in the Philippines," she said, sitting rigidly in her living room, her slender, exquisitely manicured hands clenched into fists in her lap. "Now, we're the poorest, the object of pity and charity." Sacks of rice were heaped waist-high on the floor of her paneled dining room, some for her family, the bulk for distribution to her plantation workers. Starke dismissed the notion that the sugar barons and their descendants must share in the blame for mismanaging the economy. Only Marcos was at fault. "Marcos may be a shrewd politician, but he knows nothing about economics. Benedicto is a business failure. And these two dummies are entrusted with the country's huge sugar industry. Do you wonder why we're in such trouble?"

With Marcos's mandate in his pocket, Benedicto set up a government export monopoly that in little more than a decade would drain off billions of dollars and leave the industry a dry shell. Benedicto named his creation the Philippine Exchange, then changed it to the Philippine Sugar Commission, or PHILSUCOM. Two years later, he added the National Sugar Trading Corporation, or NASUTRA, to handle domestic sales. Benedicto appointed as administrators men who'd never been planters and did not understand the industry—senior military officers, ethnic Chinese businessmen who'd contributed heavily to Marcos, and relatives of the First Family.

Under the new setup, planters were required to sell all their sugar to the monopoly, which paid them a half to a third of the price received from the United States. Marcos's Presidential Decree 579 ruled that the difference go into a "special fund of the national government subject to the disposition of the president for public purposes." Since the "special fund" was kept secret, planters looked on it as the regime's license to steal. Guillermo Araneta, vice president of a group of companies owned by his family, made it his business to track the rakeoff, but that proved impossible. "Around 1975, the president said that the money was being used to fight the Communist insurgency in Mindanao," he said one afternoon in the office of one of the family's four sugar mills outside Bacolod, the provincial capital. "Otherwise, there's been virtually no reporting, no accountability. No one knows where the money has gone."

Araneta had managed to trace an ongoing discrepancy of two to four cents a pound between what the U.S. Department of Agriculture was paying and what PHILSUCOM reported receiving and calculated that over the decade since the monopoly began operating, $1.5 billion was unaccounted for. With some opposition members of the National Assembly from Negros Occidental, Araneta attempted in 1984 to conduct hearings with the aim of documenting these discrepancies, but the effort was stopped by the Marcos parliamentary machine.

Benedicto and Marcos also profited handsomely from the construction of fourteen sugar mills in the provinces. The mills had been built in the mid 1970s by Japanese firms, which submitted bills totaling $507.6 million, 25 to 30 percent above actual cost. The difference had gone to Benedicto, who shared the wealth with his friend in Malacañang Palace. Although the mills would turn into a fiasco and a national scandal, the original concept to build them made some sense early in the martial law era. The Philippines was then attempting to fill the gap in U.S. sugar quotas still left by the embargo against Cuba. But the mills were built hastily, without such normal precautions as soil testing, in locations where production was poor, and all fourteen swiftly went bankrupt. This was a familiar pattern in the lucrative industries the president handed over to his cronies—logging, oil, tobacco, banking, and construction, to name but a few.

By the mid 1980s, Benedicto had driven the sugar industry into such dire straits that it was no longer generating much profit for himself or Marcos, let alone the planters. In an attempt to forestall disaster, the president moved in two other cronies to take control from his old fraternity *brod*. These were Cory Aquino's cousin, Eduardo Cojuangco, Jr., who owned San Miguel Corporation, the largest beer, soft drink, and processed food conglomerate in the Philippines; and Armando Gustillo, an enigmatic, Yale-educated attorney and brutal local warlord in northern Negros. Concurrently, Marcos gave in, though only superficially, to pressure from the World Bank and the International Monetary Fund to reorganize the sugar industry. All he did, in fact, was replace PHILSUCOM and NASUTRA with a new acronym, PHILSUMA, or the Philippine Sugar Marketing Corporation, an allegedly private firm. By the middle of 1985, the monopoly owed the planters of Negros some $83 million from sales made the year before. The delayed payments meant that the planters couldn't pay their workers to cut the crop in the ground, nor could they repay loans. Throughout the province, banks were foreclosing on haciendas.

Everyone was hurting; it was just a matter of degree. Hortensia Starke was tightening her belt. She had sold one of her five homes, the one in Miami, and was renting out another in Manila. Other planters were selling off spare Mercedes-Benzes, canceling annual round-the-world trips, or checking out chances of emigrating to the United States.

The rich had their ways of coping, but no alternatives were left to their workers for whom the sugar crash was an unmitigated disaster. They were the ultimate victims, literally starving in a fertile land. Negros's food shortage was directly caused by a bizarre and short-sighted social policy imposed by the sugar barons and sanctioned by the government. Called "mono-cropping," it prescribed that nothing but sugar could be grown on plantation property. If a cane worker tried to put in a few rows of sweet potatoes or beans alongside a road or in a patch outside his hut, he was subject to a fine or even physical punishment. In 1971, a group of unionized workers had appealed to several planters to loan them vacant land for short-term crops. The attempt backfired immediately, and 127 workers were arrested and charged with sedition. To the planters, the idea smacked of land reform, and as Hortensia Starke readily acknowledged, "We're not afraid of anything more than land reform." (The planters had won special exempt status for sugar plantations under Marcos's land-reform program.) Mono-cropping worked only as long as the planters were rich enough to supply food to their workers, whose lives were completely tied to the haciendas from birth until death.

Some 439,000 men worked in the cane fields and the mills that crushed the tall stalks. With their families, they constituted about 1.5 million of the province's 2 million people. Traditionally, sons followed fathers into servitude, the planters providing them with food, shelter, medical care, and limited education. Although the work was back breaking and the financial rewards pitiful, the paternalism provided a better life than most of the laborers would have been able to afford independently. But by 1985, when 300,000 workers were unemployed and seven out of ten were underfed, the cruelty of mono-cropping became apparent. Every week, five children were dying of starvation in Negros, twice as many as the year before and four times more than in 1983. Malnutrition was advancing at a similar rate.

Dr. Lourdes Espiña, the chief pediatrician of the Provincial Hospital in Bacolod, had become an unwitting expert in malnutrition and starvation. A slim, gray-haired woman whose chignon and gold-framed glasses gave her the look of a librarian, she'd been watching in bitter frustration for the past three years as the children of Negros died in increasing numbers. And she'd seen those who survived lapse into mental retardation, the result of insufficient food at a time when the brain is growing fastest, between the ages of three and six.

In a bed next to Espiña's office lay a tiny girl whose skeleton showed clearly through dark, blotchy skin. She looked no more than a year and a half, but she was five. The doctor said that the hospital probably could bring her weight up to between 60 and 75 percent of normal. But then she'd be returned to her parents, cane workers who lived fifteen miles away, and almost certainly would decline, perhaps becoming mentally retarded, blind, or both. "At least thirty percent of our cases relapse into third-degree," Espiña said.

Third-degree malnutrition, its victims little more than skin-and-bones with bloated bellies, copper-colored hair, vacant eyes, too weak even to cry, is a condition that the world had come to associate with drought-stricken Ethiopia. But in Negros, where rain was plentiful, where the land was lush and green, 25 percent of children under the age of six were already into the third-degree stage. And Dr. Espiña projected a continued doubling of the rate of malnutrition and starvation every year until the economy and the entire way of life were changed in Negros Occidental.

While most planters wore blinders, a few recognized that nothing short of a social revolution would save Negros Occidental and that if they didn't help bring about the change, the guerrillas of the New People's Army would. They knew, too, that the good days were over and there was little time left to get at least part of their money out. A very small number of them felt a sense of responsibility for their workers. Frederich Pfleider was one of these. A small-timer in the sugar business, he was fifty-six years old, a graduate of the Philippine Military Academy who'd served in Vietnam and then gotten into planting in 1969. Now, with his last year's payment from the monopoly still due, he was unable to meet his debts. The bank had foreclosed on his forty-nine-acre holding and his farmhouse, and he'd sold his jeep, his pickup, and his car. He was hanging on, though, leasing land and attempting to help his workers help themselves. "I've parceled out fifteen percent to the workers so they can plant substitute crops," he said. Putting land in the hands of the workers, in the view of Pfleider, who'd been labeled "enlightened" by cane workers and union leaders, was the last hope for Negros.

Another "enlightened" planter, Ricardo Garcia, was carrying out the largest land transfer in the province. At forty, he was handsome and gray-haired, and in his blue jeans and cowboy boots he looked more like a dashing Latin movie star than a struggling sugar farmer. Garcia ran two huge haciendas, owned by an uncle who had emigrated to Canada, and he was offering single-acre plots to his three hundred workers for the equivalent of $111 apiece. The idea was to give the workers a stake, however minuscule, in the economy and with it the ability to withstand increasingly high-pressure appeals by the New People's Army. "We've been infiltrated, and the NPA holds daily teach-ins among our workers," Garcia said. "I've sent word to the NPA, asking them to talk, since we both seem to have the same goal, to help the people. I've had no response. But they don't like what we're doing because it kills their issue: The workers are becoming landowners."

This optimistic evaluation was wishful thinking. The prospect of significant numbers of cane workers owning land in Negros was slender. Most were unable to raise the money to buy even a single acre. Certainly the local banks, pressed as they were by bankrupt planters, were in no position to risk capital on an untried experiment. But, more to the point, the real power was in the hands of a few big hacienda operators, men like Gustillo and Cojuangco, the pair assigned to salvage the failed sugar monopoly. These men were not about to sell off any land in order to redress social ills. They and a handful of others held huge properties, employed the largest number of workers, and lived by their own laws. They were not, by any measurement, "enlightened." Cojuangco operated his own 1,600-man army, a not uncommon practice among rich and powerful Filipinos. His men had been trained by Israeli mercenaries. Gustillo ran an army of 1,200 and lived behind high walls on a seaside estate fitted out with a helicopter landing pad and a dock for a high-powered speedboat, to facilitate an emergency escape. He also owned a local broadcasting station, which he used to harangue his and Marcos's enemies in the region. He wielded such enormous power that the northern portion of the province was commonly called "Gustillo Country."

As an illustration of how powerful he was, in October 1985, Gustillo unleashed militiamen of the local Civilian Home Defense Force, who were on his payroll, to crush an anti-Marcos demonstration in the market town of Escalante. The armed men opened fire from sandbagged positions, one of them atop the town hall, and killed twenty-seven demonstrators. Dozens more were injured. A hundred or so fled and were welcomed by the NPA.

As he had so often done with brilliant effect, Marcos turned the Escalante massacre around and used it to meet his own needs. He charged acting Chief of Staff Ramos with ultimate responsibility for the attack, since the CHDF technically was under the command of the armed forces, and used this as an excuse for not promoting him while General Ver was on trial in Manila.

The brutality in Escalante highlighted the rapidly eroding security situation in Negros, where the NPA was making unprecedented gains militarily and influencing members of the Church hierarchy. Father Ireneo Gordoncillo, a popular priest who everyone in Bacolod called Father Baby, made little attempt to hide his admiration for the guerrillas and some of their recent exploits. "What they've done is simply spectacular," he said. And he wasn't alone; at least four local priests had "gone into the hills" with the Communists. "There is some commonality between the Church and the NPA," said Father Baby. "Both listen to the people and both try to help."

Daily life had become desperate in Negros, and many sugar workers were driven to taking grave chances. Anelito Imalay was one of these. Imalay was twenty-eight years old, his body slight but strong with the stringy, efficient muscle that comes from swinging a long, curved *espading* blade against the tough cane fiber day after day, something he'd done since he was fourteen years old. He was paid the equivalent of seventy-five cents a day, considerably less than half the legal wage. He and his wife had three small children. Now that there was no work, he hung around the cheerless headquarters of the National Federation of Sugar Cane Workers in Bacolod, talking with others in the same situation. Imalay was blasé about displaying a gunshot wound he'd received during the Escalante massacre. He'd been lucky—two of his friends had been killed. The experience had frightened him, but he was going to take part in the next demonstration anyway. "I have nothing to lose," he said.

11

*H*IDDEN WEALTH

As I traveled repeatedly to the Philippines from my base in Tokyo after the Aquino assassination and came to know more Filipinos well, conversations frequently turned to who owned what where. I would hear references to properties that the Marcoses, their friends, relatives, and close business associates supposedly owned in the United States and other countries. Almost everyone had a story about a piece of choice real estate or a treasure trove of jewelry or a numbered Swiss bank account belonging to someone in the inner circle. During a breakfast meeting at the Mandarin Hotel in Makati in October 1984, a banker asked me offhandedly if I knew what Imelda Marcos had paid for the Crown Building, a superb, Art Deco-style skyscraper located on prime property at 730 Fifth Avenue in Manhattan. Actually, all that he said was "How much did she pay for the Crown Building?" I understood who "she" was; there was only one "she" and one "he" in the Philippines. But my banker friend could see from my blank expression that I had no idea what he was talking about, and that surprised him. "Surely you know she owns the Crown Building," he said. When I assured him that I did not, he said that it was common knowledge in Manila that the First Lady had bought the classic structure and had it completely refurbished, paying exquisite, and costly, attention to details, from taking apart and reassembling its black marble lobby to regilding the golden crown at its peak.

A few days later, a Jesuit priest mentioned just as matter-of-factly that it was widely known that the First Lady owned a "multimillion-dollar estate" on Long Island. And I heard more, concerning not just the president and his wife, but her brother, Benjamin Romualdez, who was ambassador to the United States, General Ver, Benedicto, Cojuangco, several members of the cabinet, some businessmen who bankrolled Marcos's election campaigns, and a few women who belonged to Imelda Marcos's political support group, the Blue Ladies. These people were said to hold huge investments in New York, California, Texas, Washington, D.C., and the state of Washington, in Canada, Australia, Latin America, and Europe. Sometimes the information was offered, other times it came in response to questions, though seldom with much difficulty. I was surprised at the range of those in the know—not just the elite, but taxi drivers, waitresses, and students.

At this time, with the economy stumbling, Marcos was lashing out, ascribing blame wherever he could. A chief cause of the country's problems, he claimed, was the illicit practice of "dollar-salting," taking hard currency out of the Philippines and stashing it abroad. This had been going on for years, actually, the amounts ebbing and flowing in relation to the nation's economic health and political climate. Big operators managed to keep huge amounts from ever entering the country by underreporting sales of commodities to foreign buyers and investing the difference abroad. One of the country's leading economists, Dr. Bernardo Villegas, estimated that Filipinos had removed more than $10 billion in recent years. U.S. Ambassador Stephen Bosworth signaled Washington's concern in August 1984 by saying that the Reagan administration would like to see Marcos make a strong effort to get the $10 billion back into the local economy. "If even half of that would return to the Philippines for private investment, it would make a considerable difference here," Bosworth said. Dr. Jesus P. Estanislao, Villegas's colleague at the Center for Research and Communications, a sophisticated economic think tank, estimated that the longer term drain may have been as high as $30 billion, starting in the 1950s and surging in the past five years. It might have been coincidental that the nation's foreign debt was also nearly $30 billion. But there was a clear cause and effect between the dollar drain and the country's gross national product, which had been $39.2 billion in 1982 and had dropped by more than 5 percent in 1984. Economic planning minister Vicente B. Valdepenas, Jr., said there no longer were enough dollars in the Philippines to import raw materials for industry.

William Sullivan, a onetime U.S. ambassador to the Philippines as well as to Iran, said that the siphoning off of dollars from the Philippines had damaged the nation's economy more severely than Iran had been hurt by the same kind of drain immediately before the shah was overthrown. "In the case of Iran," Sullivan said, "capital flight took place against a background of enormous foreign-exchange earnings from oil. But the Philippines can earn damn little. Every main commodity they have has gone flat."

Dollar-salting was one of those issues that President Marcos had turned around, creating an appearance of clamping down on a social evil while, in fact, he was the chief perpetrator. In 1984, Marcos had appointed a seventeen-member task force under Minister of Trade and Industry Roberto V. Ongpin to investigate dollar-salting, and every once in a while the local newspapers would carry a report of a small-time businessman being arrested while trying to smuggle out a few thousand dollars in a suitcase. Yet, the task force estimated that in 1984 alone, some $2 billion had been salted abroad, and $1 billion had left the Philippines the preceding year. It seemed evident that the investigation wasn't intended to go anywhere.

I began to wonder if there weren't a connection between the huge sums that Villegas and Estanislao were talking about and the stories of investments by the First Family and their friends. It struck me as typically Filipino that while so many people enjoyed the juicy gossip, no one had confirmed the facts. Early in December 1984, I talked with my editor at the *San Jose Mercury News,* Jonathan Krim, about the possibility of looking into the investment stories. Krim was interested in the idea but raised practical considerations. I had to admit to him that what I'd been hearing amounted to little more than rumor and that I had nothing yet that would prove anything. An investigation would require a major commitment, with only a small chance of success.

San Jose, the core of California's Silicon Valley, and the adjacent San Francisco Bay Area are major centers of expatriate Asians in general and Filipinos in particular. As a result, ever since the Aquino assassination, the *San Jose Mercury News* had devoted considerably more space to developments in the Philippines than most other newspapers in the United States. When the paper had broken the story the previous August that the Agrava Fact-Finding Board would implicate General Ver and other members of the armed forces, the news drew the attention of significant numbers of Filipino readers who came forward with additional information. Some were well connected within the expatriate community throughout the United States and were highly informed about the activities of the Marcoses and their friends at home and abroad. Krim listened to what they had to say, and a few weeks after he and I had spoken he put together some of the information we'd both gathered and passed it on to the newspaper's chief investigative reporter, Pete Carey. Carey ran some preliminary real-estate checks and said that his sources led him to believe that the stories could be proven through records available in the United States. With that, the decision was made for the two of us to begin an investigation, Carey working in California and New York and I in the Philippines. San Francisco correspondent Katherine Ellison was soon assigned to the effort, and the three of us spent five months interviewing scores of government officials, politicians, attorneys, real-estate agents, bankers, diplomats, and other knowledgeable people in both countries.

Very little documentation could be obtained in the Philippines, and much of what was available in the United States was designed to hide the real owners behind onionlike layer upon layer of dummy corporations and false fronts. Nevertheless, we confirmed much of what we'd heard, making the connections between Marcos, his cronies, and U.S. real estate. The result was a three-day series of articles that began on June 23, 1985, and was published by the *San Jose Mercury News* and other papers of the Knight-Ridder group. The articles examined the broad issue of money being funneled out of the Philippines but focused on investments in the United States by ten people: Ferdinand and Imelda Marcos; their close associates Benedicto, Cojuangco, Enrile; Energy Minister Geronimo Z. Velasco; businessmen Antonio O. Floirendo, José Yao Campos, and Rodolfo Cuenca; and senior civil servant Roman Cruz, Jr. The series was entitled "Hidden Billions; The Draining of the Philippines." It began: "As the Philippines sinks deeper into a quagmire of poverty, foreign debt and political unrest, many of its most prominent citizens are systematically draining vast amounts of wealth from their nation and hiding it overseas."

The Marcoses, like the rest, had gone out of their way to hide their investments, often putting them in the hands of seemingly casual friends or minor employees with little to recommend their being trusted with millions of dollars. Since the properties were legally in their names, such people could easily have sold and fled, but they didn't, either because they were well looked-after or because they feared the consequences. Some surrogate arrangements appeared to be based on the Filipino system of "blood debt," *utang na loob*. A lawyer in San Francisco who had been investing heavily in real estate for prominent Filipinos over the previous fifteen years was a case in point. "I 'own' more goddamn property," he said, consenting to discuss his business as long as he was not identified. "Tomorrow, if I wanted, I could sell fifty million dollars' worth of real property, get the money, and abscond. I could go to Rio and just say, 'Bye-bye, baby.' I just wouldn't, 'cause they trust me."

Another common approach was the use of offshore holding companies, many located in Caribbean tax havens that were delighted to assure owners complete anonymity. These complex arrangements, intentionally laid out like mazes to lead pursuers down dead ends, made tracing relationships between individuals and businesses extraordinarily difficult. One of those who had tried was U.S. Representative Stephen Solarz, a Democrat from Brooklyn who was a close friend and admirer of the Aquinos' and a persistent critic of Marcos. He had called on the State Department in mid 1985 to collect information on investments by Filipinos in the United States for his Asian and Pacific Affairs subcommittee. John Maisto, the State Department's director for Philippine affairs and one of the most knowledgeable specialists in the U.S. government, said that he had come up nearly empty handed in response to Solarz's request. "We found it very difficult as we checked through the U.S. government to find anything that was readily available, without calling together a task force," Maisto recalled.

But Pete Carey learned of a lawsuit that was brought in March 1984 against Imelda Marcos by a former business partner, and this became a crucial breakthrough in helping us peel back the layers concealing millions of dollars' worth of investments in the United States by the Marcos family and its inner circle. Filed in Suffolk County, New York, by Pablo E. Figueroa, an expatriate Filipino physician, the suit charged that Mrs. Marcos and two partners bought into an estate in Center Moriches, Long Island, in 1980. Figueroa had put the deal together, and he needed $1 million to buy the twelve-acre estate so that it could be developed into a $19 million resort. He turned to the First Lady, and she brought in two partners, Antonio Floirendo and Jorge Ramos, her favorite architect. The threesome owned a corporation based in Curaçao, Netherlands Antilles, called Ancor Holdings N.V., which the suit said was "controlled" by Mrs. Marcos. ("Ancor" was a little acrostic, based on Mrs. Marcos's maiden name; when reversed, the letters stood for "Romualdez Companies in Netherlands Antilles.") But, soon after Ancor and Figueroa had purchased the splendid, beachfront estate, known as Lindenmere, the First Lady gave a party there and decided that she couldn't bear to part with it. She told her associates that she would keep it for herself. What bothered Figueroa most, according to the suit, was that Mrs. Marcos also changed her mind about buying him out for $1 million, as she supposedly had promised. The suit said that Mrs. Marcos "does business in New York State systematically and continuously," that her business activities included "extensive real-estate purchasing, improving, developing and managing," and that she used various agents and fronts "to keep hidden her personal . . . involvement."

Just filing such a lawsuit was, for a Filipino, an astonishing act. It flew in the face of culture, notably the concept of *delicadeza*, or doing "the right thing." It was *delicadeza*, for example, that led Justice Agrava to sing "Happy Birthday" to Mrs. Marcos when she appeared before the Fact-Finding Board to testify. One was expected to do, and not do, certain things as they concerned the First Family. But beyond culture, Filipinos understood that good sense and the survival instinct dictated making sacrifices when doing business with the Marcoses, particularly Mrs. Marcos. Although she could be extraordinarily generous when the mood struck her, she was usually on the receiving end. A joke frequently heard in the Philippines had the First Lady looking over priceless antiques in a friend's opulent home while mentioning that she was in the "mining" business. When the friend responded with surprise, the First Lady explained, "Yes, that's mine, and that's mine, and that's . . ."

Shortly after our series of articles was published, Figueroa withdrew his suit. Neither he nor his attorney would say why.

Another Marcos-owned property we found was an estate on thirteen acres in Princeton, New Jersey. The Manila gossip that daughter Imee Marcos lived in the house when she attended Princeton University checked out. Real-estate records showed that the estate was owned by another offshore company, this one called Faylin, Ltd. The company's lawyers were a New York firm, Bernstein, Carter & Deyo, which also represented Ancor Holdings. Joseph Bernstein, senior partner in the law firm, and his brother, Ralph, were Americans who'd lived as children in the Philippines, where an uncle, a textile manufacturer named Jack Nasser, had made a lot of money and had developed a business relationship with President Marcos. This connection paid off handsomely for his nephews but would eventually land them in trouble when the Marcoses came under Solarz's scrutiny.

The introduction of the two American brothers into the trusted circle of real-estate operatives typified the international cobweb of relationships the Marcoses had spun over the years. Initially, dealings were arranged by Imelda Marcos's close friend Glyceria Tantoco, whose husband, Bienvenido, was Philippine ambassador to the Vatican. The Tantocos owned the Rustan's chain of department stores in the Philippines and the duty-free shops at Manila International Airport and in a number of exclusive hotels. Glecy Tantoco, a cold, imperious woman, frequently accompanied Mrs. Marcos on her international shopping sprees, the pair of them sweeping through the most exclusive shops of New York, Paris, Rome, and London and returning to Manila, the baggage compartment of their chartered Philippine Airlines plane loaded with treasures for themselves, their friends, and the Tantocos' retail outlets. Naturally, all this loot was admitted without customs charges, which would have amounted to millions of dollars.

In September 1981, after receiving word through Tantoco, the Bernstein brothers bought the Crown Building for $51 million and assigned it to an existing Netherlands Antilles-based shell, the Lastura Corporation. Lastura was owned by the Marcoses, though the Bernsteins later claimed that they hadn't known it at the time. The First Couple was pleased, and in November, Tantoco took the Bernsteins to meet with Mrs. Marcos at her suite in the Waldorf Towers. Imelda told the brothers she liked that they'd grown up in the Philippines and, in a motherly fashion, confided to the young men, Joseph then thirty-two and Ralph twenty-three, that Lastura was controlled by three Panamanian corporations she'd formed on behalf of her three children.

She then asked them to buy for her the old Korvette's building on Manhattan's Herald Square, at Broadway and West Thirty-fourth Street, next door to Macy's, which she and Tantoco intended to make over into a center to promote Philippine-made products. This purchase was made in February 1982, for $17 million. Imelda and Glecy later changed their plans, though, and decided to build on the site Herald Center, a ten-story, glass-encased shopping mall, to be filled with fine boutiques. The Bernsteins, who at the time were just novice developers, estimated that the project would cost $20 million. But it was to become bogged down in repeated delays and cost overruns, and by the time it was completed, in the spring of 1985, it would cost $46 million. Commercially, Herald Center was to become a white elephant, barely half-filled, its garment-district location jarringly out of step with the upscale image its owners had intended.

In March 1982, the Marcoses flew the Bernsteins to the Philippines for a month and, on April 5, gave Joseph a "declaration of trust" authorizing him to look after the First Family's real-estate dealings. The manner in which he was entrusted was indicative of the unusual ways in which the Marcoses ran their financial empire. One of the president's associates called Joseph in his room at the Manila Peninsula Hotel and dictated the declaration. Joseph took it down in longhand on a sheet of hotel stationery and signed it. When the Marcoses abandoned Malacañang Palace, a copy of this sheet of paper was left behind. It would become what Congressman Solarz would later refer to as the "smoking gun" in his investigation.

Armed with the president's authorization, the Bernsteins used another company they had created, New York Land, to acquire additional properties for their prized clients and to improve and manage the buildings the Marcoses already owned. They ordered the illumination of the Crown Building and the gilding of its crown with 1,363 ounces of twenty-three-karat gold leaf. These and other spectacular cosmetic alterations cost nearly $15 million and created in midtown Manhattan a gleaming landmark reminiscent of the ancient splendors of Asia. They spent another $6 million on antiques to tone up the interior of a $15 million town house on East Sixty-sixth Street that purportedly was owned by the Philippine government but in fact belonged to the Marcoses. At the end of 1982, the brothers bought for the First Family a building at 40 Wall Street, one of the tallest and most elegant skyscrapers in the financial district, for $71 million. For their services, the Bernsteins were paid more than $2 million a year.

Until the Marcoses fled the Philippines and the Bernsteins subsequently were charged with contempt of Congress for refusing to cooperate with the Solarz investigation, they denied doing business with the First Family or even knowing Imelda Marcos.

Another surrogate was Vilma H. Bautista. She was employed by the Philippine mission to the United Nations but actually functioned as Imelda Marcos's personal secretary in New York. Bautista also was the authorized agent for Theaventure Ltd., a Hong Kong corporation that was the registered owner of three adjoining condominiums in Olympic Tower, at 641 Fifth Avenue. When she was reached at a telephone number listed on real-estate records for the condominiums, Bautista said she had no knowledge of the properties. "There are so many names, there are so many phone numbers," she said. "This could be another Vilma Bautista."

The Marcoses themselves claimed to know nothing of New York real estate. They ignored repeated requests for a personal interview, so I sent them a registered letter. It asked whether the First Couple owned the Lindenmere estate and the three condominiums, the East Sixty-sixth Street town house, the Crown Building, Herald Center, 40 Wall Street, as well as the adjacent number 30, and another building at 29 West Fifty-seventh Street, which was where the Bernstein brothers had their offices. It also asked if Mrs. Marcos was a partner along with Floirendo in Ancor Holdings, and it cited the names of various other holding companies and front men, including Bautista. The final question was: "What are the views of President and Mrs. Marcos on Filipinos holding real-estate and other financial investments in the United States and other foreign countries, particularly at a time when the economy of the Philippines is in such dire straits?"

Their answer was telephoned to me by an aide, in much the same way that Joseph Bernstein had received his "declaration of trust." I, too, took the message down in longhand. It did not answer most of the questions, but it provided an insight into the president's thinking, always legalistic:

"Neither the President nor the First Lady owns any property in the United States. The property you mentioned on East Sixty-sixth Street in Manhattan, New York, is owned by the Philippine government.

"The building thereon was the original location of the Philippine consulate in New York and is still part of the consulate, the main office of which changed to another site on Fifth Avenue of the same city.

"The property was unutilized for awhile until the government decided to refurbish it to be used for receptions and conferences. There are also sleeping quarters on the property.

"As to the question of property and other investments in the United States and other foreign countries of Filipinos, it is the government's stand that so long as the acquisitions are legal, nobody can question the owners' right to these properties."

This last part of their answer was most telling. The question had been a moral one: How did the president and his wife feel about their countrymen owning property abroad, "salting dollars," at a time when their domestic economy needed all the support it could get? Knowing that Philippine law on overseas investing was complex and full of loopholes, tailored by Marcos for the benefit of himself and his friends, we had decided to focus on the question of morality. The Marcoses seemed to miss the point entirely.

Defense Minister Enrile was, by comparison, forthcoming. Real-estate records in San Francisco showed that he and his wife, Cristina, had bought a condominium at 2190 Broadway in 1979. The records also revealed that the couple had owned a second unit in the same building, which they sold in 1982 to a California-registered corporation, Renatsac, Inc. A somewhat less involved word game than "Ancor," "Renatsac" was Mrs. Enrile's maiden name spelled backward. Also in 1982, Renatsac, Inc., had purchased a San Francisco house at 2310 Broadway for $1.8 million.

Enrile met me in a lounge at the National Assembly. He was sixty-one at the time, an attorney who had received a master's degree at Harvard Law School, one of the wealthiest men in the Marcos regime, and thoroughly polished. We spoke briefly about national security and the Communist threat. Then I asked him if it was true that he owned a condominium in San Francisco. Without missing a beat, he acknowledged that he did. "It's true," he said. "That was bought by us when our daughter was supposed to go to school in San Francisco. This unit was available and cheap, so we bought one. It cost one hundred eighty thousand dollars. This was in the mid seventies." Six years after he bought it, the $180,000 condominium was worth an estimated $1 million. When I asked him about the $1.8 million house, though, he demurred. "No, we don't own it. It was bought by a company and has been sold. We, my wife, was acting for someone. I won't tell you who it was. It's since been sold.'' I asked him if the company was known as Renatsac, Inc. ''Renatsac was the name of a corporation my wife used,'' he acknowledged.

Although none of my questions had touched on the legality of his or any other Filipino's investments abroad, only their morality, Enrile, like the Marcoses, seized on the legal aspect. ''Financing was by a loan arranged in San Francisco,'' he said. ''There was no outflow of funds from the Philippines. This was about '82 or '83. . . . There was nothing illegal about it. . . . The money I used to buy our condo I earned when I was in private law practice. I paid taxes on it. I want to clarify that it was not from an ill-gotten source.''

I pressed the matter of morality. ''I won't pass moral judgment on those who own properties abroad,'' he said. ''It's a matter of judgment for them. In my case, it was because my daughter was going to school there. In the end, she decided not to go and went to the University of the Philippines, but we kept the property. Then my son used it when he studied at a college near San Francisco.''

Other than the one condominium, he said, he owned no other property in the United States. ''If they can show you any other property I own in the U.S., I'll give it to them.'' (Eight months later, a few days after Enrile had deserted Marcos and become a national hero, we met again and spoke for three hours. Although our conversation dealt primarily with more current events, he drew my attention back to the earlier interview and assured me again that if anyone could prove that he owned other property abroad he would give it away.)

We talked about estimates by economists on the flow of foreign currency out of the Philippines and how harmful this was to the economy. Again, Enrile said, it depended. ''We're only speculating and guessing. If the holdings are of such a magnitude as billions of dollars, I'd say it would be just to get it out of the Philippines, and I'd agree that it was harmful. But when I acquired mine the economy of the Philippines was not what it is today. It was stable and strong. I felt that investing one hundred eighty thousand dollars for the purpose I mentioned would not amount to much. If the situation then was like it is now, I wouldn't have done it.'' In fact, he added, if anyone wanted to buy his condominium, he would be willing to sell it and bring the money back to the Philippines. ''I understand, though, that the property market in the U.S. is rather soft," he added with a smile.

Enrile then sought to turn the spotlight elsewhere. With a charming half-attempt at naiveté he said, "From rumors I hear I understand that there are quite a few Filipinos who've established themselves with substantial assets in Canada, Australia, and the U.S. . . . I don't know if others will tell you, as I did, 'Yes, I own it.' Have you interviewed Mr. Benedicto? He's reputed to own a bank in California."

We knew that Roberto Benedicto was principal owner of the California-Overseas Bank in Los Angeles. He didn't want to talk about it. Nor did he want to talk about a U.S. sugar trading company, Czarnikow-Rionda, that he'd bought for $63 million in cash. Benedicto ignored dozens of telephone calls and a registered letter. According to the state superintendent of banks, the California-Overseas Bank had total assets of $133 million. Between 1976 and 1985 Benedicto and the other owners had poured more than $30 million into it. The records, of course, did not indicate where the money came from.

Antonio Floirendo, an elegant-looking, silver-haired man in his seventies, was a close associate of Imelda Marcos's and had used that relationship to lever himself upward from obscurity. Starting his career as a Ford dealer in Mindanao, Floirendo became the island's banana king. In 1977, he branched out to sugar, paying $11.7 million for three refineries, in Boston, Chicago, and New York, that had belonged to Sucrest Corporation, an American firm. He renamed the new company Revere Sugar Corporation. The banana man didn't do too well in sugar, and Revere filed for bankruptcy and shut down in 1985, declaring assets of $20.3 million.

Floirendo did well in real estate, though. In addition to being a codirector with Mrs. Marcos of Ancor Holdings, he owned a condominium in Olympic Tower, the same building where she owned three adjoining units. Floirendo's was registered in the name of a company called United Motors Corporation. In the Philippines, Floirendo owned United Motors and Equipment Corporation. Another of Floirendo's U.S. addresses was in Makiki Heights, Honolulu, where he bought a $1 million mansion in 1980, paying $800,000 in cash and signing a note for the $200,000 balance. Like most of the others on our list, Floirendo did not return calls or respond to a registered letter. But an employee of his in Manila, who gave his name only as "Mr. del Rosa," said of Revere Sugar, "It's an investment by Mr. Floirendo. . . . This company has been shut down because of poor business in sugar. . . . Everybody's losing money in sugar."

Energy Minister Geronimo Velasco couldn't have been more hospitable. I had gone to his palatial home on the coattails of a Filipino reporter, Noel de Luna of *Business Day,* who normally covered his ministry, and Velasco had assumed that I wanted to talk energy, too. Velasco, fifty-eight, was erudite and talented. Trained as a mechanical engineer, he'd been president of Dole Philippines, the pineapple-canning firm, and was the first Filipino to head a major multinational company in the country. As a uniformed maid served excellent fresh pastries and coffee, Velasco and de Luna chatted about oil and coal, and I looked around the den in which we were seated. It was decorated with statues and paintings of horses, one of his passions. Then I began to ask him about his real-estate holdings in the United States. Velasco was angry. He sputtered, "I'm not a government man. I'm a businessman first. I don't want to answer your questions. It's no secret I'm trying to get out of government. These rumors are ridiculous. There are rumors I bought this house three years ago. The truth is I'm here since 1959. I was the highest-paid executive in the Philippines."

I had asked him about a mansion that had been bought in Woodside, near San Francisco, in 1979, for $925,000 in the name of Decision Research Management Ltd., a Hong Kong corporation. One of Velasco's nephews, Alfredo de Borja, had executed a $675,000 promissory note on the property in 1979. He ran Decision Research, which managed some of Velasco's other properties, as well. Decision Research had also bought a condominium in Los Angeles in 1982 that had been assessed at $561,000. De Borja's brother, Patrick, lived in the Woodside property and described it as "a family home" where his uncle stayed when he was traveling in the area.

"I don't own any property abroad," Velasco said. "I don't own it." He was nervous. "The president will be furious with me for even talking with you! I don't want to dignify your question. I don't know anything about Decision Research Management Limited. Alfredo de Borja is my nephew, but I don't know anything about his supposedly managing my supposed overseas properties."

Then Velasco began to grumble about rumors, long prominent in Manila, that he received a cut from all the Philippines' energy imports. "I'm supposed to get three dollars a barrel of oil; four dollars a ton of coal. I've heard all these rumors, all this innuendo." He was clean, he insisted. His wealth had all been accumulated before he'd joined the government eight years earlier. Which was not to say that he was a babe in the woods, that he didn't realize that some people in and around the cabinet had made themselves wealthy by abusing the advantages of power: "I can't answer for others, not until I leave government. It's no secret I want out. The president knows it. I'm not a politician, I'm too candid."

He kidded that if I didn't refer to this interview in our series he'd "spill the beans" after he'd retired from government. The atmosphere lightened a bit, and he invited de Luna and me into the enormous living room, overlooking an Olympic-sized swimming pool, where his wife and a friend were playing a duet on gleaming, matched grand pianos. Among Velasco's talents was his superb ability as a cellist. With a little urging, he sat down with his instrument, and his wife accompanied him on the piano. They played Tchaikovsky's *The Dying Swan*.

Any discussion of wealth and power in the Philippines inevitably turned to Eduardo Cojuangco, Jr. He had long controlled the country's enormous coconut industry and in more recent years was encroaching on Roberto Benedicto's turf in sugar. Cojuangco, who was fifty when we published our series, was also the chairman of the giant brewery and food conglomerate, San Miguel Corporation. He and Cory Aquino were cousins (their fathers were brothers), and during the first ten years or so after Cory and Ninoy had married, they were very close with Cojuangco, whom everyone called Danding, and his wife, Gretchen. Almost every weekend, the two couples, along with Cory's elder sister, Teresa, and her husband, Ricardo Lopa, would go to a movie and dinner together. But then, in 1963, shortly after Ninoy had been elected governor of Tarlac province, Danding and another cousin, Ramon Cojuangco, bought controlling interest in the family-owned Philippines Bank of Commerce. Cory and Ninoy, as well as some other members of the family, felt that the takeover had been done clandestinely, and tension entered the relationship. Whatever warmth remained was wiped out entirely two years later when Danding ran for congress against Cory's younger brother, José "Peping" Cojuangco. The campaign was ugly, with Danding attacking not just Peping, but Ninoy as well. Ninoy, who was very popular in his province, campaigned intensely for Peping, and he won. Danding was bitter and from that time on worked at developing extremely close ties with the nation's new president, Ferdinand Marcos. The two men became each other's son's godfathers, and Cojuangco named his eldest son Marcos. By the time Ninoy was assassinated, Danding Cojuangco had become one of the triumverate, along with Imelda Marcos and General Ver, who advised the president on his most serious problems.

Although Cojuangco was a wealthy man by the time he became a presidential intimate, he capitalized enormously on his association with Marcos to make himself possibly the richest man in the Philippines. During the president's protracted kidney ailment, rumors circulated that Cojuangco would replace Marcos when he died. But it was rumored also that Danding didn't aspire to the throne, that he preferred to remain in the shadows, pulling the strings.

What we'd been able to confirm about Cojuangco's overseas holdings was, without doubt, the tiniest tip of the iceberg we were certain existed. If the Marcoses and the others we examined had been clever about covering their tracks, Cojuangco had been brilliant. In Australia, he owned a multimillion-dollar horse farm. In San Francisco, he ran Granex Corporation, a coconut oil refinery. Granex was a subsidiary of a Manila-based firm, United Coconut Mills, Inc., or UNICOM. Cojuangco was UNICOM's former president, so the connection was indirect. But he headed the United Coconut Planters Bank, which controlled UNICOM. That was the link.

In Los Angeles, he owned Coastal American Traders, Inc., an import-export business, although the owner of record was Helenita Soriano, who formerly had been Cojuangco's personal secretary. Coastal American Traders owned a house in Santa Monica, California, which was valued at $220,000, and, in Beverly Hills, Cojuangco's wife owned a jewelry shop, Jewelmer International, which was a branch of a corporation of the same name that she headed in Manila.

Cojuangco was notoriously wary of the press and almost never gave interviews to reporters. Thus, it was no surprise that he could not be reached by phone or letter. But an excuse offered by his public relations spokesman, Dennis Navarro, was delightful: "My boss will not be able to tackle the questions you posed. He was too busy and is now preparing to travel to Barcelona with his San Miguel basketball team."

Roman Cruz, Jr., or Jun, was a civil servant who'd done well for himself. By the time he was forty-seven, he was president of the government-owned Philippine Airlines, reporting to chairman Imelda Marcos; head of the Government Service Insurance System, or GSIS, which was intended to provide financial security for retired civil servants; and operator of the government-owned Manila Hotel, whose reconstruction had been one of the First Lady's pet projects. Responsive, intelligent, charming, Harvard-educated, Cruz was very much one of Imelda Marcos's protégés.

Intriguingly, it was Jun's father, Judge Roman Cruz, who had found Ferdinand Marcos guilty of murdering his father's political enemy, Julio Nalundasan, in 1935. One would not have imagined that Judge Cruz's son would have gone far in the Marcos regime. But Jun's older brother, J. V. Cruz, an entertaining, hard-drinking former journalist, had gotten close to Imelda and become a frequent guest at her parties. In time J. V. was appointed ambassador to Britain, a post he served largely from the Lobby Lounge of the Manila Hotel, but by then he'd introduced Jun to Mrs. Marcos. The younger Cruz was in financial difficulty, having accumulated debts in the range of $500,000 through bad investments. Mrs. Marcos took to him immediately, and in 1971 Jun was appointed general manager of the GSIS. Six months or so later, Jun had taken care of his debts and bought a mansion, complete with swimming pool and stable, in Forbes Park, Manila's most exclusive residential community. In 1973, Mrs. Marcos decided to build the Heart Center for Asia in Manila, one of her many civic projects, and the GSIS, through Cruz, provided the required $50 million. When the costly project was completed, Cruz purchased three Mercedes-Benzes and a second palatial home in the countryside.

His reputation as a superior technocrat and finance man, enhanced by Mrs. Marcos's favor, led to his appointment as head of Philippine Airlines, or PAL, in 1980. In this role, too, Cruz accommodated the First Lady who, when she flew, required her own 268-seat DC-10, so that she and her coterie could be comfortable. Calculating lost sales

as well as actual expenses, which were not reimbursed, each trip cost
PAL an estimated $3,250,000.

In the United States, Cruz was chairman of Century Bank, the Los
Angeles affiliate of the government-owned Philippine National Bank.
He also owned four lots in a California resort and a cooperative apart-
ment on San Francisco's Nob Hill.

Nob Hill was popular with Marcos's cronies. Rodolfo M. Cuenca,
who had run the government-owned Construction and Development
Corporation of the Philippines, or CDCP, was the registered owner of
a condominium there as well as two San Francisco area houses through
a corporation he headed, TRA Equities, Inc. The firm had also bought
two San Francisco office buildings for $10.3 million. On the East
Coast, he owned an apartment at 700 Park Avenue in Manhattan.

Cuenca, fifty-seven, had gone from rags to riches in a few years
by draining funds out of the CDCP until it was a dry husk, then
establishing Galleon Shipping Company, a Philippine firm with a Del-
aware-registered subsidiary in the United States, Trans-Asia Marine
Corporation. Through connections with Imelda Marcos's brother, Ambassador Romualdez, he received an $87 million guarantee from the
government's Development Bank of the Philippines to buy seven cargo
vessels. The $87 million was roughly twice the asking price.

In addition to the Marcoses and their inner circle, we found other
Filipinos who'd drained large sums of money out of their country and
invested it in the United States. One of these was Mayor Nemesio
Yabut of Makati. Yabut, who would die of a heart attack a few days
after the First Family fled Malacañang, owned a $520,000 pink-stucco
house in San Francisco's exclusive St. Francis Woods, a $900,000
apartment building, at least two condominiums, and a San Francisco
seafood restaurant known as the Old Clam House. Yabut told my
colleague Katherine Ellison that he always remembered to pay his U.S.
taxes. "I remember the story of Al Capone," he said with no apparent
sense of irony. "Al Capone was never convicted of anything but tax
evasion."

Another well-connected investor was Edna Guiyab Camcam, who
in 1980 bought an apartment building in Los Angeles valued at more
than $1 million. She also owned a second property in Los Angeles
and a house on Long Island. What made Camcam of more than passing

interest was that she was General Fabian Ver's mistress. The couple had a child, and Camcam called the general Daddy. We were unable to contact her, but Ver replied to a registered letter with a telegram in which he denied owning any property in the United States "for use of anyone."

Herminio Disini was a cousin of Imelda Marcos's, and in the late 1970s he'd been paid $11.2 million in what were termed "commissions" by Westinghouse Electric Corporation, which was building a nuclear power plant on the Bataan peninsula. Hints were floated that the president had received a cut, and Marcos was forced to punish Disini by having him divest himself of three of his companies. Disini soon left for Europe and spent much of his time living in a castle he'd bought in Austria, along with the title of the former owner, a duke. He also owned three condominiums in the same Nob Hill building where Rodolfo Cuenca owned a unit.

The series of articles detailing the overseas acquisitions of the Marcoses and their friends electrified many Filipinos. "Hidden Billions" instantly became "Hidden Wealth" and entered the Philippine lexicon. Although Filipinos themselves had been our original sources, and many had long known that their leader and his friends were bleeding the country white, they'd never been presented with the facts. That an American newspaper had done this added to the significance as far as most Filipinos were concerned. Among the sadder effects of the bastardization of their culture, and the consequential diminution of self-confidence, has been the feeling among many Filipinos that they must turn to the United States for approval or for wrist-slapping. At the same time, since the articles had originated in the *San Jose Mercury News* and not *The New York Times,* Marcos believed that he could ride out the problem. Columnists in the controlled press and members of his cabinet denegrated the paper. "Up to this point, there is no question that he can overcome this," his labor minister, Blas F. Ople, told reporters in Manila. "After all, this is not a court of law that has convicted him. These are the findings of a small regional newspaper in California." (The daily circulation of the *Mercury News* was 265,000; the combined readership of Knight-Ridder Newspapers and the papers that subscribed to its news service exceeded 18 million a day.)

The first reaction to the damaging reports came within a week, on the night of July 1, when Energy Minister Velasco sent a messenger to Marcos with his resignation: "I have, Mr. President, spent the last few days in deep soul-searching and I am convinced that we have not seen the end of this kind of virulence. The issues affecting my own integrity, no matter how unfair and unfounded, have raised questions as to my future ability to be effective. . . . I hope that my resignation will pave the way toward a new attitude on the holding of a government office, which, especially in times of crisis, must enjoy the full confidence of the people." Velasco, as he had said during our conversation at his home, wanted to get out. But Marcos could not let him go. Faced with the need for effective damage control, Marcos spent the next two days pressuring Velasco. At the end of the week the Malacañang Palace information office announced that the minister was "ready to abide by the president's decision" and would stay on.

Then the president had to deal with local newspapers that were reprinting the articles. Several antiregime publications, among them *Business Day, Veritas, Mr. and Ms.*, and *Malaya*, had published the complete series or abbreviated versions. Marcos remained silent but maneuvered his good friend Antonio Floirendo into the line of fire.

At the president's behest, the banana king threatened to sue *Malaya* and its publisher, Jose Burgos, for $11 million. Burgos was already charged with subversion in connection with articles he'd run in another publication, *We Forum*. Floirendo had his lawyers prepare an affidavit, but he merely leaked it to the government-controlled press and never filed it. Floirendo acknowledged in the affidavit owning not only Revere Sugar Corporation and the New York and Honolulu real estate, as had been reported in the articles, but he also said that he was "really the actual, beneficial and registered owner" of Ancor Holdings and, through it, the Lindenmere estate. This was intended to protect Imelda Marcos.

Besides Burgos, another anti-Marcos journalist was having trouble. Francisco Tatad, forty-five, who had broken with the president after being his information minister through the first half of the martial law period, had written a number of provocative columns in *Business Day* based on the *San Jose Mercury News* series. The government's ombudsman suddenly resurrected five five-year-old cases of graft against Tatad and had him arrested. Tatad claimed his arrest on the long-ignored charges was "a smokescreen to draw attention away from the foreign wealth scandal."

Meanwhile, Marcos's opponents had picked up the ball and were running. In an unprecedented move, opposition National Assembly members drafted a motion demanding that the president be impeached. Even though Marcos's New Society Movement had suffered losses in the assembly as a result of the May 1984 elections, he still exercised powerful control of the house, and the motion was crushed within twenty-four hours. The opposition expected this outcome, but was playing for exposure, not direct results. Salvador Laurel produced a videotape showing many of the properties we identified and had copies distributed throughout the country along with reprints of the full series of articles, translated into Tagalog and several other dialects. Groups of noisy demonstrators were dispatched by Laurel's UNIDO organization to the Manila residences of a number of those named in the series, where they made nuisances of themselves.

After three weeks of a public outcry unmatched since the Aquino assassination two years earlier, the president recognized that the hidden-wealth issue was not going to go away, and he ordered Justice Minister Estelito Mendoza to conduct an investigation into "ill-gotten, unexplained wealth or unlawfully transferred foreign exchange from the Philippines to other countries." The minister was instructed to "spare no one." With one exception. In an interview with the pro-government *Daily Express,* Information Minister Gregorio Cendaña was asked whether the Marcoses would be included in the investigation. With exquisite simplicity, he replied, "If they have no property, how can they be included?" The president had instructed Mendoza to complete his report by the middle of September. When the deadline came and went, Mendoza called a news conference and said that he'd been having a hard time since much of the information he needed was not in the Philippines. The investigation would continue, he said, "but I must emphasize that under our laws, the ownership of assets abroad is not *per se* an offense or a crime."

As "hidden wealth" continued to damage Marcos, the president uncharacteristically went on the defensive. A week after Mendoza failed to produce his report, the president told a luncheon meeting of the Manila Rotary Club that the *Mercury News* series was a "malicious lie" and that those keeping it alive "have done me wrong. They have hurt me." Even the First Lady, he complained, was being treated unchivalrously. Just a week earlier, she had gone on a religious pilgrimage to Naga City, in southeast Luzon, "to pray" and was "confronted with the videotape on the hidden wealth produced by the opposition.'' The president was unused to being challenged. If he or his friends said that something was so, then it was. Marcos told the Rotarians that Joseph Bernstein had denied knowing the First Lady and that Antonio Floirendo had said he, not the First Family, owned Lindenmere. There was nothing more to be said. ''All these statements and accusations, what does this mean?'' he asked rhetorically. ''This means this is a malicious lie. That is why we should disregard all of these.''

Over the longer run, hidden wealth provided the opposition with an issue it used for as long as Marcos remained in office. The First Family had finally been shown to have exceeded the acceptable norms of gouging Filipinos.

As harmful as the charges had become at home, they were causing Marcos equally big problems in the United States. Four months after our series was published, the *Village Voice* ran a lengthy article on the Marcos's New York property. Congressman Solarz, sensing a hot issue on his home turf, quickly started a subcommittee investigation focusing on the relationship between the Marcoses and the Bernstein brothers. The Solarz hearings would continue through the First Family's hasty departure from the Philippines, eventually eliciting a full confession from Joseph Bernstein that he and his brother had purchased and managed hundreds of millions of dollars' worth of real estate for President and Mrs. Marcos.

12

*I*NNOCENT OF THE CRIMES CHARGED

Since that day in October 1984 when the majority Agrava board decision was submitted and Marcos promised General Ver that "the rigors of judicial process will ferret out the truth and arrive at justice," the president had taken a personal hand in the assassination conspiracy trial against his friend, twenty-four other military men, and a lone civilian.

Marcos wanted Ver free and clear. He was thinking about holding presidential elections a year ahead of schedule and needed his trusted right arm, the expert in stuffing ballot boxes, stealing poll tallies, and carrying out all the dozens of tasks necessary to assure reelection. The president also was concerned about the growing strength of the military reforms movement under Ramos, Ver's acting replacement as chief of staff.

The fix was in from the start. On January 10, 1985, nearly three weeks before the trial was to begin before the three judges of the *Sandiganbayan* in the court's narrow, high-ceilinged chamber, Marcos summoned Chief Judge Manuel Pamaran along with prosecutor Manuel Herrera and his three deputies to Malacañang Palace. It was a repeat of the secret meetings the president had held with Agrava and board member Salazar. Herrera revealed later that they were taken in through a rear entrance and led to a small study were met by President Marcos, wearing pajamas, his face puffy. With his wife seated next to him, the president told them that he had been alarmed to learn that Herrera

193

had drafted a resolution calling for the indictment of the twenty-six men for first-degree murder. Marcos urged caution and advised the prosecutors "to put on a show." After two hours, he concluded the meeting, telling his callers, "Gentlemen, I'm tired. I want to rest. Thank you for coming. Thank you for your cooperation. I know how to reciprocate."

Marcos's hand was evident on the first day of the proceedings. He had told Herrera and Pamaran that he didn't want "the boys" jailed during trial but preferred that they be held under military custody or freed on bail. "The boys are frantic," he had said. Arrangements had already been made for the accused to be transferred to the penitentiary at Muntinglupa, a Manila suburb. But two hours before they were to be taken from their barracks at Villamor Air Base, the national prisons director, the Manila police chief, and the National Bureau of Investigation director suddenly announced that all their holding facilities were overcrowded. So "the boys" stayed free at their barracks throughout the trial.

Despite the meeting in Marcos's study and a subsequent telephone call from the president, Herrera, a sixty-one-year-old attorney who'd spent his entire career in government service, tried, within limits, to press his case throughout the trial. It wasn't easy. He was being intimidated, and he was frightened. At one point, when he was attempting to make contact with a key witness to the assassination, he was approached by his superior, government ombudsman Bernardo Fernandez, who warned him cryptically, "Olympus feels that you are going out of your way. You'd better watch out."

The high point in Herrera's efforts came on May 2, when he presented a witness the entire country had been waiting for since the day of the assassination. Her name was Rebecca Quijano. She had been called "the crying lady" ever since she'd walked off China Airlines Flight 811 shortly after Aquino's assassination sobbing hysterically and told waiting newsmen, "They have already killed him, yet you are not weeping." Now, with Herrera standing alongside her in the courtroom, Quijano said she had seen a man wearing the khaki uniform of the Metropolitan Command, or METROCOM, of the Philippine Constabulary walking down the service stairway immediately behind Aquino, point a handgun at the back of his head, and at that instant she had heard a shot. From her description of his uniform and his place on the stairway that man was Constable First Class Rogelio Moreno, one of Aquino's six escorts.

Quijano's testimony was the first, either at the trial or before the Agrava board, that singled out the gunman. Board counsel Andres Narvasa and four of the five members of the board had concluded that the gunman was either Moreno or his companion, Sergeant Filomeno Miranda. And deputy counsel Bienvenido Tan had pointed out in the videotape the board had commissioned that Moreno appeared to be receiving a gun as he escorted Aquino to the door of the plane.

Quijano, seated at the left of the three judges, Pamaran and the two new Marcos appointees, Bienvenido Vera Cruz and Augusto Amores, said: "I saw the METROCOM who was behind Senator Aquino aim his gun at Aquino's head and, simultaneously, I heard a shot."

Herrera asked her to stand and demonstrate what she had described, and she presented a little tableau of the shooting, pointing the index and middle fingers of her right hand slightly downward and a few inches behind the base of the skull of Ricardo Buenviaje, a deputy prosecutor playing the role of Aquino.

Quijano also told the packed courtroom that she hadn't realized Aquino was on the plane until ten minutes or so before landing, when a Japanese reporter had pointed him out. She had approached Aquino and asked him, "Why did you return? Are you not afraid?" Moments after the plane had docked, she testified, she had noticed three enlisted men enter the cabin, and as they approached Aquino she had heard him exclaim, "Oh, my God!" Like the newsmen, she had attempted to follow Aquino off the plane, but her way, too, had been blocked. "I decided to run to a window on the left side of the plane," she recalled. "I saw the man in white, Senator Aquino, with the soldiers, with about one fourth of the stairway left before the tarmac." It was then that she had seen the khaki-uniformed constable point his weapon and she'd heard the shot.

"I was startled," she testified. "I let out a shout over what I saw." She ran to her seat, then back to the window, in time to see soldiers in blue coveralls aiming rifles downward. In a quavering voice, Quijano continued her testimony: "I thought they were still shooting at him and became hysterical. . . . I could not bear to look at Senator Aquino lying there with all the blood."

She had still been hysterical when she left the plane with other passengers and was confronted by a cluster of frantic newsmen, whose view of the shooting had been blocked completely because they'd been confined to a windowless section of hallway. Quijano testified that she had begun to tell the journalists what she had seen when a man wearing a T-shirt approached her. The man grasped her shoulders and said to her, in Tagalog, "Don't make noise if you don't want to get hurt." She recalled that the man held her very tightly. "He hurt me." The man in the T-shirt was Colonel Vicente Tigas, the press officer in General Ver's Presidential Security Command and one of the twenty-six on trial. Tigas had whispered to her, "Come on, come on, let's go outside," Quijano testified. As they were approaching the airport's broad immigration hall, Tigas had met a man he knew and had told him, "Friend, it's finished."

At that point in her testimony, the courtroom's lights suddenly blacked out. Quijano, terrified, grabbed Herrera's arm and pleaded, "Don't leave me!" He told her to lower her head. TV crewmen switched on battery-operated lights, showing prosecutors ringing the witness protectively. When the power came back on after half an hour, a more composed Quijano resumed her testimony, saying she had realized that she might be in peril if Tigas and the other man had understood that she'd witnessed the shooting. "So that the man in the T-shirt and his companion would leave me alone, I told them 'I am OK. I did not see anything,' " she testified. But the experience had frightened her sufficiently that she had stayed away from the Agrava hearings.

Quijano was an attractive, college-educated, thirty-two-year-old businesswoman. Her testimony had been impressive and convincing. But her personal history was marred, and Herrera, anticipating that the defense attorneys would use this background against her, had her expose these flaws to the court. She had once used a false name to obtain a U.S. tourist visa; she had made a number of misjudgments in running her family's business, and as a result, in 1984, she'd been sued for fraud, though the case later was dismissed; she'd guaranteed an automobile loan for a friend who had not made the payments; she'd been arrested and detained for six months in Hong Kong on charges involving counterfeit currency and traveler's checks. Most importantly, perhaps, her father, Hector Quijano, who'd been the mayor of a small town and a successful local businessman, had been arrested in 1981 and confined to a cell in Camp Crame, a military installation in Quezon

City. He was found hanged there. The military claimed that he'd killed himself, but the family was skeptical. Herrera asked Quijano what effect her father's death had had on her attitude toward the Armed Forces of the Philippines. "I am not angry with all the armed forces," she replied, "only with those responsible for my father's death and with those who killed Senator Aquino."

Five defense attorneys were present in the courtroom and, surprisingly, all five turned down their right to cross-examine the witness after she had completed her three-hour testimony. The five renewed their option a month later though, on June 6, and grilled Quijano for five hours. As the cross-examination proceeded, a lawyer in the room saw that one of the judges, Vera Cruz, was rising from his seat periodically, walking to the end of the bench, and passing little slips of yellow paper to Aviation Security Command lawyer Rodolfo Jimenez and other defense attorneys who were questioning Quijano. The lawyer, Raul Gonzales, who'd taken it upon himself to monitor the proceedings at the Agrava board, was playing the same role now.

At the lunch break, Quijano confirmed what Gonzales had seen, and she told him, "That justice sitting closest to me was writing notes on a yellow pad and passing them to attorney Jimenez while he was questioning me." Gonzales was unable to retrieve any of the yellow papers, which continued to be passed throughout the afternoon session, until Ver's lawyer, Antonio Coronel, received one, tore it up, crumpled the pieces into a ball, and dropped it on the floor. After the hearing, Gonzales picked up the note, which he and Herrera pieced together. It said: "Not Dean Narvasa, but Dean Andres Narvasa. Ask more on Dean Andres Narvasa." The judge's note suggested a line of questioning for Coronel, who had been trying to get Quijano to admit that Narvasa had coached her prior to the hearing.

The defense lawyers failed to get her to make such an admission, despite their own coaching from the bench. They did manage to elicit from her confirmation that she'd attempted suicide while in detention in Hong Kong, and they were able to get her to break down and cry. But they failed to shake her original eyewitness account: "I may be the most wicked person in the world, but it cannot change what I saw—that a METROCOM soldier shot Senator Aquino."

Quijano's testimony was important to the prosecution, but more crucial was the evidence that had been gathered by the Agrava board during its eight months of hearings. This evidence, particularly the testimony by General Ver, Major General Olivas, and six enlisted men, was the crux of the case. And eighteen weeks into the trial the three-judge court threw it out, calling into play the vague wording of Presidential Decree 1886 that had created the board. They ruled that the testimony Ver and the others had given before the board was inadmissible in court because it would violate their right against self-incrimination. Herrera and his colleagues now barely had a case, since they had done almost no original investigating. They had planned on using the Agrava testimony to demonstrate the military's involvement in monitoring Aquino's return, arranging the hire of Galman, eliminating Galman's wife and girlfriend, and all the other critical details surrounding the assassination. Ver's attorney, Antonio Coronel, knew the judges' decision signaled the end of the case against his client. ''The only evidence of the prosecution is the testimony [Ver] gave before the Agrava board,'' Coronel said gleefully. Herrera could see the handwriting on the wall but still filed an appeal with the Supreme Court to have the Agrava board testimony restored.

On August 30, Supreme Court Justice Serafin R. Cuevas wrote the decision. Just a year earlier, as the case against Ver and the others was beginning, Marcos had appointed Cuevas to the bench. At the same time, the president had ordered that a $10.3 million driver's-license-production contract be granted to Felimon R. Cuevas, his brother. The two men were pillars of a Philippine religious sect, the Iglesia ni Cristo, which had contributed heavily to Marcos's party during the May 1984 National Assembly elections.

Now Justice Cuevas wrote that the three *Sandiganbayan* judges had been correct in dismissing the Agrava testimony since Ver and the others had not been advised by the board of their right not to incriminate themselves. As often occurs in Philippine jurisprudence, Cuevas cited U.S. law and based his decision on the landmark *Miranda* case, under which police officers must warn suspects of their rights when carrying out arrests. Ten justices shared the majority finding; three opposed. One of those three, Justice Claudio Teehankee, who regularly did combat with the majority of his colleagues on the loaded bench, argued that Ver and the others had been invited, not subpoenaed, to appear before the board and they had not resisted in the least. They had certainly not been arrested, he said. Indeed, wrote Teehankee, the military men "were all too eager to testify and make a strong effort to gain support from the Fact-Finding Board and the public of the military version . . . that the assassin was Galman. . . . It would have been ridiculous, if not bordering on officiousness and impropriety, to warn them as the highest-ranking military officers of their option of refusal to answer incriminatory questions and . . . of their right to remain silent."

The elimination of the Agrava testimony all but assured the outcome of the trial. But Marcos, who'd suffered an unwelcome surprise at the hands of four members of the Agrava board, was not going to take any chances this time. Some other potentially damaging testimony had to be eliminated, too. In July, the *San Francisco Examiner* had reported that U.S. Air Force personnel stationed at two Philippine air bases, Wallace and Villamor, had witnessed the scrambling of two Philippine military jets and other unusual activity on August 21, 1983, the day Aquino had flown into Manila International Airport. The implication was that an effort had been made to intercept China Airlines Flight 811 and either force it to return to Taipei or escort it to a more distant Philippine airport. If this were so, it would shed considerable light on how intensely the military had been monitoring Aquino's trip, something Ver had denied.

Responding to the reports, acting Foreign Minister Pacifico Castro had asked Ambassador Bosworth for any information the United States might have. The U.S. Air Force prepared affidavits from six American personnel who'd been on duty at the two bases that fateful Sunday. The affidavits were sworn before a notary public, authenticated by the State Department and the U.S. embassy, and delivered to the Ministry of Foreign Affairs meticulously sealed in an envelope for transfer to the prosecutors. All these details had been worked out previously by both sides. But on September 13, just two weeks after the Supreme Court assured the trashing of the Agrava testimony, Ombudsman Fernandez announced that the prosecutors would not use the affidavits. He said that they had not been properly authenticated.

For Herrera, this was the final straw. He argued with Fernandez over the admissibility of the affidavits, but when he was overruled, Herrera declined to appear in court for the rest of the trial, leaving his deputies to carry on.

The elimination of the affidavits was more telling than what they contained. Taken from the airmen two years after the events had transpired, the information varied somewhat, but all concurred that two F-5 jets had been scrambled on August 21, that there had been an unusual level of activity by Philippine air force personnel at the two bases, that the Filipinos had used U.S. radarscopes, and that certain Philippine personnel had behaved curtly to the Americans on that day. Several of the Americans stated that they'd later learned the two scrambled fighter planes were to have led the China Airlines plane to Basa Air Base, adjacent to the U.S. facility at Clark, northwest of Manila, but that the mission had failed.

A few days after Fernandez rejected the affidavits, the State Department made them public, along with a statement expressing the U.S. government's disappointment. "We cannot, of course, substitute our judgment for that of the Philippine judicial process concerning the weight or probity of the information in the affidavits," the department said. "We had hoped, however, that a rigorous examination of that information would have occurred within the judicial processes themselves."

By October, the public had lost whatever interest it may have had in the trial, and that was very little even from day one. Unlike the Agrava hearings, it attracted few followers. Nearly two years had transpired since Aquino's death, and passions had cooled. Most Filipinos had been satisfied by the majority Agrava report. The trial was anticlimactic and shed little additional light on what they already knew. Furthermore, no one expected justice from Marcos's court.

A few well-known figures spoke out against the public apathy. One was Arturo Tolentino, a member of Marcos's New Society Movement who was rated (perhaps overrated) as a free thinker and had been fired as foreign minister the previous March following a number of disagreements with the president. Tolentino, an acknowledged expert in constitutional law, said of the trial, "Whether there was influence or not, the trial is a very suspicious one, as if the prosecution or the government did not really want to prosecute the accused."

Agrava board counsel Narvasa was saddened and angered by what he'd been observing. He understood the value of the testimony he and the board had gathered and recognized that without it there was virtually no case. "Why am I and a very few others the only ones to be angry?"

he asked me over a gloomy lunch shortly before the verdict was delivered. "Why is there no rage? I don't understand my own people." He did, of course. This was a classic case of Filipinos, inured to Marcos getting his way, shrugging their shoulders in the face of the inevitable. Narvasa was carrying on, though, attempting to head off a final *Sandiganbayan* verdict based on what he considered an improper Supreme Court judgment. He was making speeches at Rotary Club luncheons and anywhere else people would listen. "They were wrong in the facts, wrong in the law," he said. "So, I won't stop. In the most respectful language of which I'm capable, I'm saying it was a wrong decision."

Narvasa's fury was in vain, and the *Sandiganbayan* announced its verdict on the morning of December 2, 1985. The entire proceeding from the suddenly crammed courtroom was carried live by government television. Court clerk Minita Nazario took two hours to read most of the ninety-page decision. Ver and the twenty-five other defendants, dressed in matching white *barongs*, rose and listened attentively to the opening: "Murder is as old as mankind . . ." The day after the Aquino assassination, President Marcos had told the world that the killing had the markings of a Communist "rub-out job." And that, judges Pamaran, Vera Cruz, and Amores had decided, was what it had been. Rolando Galman, whom the court described as "the soulless assassin," had done the foul deed on behalf of the New People's Army. General Ver and his co-accused were not merely acquitted on the grounds that guilt had not been established, which was normal judicial practice, but were found "innocent of the crimes charged."

Ver left the courtroom ringed by bodyguards, his broad face beaming, his hands clasped above his head like a boxing champion. He paused briefly to tell newsmen, "Thank God it's all over. There was never any ground for the charges against me." He later issued a formal statement in which he said he "hoped that the cloud of suspicion over me and my comrades in the military shall be forever cleared." After lunching with his wife and sons, Ver dressed in a crisp uniform and reported to Marcos at the palace. He handed over a copy of his acquittal, saluted smartly, and said, "Reporting for duty, sir." The president signed a document reappointing the general to his post as chief of staff, shook his hand, and returned the salute. Less than three hours had passed since Ver had walked out of court.

In Washington, the State Department reacted with a chilly statement that compared the ham-handed conduct and outcome of the trial with the "exemplary, thorough work" of the Agrava board and found the two "very difficult to reconcile." The official comment also addressed the hasty reinstatement of Ver as chief of staff and indicated that this cast real doubt over Marcos's "professed desire to initiate serious reforms" in the armed forces.

Anticipating such criticism, Marcos quickly announced a number of position changes in the military command, but they were almost entirely cosmetic. Lieutenant General Ramos slipped back into his pretrial position as Ver's deputy, where he was deeply depressed and practically immobile. Defense Minister Enrile maintained his appearance of personal loyalty to Marcos, but he and the young reformist officers of RAM saw this corruption and the widespread revulsion it engendered as enhancing their opportunity to get rid of Marcos. They set aside any residual concern with genuine military reform and began drafting plans for a violent rebellion, a coup d'etat.

Although the court's across-the-board acquittal was more outrageous than most people had anticipated, it raised little turbulence. Most Filipinos maintained that the Agrava board's findings had been more than they had any right to expect. But the real reason for apathy was that Marcos had succeeded in diverting attention from the courtroom to the campaign trail. He had called a presidential election.

13

SNAP ELECTIONS

Marcos had stated his intention to hold a special election during a television appearance a month earlier. Now, on the night of the acquittal, he stayed up late, signing into law Cabinet Bill Number 7, which formally set the date, February 7, 1986. Marcos's penchant for his lucky number was very much in evidence as he prepared for the most trying test of his political life.

He had been toying with the idea of "snap" elections for months. Such elections would be called on short notice, giving the incumbent the great advantage. Marcos had first floated the idea the previous August, when the parliamentary opposition had attempted to impeach him over the hidden-wealth reports. Infuriated, he had threatened in public statements to hustle the country into an election, catching the squabbling opposition off-guard and incapable of agreeing on a single candidate or orchestrating an effective campaign. With the impeachment thrown out of the National Assembly in less than twenty-four hours, the president thought better of calling early elections, though the notion, kept alive by the Reagan administration, stayed in his mind.

In mid October, Marcos met twice at Malacañang Palace with Senator Paul Laxalt, a Nevada Republican who was a longtime personal friend and adviser to President Reagan. Marcos had let it be known that the U.S. expressions of concern over political instability and popular support he'd been hearing from various American officials did not mean anything to him. He spoke only to the president of the United

States. Reagan was anxious to get through to Marcos but could not afford to be tainted by direct communication. So he dispatched his trusted friend to Manila with a handwritten letter. "That letter essentially expressed President Reagan's concern for his old friend, and they've been old friends for a long while, about what was going on in the Philippines," Laxalt said. The senator's instructions were to discuss matters that were troubling Reagan and his White House advisers. The message boiled down to two key points: Hold elections, because Americans believe that elections demonstrate democracy and will be suitably impressed; and hire a good public relations firm in Washington.

Marcos readily agreed to the second point, and in November his son-in-law, Gregorio Araneta, signed a $950,000 contract with a PR company closely tied to the Republican power structure, Black, Manafort, Stone and Kelley. The firm's job was to spruce up Marcos's shabby image on Capital Hill and in the U.S. press. But getting the president to agree to call an early election took longer.

As the silver-haired Laxalt later recalled, his conversation at Malacañang eventually came around to Marcos's political strength, how he perceived it himself, and how it was perceived in Washington. "We briefly discussed the idea of a snap presidential election earlier than the one planned for 1987," Laxalt wrote in a report. "This possibility had been previously broached to him by CIA Director William Casey. But, during our meetings, he didn't entertain it very seriously. He said there was no need for it, since he already had the support of the people. And he said it would be a costly distraction that would take him away from other things he had to do."

Laxalt remained in Manila for two days, meeting with Marcos for four hours on the first day and an hour on the second. He played a round of golf and then flew back to Washington. From the capital, Laxalt kept in touch by telephone, gradually building up a rapport that would become key during Marcos's final days in office. At the same time, Laxalt kept up pressure for snap elections. During one of their talks, Marcos asked for the impressions of influential Americans. "Well," Laxalt replied, "the biggest reaction I get around Washington is that there is almost uniform feeling that you have lost the support of your people, and that is a very pressing problem."

Toward the end of October, the two men spoke by phone again

because they were both to appear on ABC-TV's "This Week with David Brinkley" on November 3. Marcos told him that he enjoyed popular support, he could demonstrate this, and he was considering calling a snap election a year and a half ahead of schedule to prove the point. "If you are going to do that," Laxalt responded, "it would be very dramatic for you to make that announcement on the Brinkley show. It would be very effective for American consumption." Marcos took this advice.

Asked by columnist George Will, one of the program's interviewers, if he "would be willing to move up the election date, the better to renew your mandate soon, say within the next eight months or so," Marcos replied with a dash of showmanship: "Well, I understand the opposition has been asking for an election. In answer to their request I announce that I am ready to call a snap election perhaps earlier than eight months, perhaps in three months or less than that, if all these childish claims to popularity on both sides have to be settled. I think we'd better settle it by calling an election right now or, say, give everybody sixty days and to bring the issues to the people."

Marcos's announcement evidently caught the panelists by surprise, and ABC White House correspondent Sam Donaldson asked, "Are there any catches, Mr. President?" Accustomed to the skepticism of American journalists, Marcos answered expansively, but evasively, "I'm ready. I'm ready. I'm ready." Donaldson, not satisfied, pressed on, "Mr. President, are there any catches? Can everyone run in this election? If Corazon Aquino wants to run, if Senator Laurel wants to run? Everyone can run?" "Oh, yes," Marcos answered. "Anyone."

Thus, the president of the Philippines informed the people of the United States that the people of the Philippines would be voting for president a day before he told the Filipinos themselves. Not only did this demonstrate Marcos's cavalier disregard for the independence and self-respect of his own people, it also revealed how out of touch he'd become.

Reagan considered it in the best interest of U.S. policy that Marcos remain in office. The big question was whether Marcos could win another election. His record indicated that he could; he'd won two relatively legitimate contests in 1965 and 1969 and, in 1981, after martial law, was returned to a six-year term, though his 86 percent victory was blatantly fixed. (Vice President George Bush flew in for that inauguration and outraged moderate Filipinos by telling Marcos, "We stand with you, sir. . . . We love your adherence to democratic principles and the democratic processes.") Marcos still had his massive KBL machine, an almost bottomless war chest, his domination of the news outlets, and the armed forces. On the negative side, there'd been the Aquino assassination, demonstrations in the streets, the economic crisis, the poor performance of the ruling party in the 1984 National Assembly polls, the hidden-wealth exposure, and the obvious rigging of the Ver acquittal. And there was the question of his health. Nevertheless, Marcos appeared to be confident. He'd even announced on the Brinkley show that observers from the United States and other countries were welcome to oversee the polling. "Please come and just see what is happening here," he'd said. "All this talk about fraud is just sour grapes, all these poor losers." Even if the KBL hooligans had to tone down their manipulating because of the foreigners looking over their shoulders, victory by a moderate margin would seem all the more credible. So, on balance, the Reagan administration was betting that Marcos would pull it off.

Marcos himself was less certain. His commitment to the poll would waffle for weeks, until it would become too late for him to wriggle out. By taking Laxalt's advice and announcing the snap elections on American television, he revealed that his thinking had been heavily colored by Reagan's wishes. His entire cabinet had argued strongly against the election, right up until the moment he announced it.

The Marcos of preassassination days would have known better than to wander into a potential minefield when he was at his weakest, that there was no reason for him to cut short his term by more than a year and take the risk, however slight it might seem, of being defeated. He wouldn't have put his trust in outsiders, even the president of the United States, because no one, least of all foreigners, knew how to search out and assess the dangers and opportunities lurking in the nooks and crannies of Philippine politics the way the old Marcos did.

But this was a different Marcos. No longer the unerring predator, he had been secluded for years behind what his daughter Imee had called a *cordon sanitaire*. As his health had deteriorated, he'd ventured out of the cool, dim security of Malacañang Palace less and less frequently. Over the years, Imelda Marcos had had the palace completely air-conditioned and its breezy porticos glassed in, windows sealed and covered with shades, shutters, and drapes until the occupants were blinded to life on the outside. Marcos's direct sources of information were increasingly cut off, and he'd become almost totally reliant on reports filtered through his most intimate associates—Imelda, Ver, Cojuangco. But these three had their own agenda, anticipating the president's death or incapacity by preparing for Imelda to succeed him, with Ver and Cojuangco pulling the strings. As a result, even the second- and third-hand information they were passing to him was biased by their own concerns.

Marcos's actions in the days and weeks immediately following his TV announcement should have made clear that these were the shuffling, halting steps of an ailing dictator taking orders from the United States, unsure about what he needed to do to hang on to power. The principal reason that this was not seen was that most political analysts, and certainly most ordinary Filipinos, had been so impressed by Marcos's seeming infallibility over two decades that they couldn't detect the obvious.

On the Brinkley show, Marcos said the elections would be a one-on-one popularity contest between himself and an opposition challenger. He said nothing about a vice president. Marcos had abolished the vice presidency in 1972 and used to joke about being "allergic" to a number two. But two days later, in response to complaints from the State Department, he announced that there would be voting for a vice president, too. Then he began to backtrack and announced that the entire decision of whether there would be elections at all would be made by the National Assembly. Since he controlled the parliament with a 70 percent majority, there was no question that he could have it do his bidding, so by shifting the decision, he was simply buying time and gaining a small bonus through the illusion of putting democracy to work.

He also had a real need for help from the assembly. Under the constitution, special elections were to be held only if the office of the president was vacant. Thus, Marcos would have to resign, and physically leave Malacañang, before the polling could take place, and he had no intention of doing this. There was no precedent in Philippine history for an incumbent stepping down; but much more importantly, leaving office, even if only for a few weeks, would weaken his position immeasurably since he would not be able to campaign as the president.

So crucial was this point that a bitterly anti-American newspaper columnist with direct access to the president, Teodoro F. Valencia, wrote in the pro-Marcos *Daily Express* early in November, "If President Marcos were to resign to run, it would be a first time, and I predict he would lose such an election bid. He'll never do such a crazy thing just to please the Americans."

To circumvent the constitutional requirement that he leave office, Marcos put his legal mind to work. He came up with a kind of postdated resignation, promising to leave office, but only *after* the elections, presuming that he would then walk out the door and back in again as the reelected president. This meaningless assurance enraged Marcos's opponents, but by putting the decision before the National Assembly he effectively dampened their fury. The house voted to allow the president to remain in office through the snap elections.

Frustrated, eleven opposition politicians and constitutional experts filed petitions before the Supreme Court, challenging Marcos's right to stay in Malacañang. This, too, suited him. If preparations for the election went according to his plan and he felt assured of victory, there would be no difficulty in having the high court agree to his staying in power; if things looked bad, it would be just as easy to arrange for the court to determine the elections unconstitutional and call them off.

What Marcos had bet on most heavily when he decided to call the snap elections was that the opposition would not be able to bury its many hatchets and unify behind a single candidate. For nearly a year, a dozen individuals had been struggling for the right to challenge him, either in the event of a special vote or in the scheduled 1987 election. At the beginning of 1985, three influential anti-Marcos people, octogenarian Lorenzo Tañada, gold-mining executive Jaime Ongpin, and Cory Aquino, had formed themselves into what they called a Conveners Group, to convene opposition presidential aspirants if and when Marcos called elections or if he died and left the office vacant. All these would-be candidates would cast a secret ballot to choose a single challenger, and, in case of a deadlock, the three Conveners would select the candidate. The Conveners were outside the normal channels of Philippine politics; they were more at home with the protest associations with catchy acronyms.

Their list of possible candidates included United Nationalist Democratic Organization leader Salvador Laurel; Eva Estrada Kalaw, a veteran Marcos antagonist and former Liberal Party leader; arch nationalist José Diokno; Jovito Salonga, who had recently returned to Manila after spending four years in the United States; Aquilino Pimentel, who had led the political grouping of the Pilipino Democratic Party and Laban, called PDP-Laban; and Ramon Mitra, a large, effusive National Assembly member distinguished by a full, gray beard. Immediately and as expected, the opposition fragmented. Kalaw and Laurel backed away. They were not comfortable with the new wave, and Laurel, whose UNIDO was the most powerful opposition organization, formed an alternative to the Conveners, the National Unification Committee. The NUC reflected the old line and, dominated as it was by UNIDO, quickly chose Laurel to face Marcos.

The Conveners, meanwhile, were coming to the conclusion that the only viable candidate could be Cory Aquino. Jimmy Ongpin, as the president of Benguet Mining was known, had actively been promoting her since the spring of 1985, but although he was extremely well regarded in the Philippine business community and by top American officials, Ongpin had difficulty getting many people to consider Cory as a serious challenger to Marcos. There were all the obvious objections: She was totally inexperienced, had never run for any political office; she was so soft-spoken and self-effacing that few outside her immediate circle of friends and relatives knew whether she had the quick intelligence necessary for a candidate; and she was a woman in a male-dominated society. True, she had the magic of the Aquino name and the image of the martyr's widow, but it was hard to imagine that those assets would be sufficient. And, what's more, Cory had given no indication that she was even remotely interested in running.

But Ongpin took the opposite approach. He insisted that Cory's greatest strength was what others were misconstruing as her weakness, that her very lack of political cunning would make her welcome to a population sickened by Marcos's wheelings and dealings. She was refreshing, the antithesis of the Filipino politician. And Ongpin had a particular aversion to politicians. His elder brother Roberto, or Bobby, was Marcos's minister of trade and industry, and the two had feuded for years. Their disagreement was based on long-term sibling rivalry as well as Bobby's implementing policies to which Jimmy took exception as a businessman. Jimmy Ongpin had stayed out of the political fray for as long as he possibly could after the Aquino assassination, even though his wife and children were marching in the streets of Makati. Finally, during a rain-drenched demonstration on October 7, 1984, more than a year after the killing, he picked up a microphone and told a crowd of ten thousand circling a monument between Manila and Quezon City, "I've come here today because I've finally convinced myself that I don't have more important things to do. In fact, I have nothing more important to do than stand here and be counted." He didn't say so, but a big part of his reason for being there was that the anti-Marcos movement was becoming dominated by Communist-front organizations. And after being forced to pay "taxes" to guerrillas threatening his company's mining sites for several years, Ongpin was as worried by the Communists as he was by Marcos.

So strong was Ongpin's distaste for politicians that shortly after Ninoy Aquino was killed he said that he never would have supported him in a race against Marcos: "Everything I know about him tells me he was no better than Marcos, perhaps worse, just as ruthless and brutal." Doy Laurel, in his judgment, wouldn't be much better; he had a "playboy" reputation and wasn't taken very seriously. But Cory was another matter. Despite having been Ninoy's wife for twenty-nine years, she hadn't acquired his baser instincts, and he knew her to be bright and a quick study. Furthermore, she would be assisted by some of the most astute and capable technocrats, educators, lawyers, managers, and clergymen outside the existing political sphere—in other words, people like Ongpin himself.

But Cory wasn't responding to pressure from her fellow Conveners. Four of her children were afraid of the risks, and they had advised her against running; only the youngest, Kris, a teenager who seemed to revel in public approval, as her father had, liked the idea. Cory recognized that the other two Conveners wanted to use her as a symbol, and she resented that. After an initial period of reticence, she stood up to them and argued that she would not be manipulated, that she would make her own decisions. And the more she protested, the more she showed those around her, and herself, that she was capable of being a serious candidate. Slowly, she came to accept the idea: "If the nation wants me, who am I to argue?" Her heart still wasn't in it, though, and she publicly rejected all appeals, calling herself "just a simple housewife." Showing contrasting public and private faces turned out to be an exceptionally wise tactic. It made her seem all the more desirable, and people started to think of her as the best possible alternative to Marcos.

Then Aquino picked up support from one of Laurel's most powerful backers. In June 1985, when Laurel had himself nominated by the NUC, seventy-two-year-old retired Supreme Court Justice and National Assembly member Celia Muñoz Palma deserted him and joined Aquino. She quickly became one of Cory's closest advisers and added her voice to those of Ongpin and Tañada, urging her to run. But Aquino set a demand. She would run only if a million people petitioned her. That, too, turned out to be a wise tactic as it effectively launched her campaign before it had been declared.

What was really holding Cory back was that she was waiting for a *sign*. Mysticism is an intrinsic part of religion in the Philippines, probably more so than in most countries, and Cory was intensely religious. She prayed frequently, seeking to communicate with Ninoy. She often wondered aloud, what would Ninoy have done? She discussed her prayers with her mother-in-law, *Doña* Aurora, with Cardinal Jaime Sin, friends, and journalists who were tracking her. In many countries, a potential presidential candidate who confided that she was praying for a sign from her dead husband before she could make up her mind would draw at least raised eyebrows; in the Philippines, her sincere religiosity was taken as inspirational, another indication of her being Marcos's opposite. *Doña* Aurora recalled that soon after Marcos announced the snap elections on the Brinkley show, Cory told her that she remembered something Ninoy had said: "It's ringing in my ears, what Ninoy said—'If during my lifetime I could have done something and didn't do it . . .' It's ringing in my ears."

Several weeks later, a priest recommended that Cory go on a retreat with an order of nuns called the Pink Sisters. She spent a day with them, praying, and then told her mother-in-law that she thought she would run and that her campaign would be based on her faith in God. "The people will believe me, Mommy," she said. "I am a victim; we are victims of this regime. We have suffered a lot. I can say that I am with them in their sufferings. My sincerity will be real and will make people free from fear." Then she went to Cardinal Sin and told him that while she'd been praying with the nuns, she had received the sign she had been seeking: "Cardinal, Ninoy is inspiring me. It seems that he is talking to me, telling me that I should run." Sin urged her to move cautiously. She agreed and did not announce her candidacy.

Ninoy's old newspaper boss, Joaquin Roces, the former publisher of *The Manila Times,* took on himself the task of rounding up the million signatures. The well-photographed sight of Roces, white-haired and frail, pushing a shopping cart through the streets of the capital, collecting sheets of paper signed by citizens backing Cory for president, stirred emotions around the country and produced more support for her. By the end of November, Roces and others had amassed 1.2 million signatures.

On December 3, the day after the *Sandiganbayan* had declared Ver and the other military men innocent of murdering her husband and Marcos had signed the election bill into law, Cory Aquino announced that she would run against the man she called "my number one suspect." In her declaration she said, "There are so many victims of the Marcos dictatorship. I know very well that I am not the victim who has suffered the most. But I am perhaps the best known."

Now, as Marcos had been betting, the opposition had two possible candidates. Doy Laurel was as anxious to run as Cory Aquino had been reluctant. Laurel might have been prepared to stand in Ninoy's shadow, but he was not willing to accept a position subservient to Cory. He was a professional, a politician from a family of politicians, who'd been preparing for this moment most of his life, building a support base, slugging it out in the tough game he'd chosen for a career. She was an amateur and, to make matters worse, a woman, who'd fallen into circumstances not at all of her making, and the thought of her snatching the prize out of his hands made him livid.

Laurel worked hard at maintaining a manly image. At fifty-five, he was good-looking, and a recent hair transplant gave him a more youthful appearance; he seemed fit and liked to roll his sleeves above his biceps. He and his wife, Celia, had eight children, all of them talented artists, actors, and singers. Doy would have had to swallow hard to run as Cory's vice-presidential candidate.

But that was what his advisers, and Cory's, were urging him to do. They reasoned with him, conceding that UNIDO held nearly all the opposition seats in the National Assembly, that it ran a machine second only to the KBL, and that he'd probably give Marcos a pretty fair run for his money. But, it was just as true, and more important, that a new force was infusing the country, that people wanted some kind of moral rejuvenation. This wasn't his moment, they said; it was Cory's, and only she could beat Marcos.

Laurel wasn't convinced. It wasn't that he was venal or foolish. But he didn't want to be shut out of what he believed to be his best crack at the job he coveted. So, he decided to tough it out. He and Cory and their advisers met repeatedly, all of them grimly aware that the longer they were in disagreement, the more the challenge to Marcos would suffer. Slowly, the tide turned against Laurel. One of his most reliable backers, former Senator Francisco Rodrigo, to whom Ninoy had written years earlier about his religious rebirth in prison, warned him that if the two of them ran independently against Marcos they would split the opposition votes, and the president would certainly be reelected. Laurel saw the simple wisdom in that and acknowledged privately to Rodrigo that if "the Marcos dictatorship" were to be toppled, he and Cory would have to join forces.

Laurel wasn't entirely without weapons, though. On December 5, he and the deputy chief of mission of the U.S. embassy, a highly experienced negotiator by the name of Philip Kaplan, had met quietly, and Laurel had come away believing that the Americans favored him over Aquino. He was particularly struck by Kaplan's mentioning that the Reagan administration was pleased by his plain talk in favor of retaining the U.S. military bases and wary of Aquino's uncertain stance. Kaplan had said that he knew Cory's personal views were decidedly pro-American, but that she had to bow to the nationalistic pressures of Ninoy's old Laban organization. This calculated stroking stiffened Laurel's resolve, and he began bargaining for all the leverage he could squeeze from Aquino.

What he had in mind was accepting the secondary position, but only if Cory would forsake Laban and run under the banner of UNIDO. That much he let leak out. More quietly, though, he was attempting to wrest considerable personal power. He wanted to be prime minister and to hold another major cabinet ministry, as well as the vice presidency, and he wanted final say over all cabinet appointments. Aquino's people balked, sensing that what Laurel really wanted was for her to be president in name only, with him calling the shots.

Time was running short; the deadline for filing candidacies with COMELEC, the Commission on Elections, was midnight of Wednesday, December 11. With much of the backroom negotiating being leaked to local newspapers by one side or the other, the day-by-day tribulations of the opposition became something of an embarrassing soap opera, and Marcos's supporters were gloating.

Only days remained when Aquino proposed that they form a co-alition of UNIDO and Laban, similar to one that had worked so well during the 1984 National Assembly elections. Laurel objected, arguing that under Philippine law voters would be permitted to split their ballots, so a vote for Cory as president wouldn't necessarily count as a vote for Doy as vice president.

On Sunday morning, December 8, Laurel called a press conference at his family's spacious and well-guarded residential compound in suburban Mandaluyong. Word had been circulated among local and foreign journalists that Laurel and Aquino had finally worked out their differences and the two candidates were going to announce a joint ticket with him in the vice-presidential slot. But when newsmen were shown into the sunny backyard they found it hung with banners pro-claiming DOY OR DIE! and other slogans supporting Laurel alone. A few of Aquino's workers were seated among the puzzled reporters but said they didn't know where Cory was. Drama heightened when, just as Laurel stepped before a microphone, the power failed and he darkly suggested "sabotage." When the power came back on half an hour later, Laurel began by saying he had told Aquino he was prepared to "make the sacrifice" and run as her vice president as long as she would represent UNIDO. She had agreed, he said, but earlier that morning she had come back to his house for their eighth meeting and, instead of preparing a joint statement, told him she was "not willing" to be UNIDO's candidate. Therefore, Laurel said, "tomorrow, I am filing my certificate of candidacy for the presidency of our republic." UNIDO workers burst into applause and cheering, and fireworks erupted in the garden.

A man wearing the black, oval-shaped, velvet pillbox hat that designates many Muslims in Southeast Asia stood up as the news conference dissolved and, shaking his head sadly, said, "Marcos must be rejoicing right now." He was Abraham Rasul, a leader of the Muslim Federal Party, a UNIDO component. Laurel's intransigence had disappointed him so much that he'd made up his mind on the spot to break away and support Aquino.

Later in the day, in the driveway of her home on Times Street,

Aquino spoke for a few minutes to an impromptu news conference. She denied that she had ever agreed to be the UNIDO candidate and said that the best she could do was represent both parties. She hoped there was still room for working out a "grand coalition." Then she excused herself, saying with a wan smile that she'd been up all night and "this is the tiredest I've ever been in my life."

The next afternoon, as Laurel had promised, he went to COMELEC headquarters in Intramuros and registered as the UNIDO candidate for president. He did not name a vice-presidential running mate. Before filing, he had told a breakfast meeting of politicians and newsmen that the tables were turned; if Cory wanted to run with him, she was welcome, but he would hold the number-one position. The line of questioning over breakfast had been cold, and it seemed evident that many Filipinos were put off by Laurel's ambitions. Tactically, though, his moves were effective. Although Aquino clearly had to be the presidential candidate, she needed Laurel's strengths to complement her weaknesses. He had taken the advantage, and she was pushed to the wall. She was going to have to meet some of his demands.

On Wednesday morning, two days after Laurel had filed, Marcos was formally nominated by the KBL. The affair, at the Manila Hotel, was a reproduction in miniature of an American political convention, with brass bands, balloons, and red, white, and blue streamers fluttering inside and out. Crowds had been bused in, wearing identical red, white, and blue T-shirts emblazoned with KBL. On cue, they chanted the president's war cry, indicative of a politician with little new to offer: "Marcos, Marcos, Marcos *Pa Rin!*"—"It's still Marcos!" Some of the banners hung across the entrance seemed ironic, presumably without intent, such as the one that proclaimed: THE PHILIPPINES IS OUR COUNTRY—AND OURS ALONE! MARCOS-MARCOS.

Another was the unearthed theme of former President Richard M. Nixon's last campaign: PRESIDENT MARCOS. NOW MORE THAN EVER.

Inside the hotel's main ballroom, the Fiesta Pavilion, some 1,800 delegates sat quietly, waiting for Marcos to appear. The spontaneous, raucous hoopla that normally dominates such a gathering was markedly diluted, and the unenthusiastic mood was accentuated by the great expense to which the ruling party had gone. Fat propaganda kits were passed out to all comers. Slick folders were stuffed with comic books featuring a youthful Ferdinand Marcos in jungle fatigues, wielding an enormous machine gun, a ferocious snarl on his face, his muscles bulging. (Sylvester Stallone as Rambo was packing them in at Manila theaters, and the resemblance wasn't coincidental.) The president took enormous pride in his war record and had always made it a major feature of his campaigning. Another booklet addressed hidden wealth and said that the unfounded allegations had been made by the *San Jose Mercury News*, "a paper of minor reputation in California."

The front of the ballroom was hung with an enormous color blow-up of Marcos wearing a brilliantly striped, short-sleeve shirt that buttoned around the hips and was called a shirt-jac. His face was beaming, his arms spread in jubilation. The picture had been taken during the 1965 election campaign.

Imelda Marcos entered the ballroom with her white-haired brother, Ambassador Romualdez, and in her address set the tone for her husband by complaining that "during the last three years, forces have conspired against us." She also took credit for placing Metro Manila "among the great cities of the world," having overseen the planting of seven trees per citizen, which now were "giving oxygen to the City of Man." Mrs. Marcos would campaign intensively in the weeks ahead, traveling to far-flung locations, entertaining audiences with songs in a variety of dialects, and delivering stinging attacks on her husband's opponent.

When the president finally entered the Fiesta Pavilion, he was wearing his same lucky shirt-jac, but he was being held in the arms of his security men. Too weak to walk through a crowd, he was carried to the stage, where he waved mechanically and blotted at his bleary eyes with a wad of tissues, a scene that would become familiar in the next two months. To Marcos's right stood his wife, taller and much more vigorous looking; to his left, older and shorter, but with the musculature of a bantamweight boxer, his dismissed foreign minister, Arturo Tolentino.

Once the president started speaking, though, the old aggressiveness began picking up. These snap elections, he told the party faithful, weren't necessary, but he wanted a victory in order to strengthen the government's hand. "Let us submit ourselves freely and openly to the test of popular support," he urged. "Let's invite the opposition, if they dare, to submit themselves as openly." But the opposition, he went on, had nothing constructive to offer the country. It was a negative force, intent on destroying everything that Marcos had built over the past two decades, legalizing the Communist Party, and returning economic control to the oligarchs. These charges would be the dominant theme of his campaign.

The climax of the convention was Marcos's introduction of Tolentino as his running mate. There was little surprise since the idea had been floated in the local newspapers for a week. Still, some skeptics had insisted until the last moment that Marcos would choose his wife to run with him. Suspicion of Mrs. Marcos was so deep that many Filipinos believed she and the president had cooked up a scheme in which he would secretly withdraw from the ticket on election day, giving way to her, and millions of innocent voters would be duped as they unknowingly cast their ballots for "Marcos." The choice of Tolentino seemed to make sense. As one of just six KBL candidates to win the 1984 National Assembly elections in Metro Manila, he was a recognized vote-getter throughout much of the Tagalog-speaking region of Luzon, the archipelago's major island, an area that accounted for 38 percent of the 27 million qualified voters in the country. And his repeated displays of independence should have dispelled any question that he was a Marcos lapdog. Tolentino stressed this in his acceptance speech: "I've been called an even more effective critic of the president than the opposition itself. There is no more need for the opposition because the opposition is carried by Mr. Marcos."

But there was something bizarre about Tolentino's agreeing to run with the president. He was seventy-five years old and had been foreign minister for just eight months when he'd publicly criticized Marcos the previous March for retaining his dictatorial decree-making powers and for refusing to name a vice president. What was not widely known was that the real disagreement was over a seemingly innocuous diplomatic appointment. Imelda Marcos had wanted the former senior vice president of the Philippine National Bank in New York, a man named Oscar Cariño, transferred to Switzerland. Cariño had made himself very useful to the First Lady by arranging huge disbursements of cash, as high as $500,000 at a time, when she was visiting New York. Now, she wanted him assigned to a diplomatic post in Berne, where he could be of similar value to her. Tolentino refused, insisting that as foreign minister, he, and not the president or the First Lady, had the power to make such appointments, and instead dispatched Cariño to Toronto as consul general. Tolentino was fired. More recently, he had filed one of the eleven petitions before the Supreme Court challenging Marcos's right to run in the snap election without resigning first. Just two weeks before his moment in the Fiesta Pavilion, Tolentino had told a meeting of the Makati Business Club, "If Mr. Marcos is going to run in a snap election, where I believe he is not qualified to run, certainly I will be mentally dishonest if I support him. But I do not have that vice; so I will not support him." Now this supposed prickly individualist was standing alongside Marcos, clasping the president's hand over their heads, agreeing to be his running mate. The president's seemingly cunning idea was producing a bad odor, and the belief spread that somehow, for some reason that was not clear, Marcos had Tolentino under his thumb.

Nevertheless, Marcos and Tolentino had forged their unity and filed their ticket while Laurel and Aquino seemed irreconcilably split. As the KBL was cheering the new team, Aquino had driven in a honking motorcade to COMELEC headquarters and filed her candidacy for president, without a party affiliation. She had been swamped by government workers who cheered her and tossed confetti. When reporters had asked if she would say something, she replied, "Not yet," indicating that the door remained ajar.

If the opposition was to unite, the deadline was just hours away. Aquino drove from Intramuros to Cardinal Sin's villa. Laurel met her there, and the two of them spoke with the prelate. He had grown enthusiastic about Aquino's chances against Marcos and was reveling in the thought of a "simple housewife" toppling the powerful old pro. But he also understood that she could not win unless Laurel were to join forces with her. Sin exerted all the pressure he could on the two of them to form a team with Cory for president and Doy the number-two position. From Villa San Miguel, the two drove to the home of Aquino's mother-in-law and met with several of their close advisers, who told them that forty opposition members of the National Assembly were threatening to withdraw support from both candidates unless they ran on a unified ticket. That did it. Aquino and Laurel agreed. They would run together under the UNIDO banner.

At 11:00 P.M., quite literally the eleventh hour, they went separately to COMELEC and altered their registrations. Aquino, smiling broadly, was swamped by reporters as she emerged from the old building. "I'm happy," she told them, "very happy. Our chances are excellent. Unity means victory.'' Hustled into a car by aides, she replied to one question: There had been ''no conditions'' to the union, she claimed. This was misleading. Laurel had exacted assurances that he would be named prime minister and foreign minister if they won. When Laurel emerged a few minutes later, he looked content and told the newsmen that ''I decided to give way to Cory. Somebody had to give way. The key is to unite for the higher interest of the nation, to get rid of the dictatorship.''

The fifty-seven-day campaign officially got under way the next morning. The challengers were off and running, setting a breakneck pace that they would maintain throughout. Aquino headquarters, set up in the Cojuangco Building, her family's business center in Makati, was bursting with yellow-outfitted volunteers. Many of them were women, often confused, but they were enthusiastic, well-meaning, and hardworking. Marcos was slow off the mark. He had not ordered disbursement of the vast amounts of money that always fueled a Marcos campaign. His party headquarters, a two-story, colonial-era building fronting on Roxas Boulevard, was quiet, its inhabitants wondering aloud when ''the boss'' would issue them orders. By forming a unified ticket at the last minute, Aquino and Laurel had stunned Marcos. He had not expected them to get together. But, as always, the president had something legalistic up his sleeve.

Even before Aquino and Laurel had joined forces, Marcos had instructed aides to look into the possibility of canceling the elections. He had in mind getting the Supreme Court to replace the presidential poll with a nonbinding referendum on his administration and permitting only the vice-presidential election to go ahead. The president's inner circle of legal and political advisers drafted a secret, two-page memorandum that addressed this question, based on the eleven petitions already filed before the court challenging the constitutionality of the election. The men who prepared the study were Marcos's four presidential assistants, Manuel Lazaro, Juan Tuvera, Mariano Ruiz, and Joaquin Venus, and Political Affairs Minister Leonardo B. Perez, who was also chairman of the National Assembly's Committee on Revision of Laws and Codes and Constitutional Amendments. Their memo was a remarkable example of how Marcos influenced the highest court in the land. It began with two questions: ''Can the Supreme Court declare presidential election unconstitutional and vice-presidential election constitutional? If so, how should the decision be written?''

The document advised Marcos that the court could invalidate the presidential poll on the basis of the eleven petitions, but that none of them had mentioned a vice-presidential contest. (It hadn't been set at the time the petitions were filed.) Therefore, the president's advisers told him, ''The Supreme Court, in line with its limited authority to try and decide *actual* cases and controversies, is not called to pass upon the constitutionality of the said law insofar as it calls for a special election on vice-presidency.''

The memo also dealt with the issue of Marcos replacing the presidential balloting with a nonbinding referendum. It asked, ''After Supreme Court declares presidential election unconstitutional, can FM use February 7 election as a referendum on his government and as a vice-presidential election only?'' The answer to this, too, was affirmative and concluded, ''There is no legal impediment.''

In order to deflect the inevitable attacks once the election was canceled and to lend maximum credibility, the president and his advisers decided that they would attempt to have the Supreme Court's decision written by the most independent-minded of the justices, Claudio Teehankee. Although Teehankee was a Marcos appointee, he frequently voted against the president's wishes and was popularly identified with the opposition. For his pains, he'd twice been passed over for promotion to chief justice. The president and his aides presumed that they would be able to get the renegade justice to write the judgment since Teehankee normally based his decisions on the law, rather than on political considerations, and for Marcos to remain in office during the special elections clearly was unconstitutional. Thus, the president and his men reasoned, Teehankee, by his strict adherence to the constitution, would be compelled to help Marcos.

The aides had submitted the memorandum to Marcos in the middle of December, just a few days after the campaign was launched. On December 17, the Supreme Court held its first hearings on the petitions. The same day, the four presidential assistants presented Marcos with a starkly pessimistic assessment of how the election was shaping up. The analysis found that in the country's most populous areas, he could expect to win only in northern Luzon, his home territory, where his margin of victory would be an overwhelming nine-to-one. Everywhere else, the outlook was grim: In central Luzon, he would lose seven-to-three, or with extraordinary effort, six-to-four; in Metro Manila, he would lose four-to-one; in southern Luzon, he would lose nine-to-one; in the Bicol region, in the far south of Luzon, he would lose nine-to-one; in the western Visasyan island group, he would lose three-to-two. These figures devastated Marcos, and he reacted by exerting maximum influence on the Supreme Court to cancel the election.

The full bench of the Philippine Supreme Court comprised thirteen justices, all of them appointed by Marcos, with one on leave at the time. Ten votes would be required to cancel. On December 18, the justices took a secret head count and found that nine "manifested agreement" on a decision to cancel the presidential contest while allowing the vote to go on for the vice presidency. The three who were opposed were Teehankee, Vicente Abad Santos, a relatively independent thinker, and Lorenzo Relova, who had a moderate record of voting his conscience. Teehankee and Abad Santos simply could not be budged. Rather than make a straightforward constitutional decision, they had decided that the issue was political. The people of the Philippines clearly had indicated their will to hold elections for president and vice president. This meant that Relova was Marcos's last opportunity. Under normal circumstances, it was conceivable that the president would have been able to twist his arm. But Relova was scheduled to retire in another two months, and he had made up his mind to hold firm. He told his colleagues that he believed the presidential poll would be constitutional.

The president was stymied. Aquino's campaign was building steam throughout the country, and his was barely rolling. Word was spreading that Marcos wanted to get out of the contest. He now found himself in a spot where the court was about to vote nine-to-three against him. Should this happen, he would lose great face, the three dissenting justices would appear as heroes for standing up to him, and Aquino would gain further strength. Attempting to rescue the rapidly deteriorating situation, Marcos reckoned that a split decision in favor of the elections would be viewed, particularly in the United States, as an indicator that he did not control the judiciary. This was small comfort, but it was better than the alternative. Through his aides, he instructed the nine justices who had lined up with him to vote as they saw fit. The final decision, announced on December 19, was seven in favor of the elections and five against.

A week later, Teehankee explained what had taken place. A witty, open man who always was ready to banter in the hallways or in the parking lot of the high court, Teehankee was somewhat reticent about elaborating on the details of direct intervention by Marcos in the court's affairs. But his brief comment was eloquent testimony to how corrupted the judiciary had become during the Marcos years: "The change from when we took the informal head count to the actual voting was plain. I'm not privy to why they actually changed, but if you check their voting records, it's safe to assume that it was a result of a shift in pressure from on high. In some cases, you know, loyalty is so total that no pressure is required."

Chief Justice Ramon Aquino was infuriated by Teehankee's remarks. "We simply discussed and then we voted," he protested. "It's not true that the count was first nine-to-three. There was only one voting, and it was seven-to-five. There was no informal head count. Absolutely untrue! A canard! A brazen lie! A vicious lie! A brazen lie! There was no pressure whatsoever. There are always malicious rumors which are maliciously intended to degrade the court. That's part of the game-plan here. I don't pay attention to them. There was absolutely no pressure. The justices expressed themselves individually. This makes me mad. We're not amenable to pressure."

The rebellion by the three justices was a jarring development and a precursor of what lay ahead for the failing Marcos. Their stand against his wishes was the first of significance since the imposition of martial law, and it ensnared Marcos in a trap of his own making.

14

CO-RY! CO-RY! CO-RY!

As an opponent, Cory Aquino befuddled the president. She was the antithesis of himself and his wife. Filipinos who had known the Marcoses and the Aquinos well in the early days used to say that the two men were much like each other; what made them different was their women. Cory, calm, sure of who and what she was, exerted a moderating influence on Ninoy. Imelda, outspoken, insecure, burning with dreams of wealth, fueled Marcos's ambition.

Corazon Cojuangco Aquino was born on January 25, 1933, into one of the country's wealthiest families, their great fortune built by thousands of impoverished laborers who raised sugar and rice on the Cojuangco's 15,000 acres in Tarlac province. When Cory was thirteen, she left the grandeur of the family seat, Hacienda Luisita, and was sent to the United States to be educated, as were her three sisters and two brothers. She remained in America for seven years, attending convent schools and then graduating from the College of Mount St. Vincent, a small women's institution in the Bronx run by the Sisters of Charity, with a degree in French and mathematics. She chose those subjects, she said, "because I wanted to be different." When she returned to the Philippines, she enrolled in law school but soon succumbed to social norms and quit to marry Ninoy.

The great affluence into which she'd been born and the discipline she learned from the nuns made her comfortable with power and helped her maintain control under stress. Coming from a background in which she was naturally treated with deference by thousands of plantation workers, she was completely at ease in the midst of masses of poor Filipinos. "The very fact that I was born privileged carries with it certain obligations," she said during the campaign. "And if I were just concerned for myself, I wouldn't even have bothered coming back to the Philippines or to continue to live here after the assassination of my husband, much less be so actively involved." Unlike Imelda Romualdez Marcos, she didn't sing to campaign crowds or distribute little gifts to establish rapport.

At first, President Marcos tried a lofty, superior approach, treating Aquino as merely a woman, someone not to be taken seriously. "My conversations with ladies have always been pleasant; I presume I will survive this encounter," he said dryly when she challenged him to an American-style televised debate. (He never agreed to the confrontation.) When the electorate refused to be swayed by that approach, Marcos started attacking her for being inexperienced. Her response was a masterful speech, probably the most damaging of her counter-assaults: "I concede that I cannot match Mr. Marcos when it comes to experience. I admit that I have no experience in cheating, stealing, lying, or assassinating political opponents." Stung, the president turned to one of his more predictable avenues of attack; he accused her and her advisers of being Communists. Aquino wisely ignored the slur, and it fizzled out.

With few traditional means open to him, Marcos unleashed his wife, who demeaned Cory's femininity and professed to be aghast that she was running against a man for political office. Cory, said Imelda, was the "complete opposite of what a woman should be." The ideal woman, she said, was one who was "gentle, who does not challenge a man, but who keeps her criticisms to herself and teaches her husband only in the bedroom." Not only was Cory ignoring these basics of womanly behavior, Imelda said, but she even failed to beautify herself with cosmetics. With Imelda herself so obviously powerful in a sphere dominated by men, Aquino again shrugged off most of those allegations. But she did begin wearing a touch of lipstick and blue eyeshadow.

Cory would have been a daunting opponent for any politician. She and her advisers had made the most of her symbolism as the agrieved widow of a martyr. She was portrayed as pure, honest, deeply religious, almost saintly.

She didn't speak well to the people, though. In the beginning of the campaign, speeches prepared for her tended to be overly long and drearily academic. In time, the quality of the words improved markedly, but her ability to deliver them with any power never grew. Her set piece was a recollection of how she had stood before Ninoy's open coffin and vowed to him that she would "continue your fight." Her small, nasal voice and singsong delivery were those of the convent girl she'd been. There was no fury, no fire in the belly. Dressed demurely in the simplest yellow frocks—always yellow—she might have been delivering a ninth-grade civics report.

After island-hopping in small, private planes, she would join low-budget, horn-honking motorcades and bump along country roads from town to town, between columns of cheering, waving villagers. They held up anything yellow they could find: underpants, ribbons, drying banana leaves, and chanted, "Co-ry! Co-ry! Co-ry!" She would stand in the back of a jeep or a truck, smiling and waving both hands, the index fingers and thumbs spread into an L for *laban,* or "fight." Aquino was the first presidential candidate in more than a decade to go to some of the remote places she chose, particularly in troubled Mindanao, and just her being there was a major event in the lives of hundreds of thousands of people. The motorcades would pull up at a roadside market, and she and Laurel would mount a ladder onto a makeshift platform, ringed by cheering, laughing people. Many had walked for hours to see her.

Typically, Laurel, dressed in UNIDO's color, green, would open with a fire-and-brimstone denunciation of the Marcos dictatorship, cronies, and hidden wealth. The crowds ate it up, shouting back to him in unison when he provoked them to demand Marcos's departure. Then Aquino would step up to the microphone and go through her little talk. The effect was similar to letting the air out of a balloon. Within minutes, people on the edges of the crowd would begin drifting away, seeking shade or a cool drink. She couldn't hold their attention. Yet, it didn't seem to matter. They were enamored of her image. "She's so brave to stand up against Marcos," said a young nurse who'd slipped away from work at a hospital outside Davao, in Mindanao. "Doy sounds very macho, but she's the one with real courage. That's why I'm going to vote for her."

Tension between Doy and Cory rose as the campaign proceeded. He thought that because she couldn't hold the attention of the crowds she wouldn't get their votes. She had her own gut instinct, although this may have been nothing more than her being hypnotized by the constant chanting of her name. Some of her advisers were not persuaded that the shouts would translate to votes; they knew that Marcos, with his almost limitless funds, had the power to buy votes and the thugs who could frighten people into changing their minds. But Cory believed that those who turned out to cheer for her would turn out on election day to vote for her. In Davao, 150,000 people spilled into the streets on a drizzly day, showering her with confetti, chanting late into the night, and when she returned to Manila she told her children that the experience had convinced her that she was going to win. She was sure that she was right, that she had a special symbiotic relationship with the masses, and that everyone else was wrong. She stopped listening to those around her. "My only input is to pass her little notes," Laurel complained after giving the warm-up speech in the small southern Mindanao town of Digos. "It's a problem."

Others in her coterie had similar complaints. "I'd say I'm lucky if she pays attention to ten percent of what I tell her," groused Jimmy Ongpin, who had put together a seven-member group of advisers, including some of the country's most brilliant businessmen, academics, professionals, and clergymen, which came to be known as her "Council of Trent." At first, she was a blank slate on which the council members wrote; she simply mouthed their words. But that quickly changed as she became intoxicated by the crowds. She demonstrated that she had a mind of her own, and a spine of steel, though some of her instructors doubted that her strong will reflected real strength. They knew she had major weaknesses, that there were great gaps in her knowledge.

The fundamental task of the "Council of Trent," named for the sixteenth-century body that restored confidence to the Catholic Church in the face of nascent Protestantism, was to conduct crash courses for Aquino in a variety of disciplines, particularly economics, her weakest area of understanding. Marcos sniped at the effort: "There is simply no way for anyone to cram for the presidency. It provides no time for schooling. Once you get in, you're in the driver's seat, and fifty-four million people will be riding on your ability to drive." Aquino's old family friend, millionaire banker and businessman Enrique Zobel, was swayed by Marcos's argument, and he shocked Aquino, and much of the business community, by announcing that he was withdrawing his support from her to back Marcos, with whom he had been at odds for years. "Good intentions and emotions alone just aren't enough to get the nation's engine going," he said. Cory was deeply disturbed by Zobel's defection, but she quickly neutered his criticism: "Well, I agree with him that substance is critical. But then, with Marcos, there is no possible way whereby he can rule this country, because he just can't win back the confidence of the Filipino people. I mean, from all indications, they just can't see Marcos as bringing about the changes they are looking for because it was he in the first place who brought about all of these problems." The campaign moved onward with no real issues as far as most Filipinos were concerned; it was even something less than a personality contest. Aquino's argument for dumping Marcos couldn't have been more basic: "Enough is enough!" For his part, the president tried to drum up fear by Red-baiting, but few bit.

In Washington, though, there were issues. The Reagan administration fretted that she was soft on the Communists and might close the bases. Black, Manafort, Stone and Kelley, the Washington public relations firm Marcos had hired, organized trips to the Philippines for influential American conservatives, such as syndicated columnist Robert Novak. They arrived antagonistic, with preconceived agendas, demanding to know what her position was on the bases. She answered them honestly: "I am for the eventual removal of the bases. But, like my husband, I have not set any particular date. As far as aid in connection with the bases is concerned, I will reserve my options on that. I will just clearly state what we demand when negotiations take place." Most went back and reported that she was anti-bases.

A similar exercise took place on the question of how she would deal with the outlawed Communist Party of the Philippines. Again, she was frank: "I am for a free market of ideas and leave it to the Filipino people to make their choice. I have no illusions about the hard core, you know, continuing to be that. But, those who have just joined the Communists because they have been abused by the military or as a temporary shelter from the Marcos forces, these are the people I hope to attract." The results on this, too, were predictable, and the conservatives reported that she was soft on Communism. Few seemed to pay any attention to the fact that the CPP was not supporting her; to the contrary, the party had distanced itself from her campaign and was calling on its backers, perhaps a million strong, to boycott the elections.

Aquino was neither anti-bases nor soft on Communism; given her background and her education, it would be unlikely for her to be anything other than pro-American and anti-Communist. She was realistic, though. No patriot, not even Marcos, honestly would say that the bases should remain in the Philippines in perpetuity. And, at one level, it made good sense to play hard-to-get, to keep the United States on its toes, to strengthen Philippine bargaining power for 1991, the time to negotiate a new agreement and raise the "aid," or "rent," Washington paid for the facilities. However, by being so forthright, she raised questions among Washington conservatives and deprived herself of support early on. As for the Communist issue, she could have pretended, as Marcos had been doing, that they didn't amount to a significant force and that she would continue to suppress them. This might have soothed Reagan and some others in the White House, but those in the State Department and at the embassy in Manila who understood what was going on in the Philippines quietly acknowledged that, as she advocated, it would be better to open discussions with the CPP.

After Marcos's attempts to tie Aquino to the Communists failed, he reverted to an older approach, charging that as a member of a rich, traditional, landed family, she would return power to the oligarchs, those he'd eliminated during martial law. Camera crews from the government's Channel 4 were dispatched to Hacienda Luisita, where they interviewed laborers who complained that they were mistreated by the Cojuangco family. Marcos charged that the family had not abided by land-reform regulations he'd imposed during martial law, and the family argued that sugar plantations had not been affected by land reform. The family was technically correct. But the Cojuangcos, and Cory, were vulnerable to this charge since their 3,500 laborers, like all plantation workers, were exploited. Still, the notion that landed aristocrats like the Cojuangcos were both right-wing oligarchs and Communists, as Marcos claimed, was too much for many Filipinos to swallow. Aquino had unleashed passions they had kept pent up for years, and those who were falling into line behind her weren't affected by what Marcos said, or what she said, for that matter. They were voting their emotions.

Because of poor health, Marcos frequently was forced to fire off his charges from the palace, waging a televised campaign while his opponents were out pressing flesh. While the president canceled trip after trip to various distant locations, usually citing "bad weather" or "affairs of state," the challengers worked twenty-hour days, every day, and traveled to almost every one of the country's seventy-three provinces. It was a once-in-a-lifetime performance, generated by an evangelical will to drive Marcos out of office.

Imelda Marcos and Arturo Tolentino took their own show on the road, campaigning with vigor in the president's stead. In her strong, clear voice, Imelda sang in local dialects and passed out trinkets, sometimes even taking a watch off her wrist and presenting it to a poor woman in the crowd. Tolentino was an astonishing performer, a powerful speaker in Tagalog, with the athletic physique of a man less than half his age, the result of weight lifting and jogging. They put on a good performance, this odd couple, backed by bands and cheerleaders, but usually there was the sense that this was just another circus, that those watching were having fun but not making a political choice. The crowds usually were substantial, and when the president himself appeared, local KBL personnel saw to it that the numbers were huge. On repeated occasions, thousands were bused to stadiums, herded in, and the gates locked behind them to keep them from fading away once they'd received their T-shirts and cash payments, usually a dollar or so for the day, not insignificant in their subsistence economy. If it wasn't possible to round up a huge crowd, the government-run TV cameras were set at angles that made the numbers appear much greater.

In sharp contrast, the Aquino crowds were natural and enthusiastic. They made their own way to rallies, spending their own money on paraphernalia or using makeshift materials, shouting with unrestrained excitement. In an attempt to counter the spread of this enthusiasm, Information Minister Gregorio Cendaña instructed broadcasters and editors to downplay numbers.

With travel in the Philippines so difficult and so time-consuming, control of news outlets was a powerful weapon. So Marcos blocked their use by his opponent. For the first six weeks of the two-month campaign, Aquino was able to get almost no access to television stations, either with paid advertisements or during newscasts. The station able to reach farthest throughout the archipelago was Channel 4, which didn't attempt to hide the fact that it existed to promote Marcos. "We make no bones that this is a government station and we're supposed to broadcast news about the government and the president," said the station's news director, Jess Matubis. "If we follow this policy, how can we say things that are detrimental to the government? Will any government allow itself to be torn down?" Matubis, a gray-faced man who seemed incapable of smiling, either on camera or off, appeared baffled by questions about the public's right to hear both sides of the campaign, particularly considering that taxes paid for the channel's budget. He merely shrugged his shoulders and said, "I suppose you could look at it that way."

An independent research organization, Philippine Monitoring Services, Inc., conducted a survey that revealed that in the four weeks from the opening of the campaign on December 11 until January 7, Channel 4 devoted twenty-six hours of special programs entirely to the ruling party's convention and to Marcos's campaign rallies. There was nothing for Aquino. Near the end of January, Rene Saguisag, a Harvard-educated civil-rights attorney who had taken on the job of Aquino's campaign spokesman, said, "Our score is still zero."

At other TV stations, the score was almost as lopsided. Three of Manila's four private channels, 2, 9, and 13, were operated by Kanlaon Broadcasting System, owned by Marcos's sugar-baron associate, Roberto S. Benedicto. All three KBS stations were dominated by Marcos commercials and news favorable to the president, while paying almost no attention to Aquino. The fourth private station, Channel 7, was owned by the Greater Manila Radio and Television Arts Corporation, a firm controlled by Gilberto Duavit, a former sports minister in the Marcos cabinet and a leader of the KBL. In the first month of the campaign, Channel 7 presented relatively balanced programming, under the instruction of Tina Monzon Palma, who was anchorwoman of the evening newscast and the station's news director. Information Minister Cendaña decided that Monzon Palma was "tilting toward the opposition." She was relieved of her duties as news director, and Channel 7 no longer offered viewers balanced fare.

Under pressure from the U.S. Congress, which had commissioned its own study by Boston University's Center for Democracy, the Marcos regime said that whether "a sitting president, owing to his peculiar position," required wider coverage than his opponent was a question to be decided by the Commission on Elections. Aquino's lawyers took the case to COMELEC, where it remained. "We started out trying for equal time," said Saguisag with just a week to go in the campaign. "Then we cut our request down to six hours. Now, we'll settle for anything we can get." Only in the final days did the TV stations give Aquino a break, largely to satisfy U.S. protestations.

Aquino's people had greater success in getting their paid spot announcements on radio stations around the country, but not in convincing popular commentators to conduct programs airing their candidate's views. The Church-backed Radio Veritas was the sole exception. It was unabashedly pro-Aquino and drew numbers far in excess of its norm because it provided the only real alternative to the government-dominated media.

Newspapers provided some variety. The four major Manila dailies continued to be overwhelmingly dominated by pro-Marcos coverage and splashed articles favorable to the president across their front pages. Stories about Aquino usually were buried inside and, on the rare occasions when they were printed on the front pages, were confined to the lower half, where they received considerably less attention from readers. The much smaller alternative papers, *Malaya* and *Business Day,* gave prominent coverage to the Aquino campaign and freely attacked the president. The net result was that papers on both sides were so biased that people had to read several, add the information to the latest rumors, and then make a personal decision as to what might have been true.

Another area of the campaign in which Aquino found herself at a severe disadvantage was funding. Her brother Peping Cojuangco had raised money from some powerful local backers and from expatriate Filipinos in the United States while Jimmy Ongpin and his associates had tapped friends in the Manila business community. But what they'd come up with was penny ante compared with Marcos, who was able to tap the national treasury and a network of multimillionaire cronies.

Yet, the president had moved slowly in disbursing funds, uncertain of whether he'd be able to slide out of the election completely. His friends had brought their money back from overseas, where it had been salted away. At the end of December, the Central Bank's balance-of-payments report suddenly showed the presence of a mysterious $654 million listed under "errors and omissions." Bank Governor Jose B.

Fernandez said he had no explanation, but financial specialists reasoned that the entry was the footprint of dollars summoned back to help fund the campaign.

Finally, on Sunday, January 26, just ten days before the election, the money began to flow. Marcos called a meeting of 350 regional party leaders at Malacañang Palace. He was sick and depressed and spoke with only a handful of them in his private study. The majority had to be content with meeting the First Lady, Tolentino, and members of the cabinet. J. V. Cruz, the ambassador to Britain who was campaigning full time, good-humoredly described the occasion as "envelope day."

The packets of money that were handed out, some containing enormous sums, were earmarked for vote-buying. Thousands of voters would receive a few pesos each, but the bulk would go in larger payments to poll officials. In areas where Aquino looked strongest the amounts were highest, ranging from the equivalent of $2,000 for officials charged with tallying regional ballot returns to $5 for a single vote. So common had the practice of vote-buying become under Marcos that Cardinal Sin had advised Catholics that it would not be a sin "to take the money and vote your conscience." A significant number of the KBL officials who'd been at Malacañang that Sunday found the atmosphere and outlook so gloomy that later they admitted distributing very little of the money, instead keeping it in expectation that this would be their last "envelope day."

The president's problems mounted when his cherished war record was questioned. There was no more basic element of Marcos's public persona than the chestful of medals he'd been awarded, among them the Distinguished Service Cross supposedly presented personally by General MacArthur for single-handedly delaying the fall of Bataan by three months. The twenty-seven medals made him the most decorated war hero in the history of the nation, "the Philippine Audie Murphy," as newspapers of the day put it.

The centerpiece of Marcos's heroics was a guerrilla organization, called *Ang Mga Maharlika*, which means "the Free Men," or "the Noblemen." He claimed that he and other daring agents of the 8,200-man *Maharlika* had harassed the Japanese occupiers of Manila between 1942 and 1944, at great risk to their own lives, 30 percent of them having been killed. Marcos's war stories had been a major part of his original campaign for the presidency, and he continued to recount them through the current race. It was essential to him that the public believe him a great hero. He had named Luzon's main north-south highway, the government-owned broadcasting network, and a hall in the presidential palace *Maharlika*.

But during the summer of 1985, an American historian by the name of Alfred W. McCoy found in the National Archives in Washington a file that "stunned" him. McCoy, whose wife was a Filipina, had spent half a year researching Marcos's record for a book he was planning on World War II in the Philippines. The file contained documents that had been declassified twenty-five years earlier but never released, and they showed that most of Marcos's guerrilla exploits were imaginary. His official claims that he had founded a unit called *Maharlika* and that this organization had been a major force in helping overcome the Japanese were "fraudulent" and "absurd," the U.S. Army had concluded. The U.S. Veterans Administration, with the help of the Philippine army, also had found that some of the men who claimed membership in *Maharlika* had actually committed atrocities against Filipino civilians and had sold contraband to the Japanese. Marcos had sought U.S. recognition of the unit so that he and the others could receive back pay and benefits, the V.A. had determined.

McCoy wrote a highly detailed article for *The National Times,* a newspaper in Australia, where he taught, and he shared his findings with *The New York Times* and *The Washington Post*. The *Times'* article appeared in Manila papers on January 24, just two weeks before election day, under blaring headlines, among them, MARCOS FAKE HERO, U.S. ARMY CONCLUDES; GUERRILLA EXPLOITS "ABSURD, DISTORTED."

The stories hit Marcos hard, "like a blow to the solar plexus," according to J. V. Cruz. The president was now in a corner, having to defend the core of his reputation. The evening that the story broke, Marcos addressed a rally of some 40,000 residents of Tondo, the capital's most squalid slum: "My opponents now say that Marcos is not a genuine guerrilla, that he did not really fight. I don't know where they get such foolishness. You who are in Tondo and fought under me, you be the ones to answer these crazy individuals, especially the foreign press. They are all going crazy." Some men cheered, but many more looked embarrassed and stared at their feet.

The assault on Marcos's war record emboldened Aquino, and she shifted into a more aggressive posture. "I'm mad," she said. "This man is an inveterate liar. He must be stopped, and I intend to stop him." As she went on the attack, the president became more of a tragic figure; he seemed not to comprehend what was happening. "This campaign has become unworldly, unreal," he said with a touch of melancholy wonder. "It's like looking through a kaleidoscope, like looking at strange images you see under water." He had found himself in the midst of a bad dream and wanted desperately for it to end: "Very soon I'll be back in my lonely office to face the problems that face the nation."

The president couldn't come to terms with the possibility that he might be voted out of office. "The idea of losing has never entered my mind," he said, and most people reckoned that, one way or another, he would manage to win. That would mean cheating. The United States was demanding "free and fair" elections or, more importantly, the impression of such elections. Congress had authorized Senator Richard G. Lugar, a Republican from Indiana who was chairman of the Foreign Relations Committee, to lead a delegation of twenty poll-watchers to the Philippines. A second team of international observers was coming, and a thousand journalists from all over the world were pouring into the country. Filipinos hoped that the presence of these outsiders would embarrass the KBL toughs into toning down the use of "guns, goons, and gold" that typified electioneering in the Philippines.

But the notion of the elections being truly "free and fair" was viewed as an example of American naiveté. "Doesn't your president have a clue about what's been going on in this country?" Jimmy Ongpin asked in frustrated disbelief. "It amazes me that the U.S. government can continue talking about 'free and fair' as if you have to wait for election day. They know free and fair elections are damned-near impossible."

All Filipinos knew there would be cheating; the only question was how much. Conversations about the anticipated outcome took on a bizarre quality, laced with innovative terms, including "wholesale" and "retail" fraud, and how many votes were "cheatable." The "cheating factor" became a serious element in all analyses. The head of a nonprofit social-research organization, Dr. Mahar Mangahas, produced a study indicating that Marcos "will have to cheat at least 16 percent, or 3.9 million votes, in order to get 51 percent of the total and win." Mangahas had conducted a nationwide survey the preceding June in which he'd found that the public's "satisfaction rate" with Marcos had plummeted to 44 percent from a high of nearly 90 percent shortly before the Aquino assassination. Now, since the acquittal of General Ver and the emergence of Cory Aquino, Mangahas estimated, the president's popularity had dropped to "no more than upper thirties."

Dr. Emanuel V. Soriano, a former president of the University of the Philippines and a member of Aquino's "Council of Trent," said that Marcos would have to limit the cheating in order not to overly offend the sensibilities of the outside world. "Our gut feeling is that Marcos won't try to win by a landslide," he said. "He's got a serious credibility problem." This put the president in the difficult position of having to fine-tune his cheating at a time when the cohesiveness of the KBL was in doubt because numerous party members were worrying about their own futures more than Marcos's. "As a result," said Soriano, "his people may overcheat or undercheat."

Cheating was the paramount concern of José Concepcion and his National Citizens Movement for Free Elections. NAMFREL had been successful in curbing the numbers of "flying voters" and limiting ballot-box stuffing in the May 1984 parliamentary elections, enabling the opposition to score an unprecedented gain. But this time around, with the stakes so much higher, the challenge would be immeasurably greater. On election day, NAMFREL would field some 500,000 workers nationwide, identifiable by white vests stenciled with a lit candle, but Concepcion had few illusions about their ability to block the massive fraud he expected. "The KBL will try to cheat in every way possible—soft cheating and hard cheating, attacking the electoral system at every point where it may be vulnerable," he said.

Lighting and relighting his trademark large, green stogie without pausing in his rapid-fire monologue, Concepcion portrayed NAMFREL as unbiased, a citizen's watchdog, its sole task to assure clean polling. But in this he was being disingenuous. NAMFREL was as much pro-Aquino as COMELEC was pro-Marcos. At a NAMFREL training session in San Fernando, capital of northern La Union province, of more than one hundred volunteers, only one confided to me that he planned to vote for Marcos. One of NAMFREL's major objectives was to monitor COMELEC, to assure that the government organization conducted a fast and honest count of the returns and that it dealt fairly with protests once the polling was completed. Concepcion said that he was more worried about sophisticated fraud, especially attempts to tamper with the election return forms, than with ballot-box stuffing, which required the acquiescence of too many people.

This concern was justified. In mid January, an Aquino spy within COMELEC prepared four memos detailing how Ambassador to the United States Benjamin Romualdez, the First Lady's brother, had co-opted COMELEC commissioner Jaime Opinion and several lower-ranking officials and was setting up plans to falsify returns. Under COMELEC regulations, tallies of paper ballots cast at each of the ninety thousand polling stations were to be entered on return forms previously affixed with secret marks by representatives of both parties. According to one of the memos, the original return forms were being stolen once the secret marks were applied. They were being photo-copied and filled in with faked totals and the forged signatures of voting inspectors even before election day. The short-term objective was to deliver inflated Marcos returns to Manila so that the president could be proclaimed the winner as quickly as possible. Although the opposition would be able to show later, from carbon copies of the originals, that forgeries had been submitted, the protest process could take years to resolve. Meanwhile Marcos would be president.

COMELEC chairman Victorino A. Savellano angrily denied claims that he or any of his fellow commissioners, all of whom were appointed by Marcos, were under the control of the ruling party. In his office at COMELEC headquarters in Intramuros, seated beneath full-color por-traits of the Marcoses and enlarged photographs of himself with the president, Savellano insisted that he was his own man. "None of us sides with any party. We submit ourselves to the searching scrutiny of the public. I don't know where they get the idea that, just because you are appointed by the president, you owe loyalty to the president."

While Concepcion and Savellano were dueling with each other over questions of which of their organizations would be able to use government lines of communication from provincial vote headquarters to Manila and which would be permitted to carry out an official "quick count" of returns, Marcos was committing the military to the final phase of his campaign.

Ever since the *Sandiganbayan* had acquitted General Ver, the president had been toying with the United States, indicating that he would retire his most trusted military aide before the elections. But on January 21, with two weeks left before election day, the president stripped away the pretense when he told a luncheon meeting of the Makati Business Club that Ver was not retiring after all. "You can't change the chief of staff with a snap of your fingers," Marcos said. During Ver's leave of absence, "factionalism and problems" had developed in the armed forces, and now not enough time remained to replace him before the elections. There was more than a grain of truth in what the president had said; the military was fragmenting. But Ver's leave was not the cause. Rather, the trouble stemmed from Marcos's long-term misuse of the armed forces—just as he was preparing to misuse them again—compounded by Ver's implication in the Aquino assassination. By refusing to replace Ver before the elections, the president was further alienating the young reformist officers.

A week later, Marcos reversed an earlier commitment to keep the troops "in barracks" during the polls and ordered them to provide "security" for the elections. COMELEC approved the involvement of the troops on February 3, sending a chill of apprehension through the Aquino camp. Ramon H. Felipe, Jr., the sole COMELEC dissenter, protested that "it would now be easy for partisan military personnel to coerce or threaten voters to vote one way or the other on election day by hiding under the mantle of the deputation order." But Chairman Savellano said that one of the armed forces' key functions would be to "make available land, air, and water transportation facilities, communications systems, and other equipment" for returning the election results to Manila. Thus, as in past elections, the military would be perfectly situated to substitute ballot boxes, exchange return forms, and otherwise help cheat. Even more basically, Marcos and Ver knew that the mere presence of armed troops in the vicinity of polling stations was sufficient to intimidate many people who might have planned to vote for Aquino.

Cory Aquino wrapped up her campaign on Tuesday, February 4. A vast crowd, perhaps as many as half a million people, surged into Manila's bayfront Luneta park and spilled into surrounding streets, snarling traffic in great knots, paralyzing much of the city. Because the government refused to permit her to speak from the concrete grandstand at the front of the park, Aquino stood on a makeshift platform near the back. The sound system was inadequate, carrying her voice to a relative handful only, yet almost no one left, and the enormous throng stayed for six hours, shouting over and over again their support for Aquino and their insistence that Marcos leave office. Aquino characteristically invoked religion into the sustained, high-pitched emotion of the rally. Her delivery, as usual, was flat, but she showed once again that in spirit she was attuned to most Filipinos:

"Rarely has a nation been given an opportunity like this. It is certain our freedom will come. We have a chance to make history. Let us pray that we have peaceful and honest elections so that by Christ we can forgive our enemies.

"Mr. Marcos has committed many sins against the people. His sins against me and my family only prove that Marcos has no respect for the dignity of the people, no conscience, no morals, no soul. I am convinced that Mr. Marcos and his regime are truly evil and have systematically plundered our country and our people.

"Marcos said I don't have the strength to be president. I recall the trials I've had since Ninoy's arrest, his incarceration, and his assassination. I have accepted all the trials from God. I can accept the challenge of the presidency."

The president closed out his race the next evening, Wednesday, February 5, in the same park, but it rained, and what was intended to be a blazing climax, complete with a dazzling laser light show and entertainment by some of the biggest names in the country, deteriorated into an embarrassing fiasco. By the time Marcos stood before a microphone on the concrete grandstand at the front of the park, no more than 12,000 people remained on the soggy Luneta grounds, most of them clustered in the area directly in front of him. Perhaps because he couldn't see the empty space behind them, the president exaggerated the turnout beyond reason in a speech that glorified his achievements over two decades:

"We have changed the indifferent and uncommitted Filipino soul into a soul that is vibrant and dynamic, as you can see in this almost, perhaps one million people who squished through the rain in order to attend a rally of the KBL."

Because numbers meant so much in the propaganda battle, the

government TV announcers kept up the ruse. "Despite the downpour," said one commentator, "everyone has kept his place in this huge crowd of one million." Cameras mounted on aerial ladders provided by the Manila Fire Department focused only on the people in front of the grandstand.

With the two Luneta park rallies, the campaign was over. According to law, there would now be a twenty-four-hour break, to allow passions to cool. Then, at 7:00 A.M. on Friday, February 7, the polls would open.

15

*N*OT ACCORDING TO HOYLE

On election day, an event transpiring halfway around the world went largely unnoticed in the Philippines. In Port-au-Prince, Haiti's President-for-Life Jean-Claude ("Baby Doc") Duvalier and his wife, Michele, fled into the predawn skies aboard a U.S. C-141 transport plane bound for France. Duvalier and his late father, François ("Papa Doc"), had ruled the tiny, poverty-wracked Caribbean nation for twenty-eight years. The sudden end of their corrupt, repressive dynasty would, in a day or so, infuse many Filipinos with optimism for change in their own country. But first they had to vote.

Filipinos took the business of voting very seriously, and by the time the sun rose, long lines had formed outside polling stations. Some 26 million people turned out, more than 95 percent of those registered. At a grammar school in the Manila suburb of Pasay, a housewife named Vida Balboa dramatically summarized the feelings of many when she said, "Today could be liberation day or it could be the start of civil war." As the day wore on Balboa and millions more found themselves enmeshed in every manner of intentional confusion, cheating, and intimidation, and many wound up not being able to vote at all.

One of the first signs that something was wrong was the discovery at thousands of voting centers that names were missing from registration lists. As would-be voters entered the schools being used as polling stations, they looked fruitlessly for their names posted on classroom doors. Muttering turned to uproar, tempers rose, and the lines grew longer. But most people stuck it out. Gray-haired Mrs. Justa had brought her noodle-vending cart with her and had been waiting on line for nearly three hours. She was losing business, she was perspiring and irritable. "They want us to spend all day waiting here and then go home without voting," she said, "but I'm not leaving until they let me vote." Those around her nodded in agreement.

Large-scale tampering with registration lists was a new tactic for the KBL machine and, while simple, proved to be very effective, freeing Marcos workers from the risky business of cooking up huge numbers. Some 3 million people throughout the country lost the chance to vote just because they couldn't find their names. The disenfranchisement was concentrated in areas known to be Aquino strongholds, such as Metro Manila, where she lost an estimated 1 million votes. There had been no attempt to eliminate only Aquino supporters from the registration lists, but the assumption was that a majority of those whose names were missing would have voted for her.

Workers in almost every precinct had stories to tell, and most of them were similar. "The instructions seem to be to tamper with everything," said Salvador Lacson, an Aquino organizer at the Guadalupe Nueva Elementary School, on the south side of Manila, where an angry crush of people had backed up for two blocks. Farther south, at the Bayanon Elementary School in Muntinglupa, NAMFREL volunteer Victoria Pertierra, dressed in white slacks, a plaid shirt, and her official white vest, said that entire registration lists were missing. In the town of San Fernando, in Pampanga province, forty miles north of Manila, NAMFREL workers calculated that at least three hundred voters hadn't been able to find their names at Dolores Elementary School, a low wooden building on the old MacArthur Highway. The local COMELEC chairman hadn't come to the school, and since he had the master list, there was no way to know how many voters were registered. Henry Carreon found his name. He also found that someone else had already voted for him.

At Samal, on the Bataan peninsula, NAMFREL attorney Juan Federico said that 10 percent of the town's voters had been turned away because their names couldn't be found. Those who were allowed to vote were forced to sign four different registration books, although COMELEC chairman Savellano had been on the radio that morning, advising people that they were supposed to sign only one. "The whole point of the exercise seems to be to slow things down and keep large numbers from voting, one way or another," Federico said.

The Marcos forces used a variety of techniques, cunning as well as violent. Alfredo Pio de Rado, a NAMFREL attorney, discovered that the "indelible" blue stain applied to the fingernail of each voter at Bayanon School came off easily with nail-polish remover. "We reported it to the school principal, but he showed us the label, which said it was official COMELEC ink, and he just walked away," de Rado said. Maria Luisa Sison, a young woman who was waiting in line at the school, said she'd seen five "flying voters" come in and cast their ballots. "They were under age and they used names that weren't their own," she said. How could she be so certain? "One of them was my own brother, Hilario."

In the financial district of Makati, six armed men burst into the large Guadalupe Elementary School, fired their weapons wildly, and beat up three NAMFREL volunteers, smashing heavy folding chairs over their heads. Police officers standing outside the school paid no attention to the gunshots and the screaming. Finally, after the NAMFREL people had locked themselves inside a room with a heap of ballot boxes and the gunmen fled, the police walked casually into the building. "According to them," said Captain Rudolfo Reodique, tipping his head toward a cluster of badly shaken NAMFREL workers, "there was some trouble, some shooting. We had to get an order to enter the building. Our communications system isn't too good."

Bienvenido Tan, the lawyer who had served on the Agrava Fact-Finding Board, was there and had attempted to photograph one of the armed men. "This goon raised a chair over my head and said, 'Go ahead, take my picture, I dare you,' " Tan said. "Then they started shouting, 'All NAMFRELs, out!' People were screaming for help. I ran out and pleaded with the police to come in, but they didn't answer me. That was really the frightening part." As Tan was talking, José Concepcion came bustling into the school, his face streaming with sweat, his cigar cold and soggy. "There's chaos all over the city," he reported.

The pro-Marcos effort in Makati, where Mayor Yabut was grievously ill, was carried out by toughs under the mayor's son, Ricardo. The outcome in Makati was crucial; as a wellspring of middle-class opposition, it could be expected to vote heavily for Aquino, and this would be humiliating, and perhaps numerically devastating, to Marcos. It was therefore determined to ignore the foreign observers who were scrutinizing Makati microscopically and go for broke. In the town's Tejeros neighborhood, ward boss Lito de Guzman led thirty armed men into a school, storming past women who'd set up a makeshift altar where they were saying the rosary, forced out 250 NAMFREL workers at gunpoint, seized boxes containing some 30,000 ballots, and fled. A similar incident took place in the nearby neighborhood of Pinagkaisahan, where Dr. Oscar Santos, a local physician, said, "I don't think world opinion matters to Marcos anymore—just staying in power."

The pace of interference picked up after the 3:00 P.M. poll-closing time. At the Bayanon school in Muntinglupa, four or five men carrying M-16 rifles burst into the building firing into the air. They snatched two locked ballot boxes from a classroom, scooped handfuls of ballots out of other boxes, and ran off with them, passing several uniformed policemen who watched calmly. Earline Dionisio, a poll clerk, crawled under the table when the shooting began. She and other workers were so terrorized that they refused to count the remaining ballots at the school and called for police to escort them to the nearby municipal building. While they waited they sat on the ballot boxes, as they'd been instructed by NAMFREL. When they finally were taken to the municipal building, they reconsidered and, fearing more trouble, knelt on the ground and counted.

At several small towns in Bataan, trucks filled with combat-armed marines roared along the dusty streets. In the central Luzon city of Cebu, attorneys working for the opposition reported convoys of armed men in civilian dress, their faces covered with bandanas, driving into rural areas. In Tarlac, Aquino's home province, armed men roamed the streets. With other gunmen reported prowling around her family's plantation, Hacienda Luisita, Aquino was whisked by car back to her house in Quezon City as soon as she finished voting. She and other members of the family had begun the day on the estate at 5:30 A.M. with prayers in a private chapel. "They're good Catholics and they prayed hard," said a family friend. "They know many people will die today."

How many people were killed throughout the country on election day was uncertain, possibly thirty. The toll since the start of the campaign two months earlier was around one hundred.

Senator Lugar and members of his official U.S. observer team were dismayed by much of what they saw, but the pattern was spotty. In some places balloting appeared to be proceeding without interference. He and his team, shuttling from one polling place to another aboard a gleaming, white U.S. Navy helicopter, witnessed confusion, but not necessarily blatant cheating. "The thing is not that far out of kilter" was Lugar's early assessment. "I felt that the voting proceeded smoothly." He seemed to want to give Marcos the benefit of the doubt. But that doubt continued to gnaw at the Indiana legislator, and he realized that what was going on bore little resemblance to elections as he and millions of Americans knew them. He visited a voting station in rural Pampanga province where poll watchers complained that four thousand blank ballots had disappeared. At the De la Paz-North station just outside the provincial capital, San Fernando, he noticed that poll watchers were wearing Marcos T-shirts. "Isn't that against the law?" he asked. A hurried consultation resulted in the clerks being sent home to change. At another station, Lugar saw an Aquino worker show up bloodied and bandaged, saying he'd been beaten by Marcos people. The senator reconsidered to a degree. "It's not all according to Hoyle," he acknowledged.

That night, back at the Manila Hotel, Lugar grew increasingly restive as reports poured in of further abuses and of the regime refusing to allow NAMFREL volunteers to observe official tallying and report the results to their own headquarters. And the COMELEC count was dragging. Lugar decided that he'd have to say something; his earlier optimism and subsequent silence were being exploited by Marcos as a sign of official American approval. The president had already been on television, announcing that the foreign observers "were certainly convinced that the elections have been honest and clean." Lugar knew that his assessment would count heavily in congressional debate on the future of U.S. military and economic aid to the Philippines. Shortly after 10:00 P.M., the gray-haired, conservative Republican walked out of the hotel's towering teak doors, and aides assembled an impromptu news conference beneath the glass canopy over the entrance. "I'm deeply disturbed by the delay in the count," he said. "One of the scenarios we anticipated . . . was if the government was worried by the results, it might try to bring things to a halt. . . . There's a serious pattern, a very serious pattern, of influence. I plead with whoever is holding up the count to free it, let it go, so we can see what the will of the people is.''

The COMELEC count being conducted at the cavernous Philippine International Convention Center on Manila Bay was lagging nearly 50 percent behind the unofficial count being conducted by NAMFREL at the La Salle University gymnasium in suburban Green Hills. The two organizations were supposed to have cooperated in what was being called Operation Quick Count. Drawing on the large number of NAMFREL volunteers and the government communications network available to COMELEC, Operation Quick Count was intended to give the country and the world a final tally within forty-eight hours after the polls closed. But, from the start of discussions well before election day, it became clear that COMELEC had no intention of cooperating. In the end, the two organizations conducted independent counts.

With almost every NAMFREL volunteer an admitted Aquino partisan, it was natural that its count would be biased in her favor, though the extent of this slant seemed relatively limited. The COMELEC count was not only biased in favor of Marcos, but was being intentionally slowed down so that fraudulent tally sheets could be substituted for the genuine ones.

Intriguingly, though, in the early stages both tallies showed Aquino marginally ahead of the president. This, Marcos knew, could become terribly dangerous. Once people came to see that his opponent was leading, a surge in his favor would be difficult to force down their throats, even if it was legitimate. Aquino and her advisers understood this as well. So, both candidates moved quickly to establish their claims to victory, and both declared themselves winners just hours after the polls closed. Saturday morning's newspapers heightened the confusion, with the progovernment dailies declaring Marcos the winner, and the opposition papers, Aquino.

Aquino appeared at a news conference on Saturday and was introduced by an aide as the president-elect of the Philippines. ''My victory is irreversible,'' she said, and insisted that she would not abide by any contrary findings by COMELEC or the National Assembly, which had the ultimate responsibility of proclaiming the winner. Setting the stage for protest if Marcos was proclaimed, Aquino said, ''If it is evident to me that I am being cheated out of an election, I will not accept anybody's proclamation.'' Charging that her ''margin of victory'' had already been severely reduced by fraud and intimidation, she called on Marcos to resign. It was a clever tactic; even if Marcos were to win legitimately, Aquino had already told the country and the world that it was illegitimate, and millions were ready to believe her.

Desperate to demonstrate that he was in control of the mechanisms of government, Marcos called a news conference at Malacañang Palace the same day and said that he was considering voiding the elections. His approach was at least as clever as Aquino's. If she continued to cry ''fraud,'' he could simply acknowledge that there had indeed been fraud and that the elections therefore were invalid—and then remain in office until the regularly scheduled elections in 1987. ''These are matters which I have thought seriously about, and as of now I am trying to play it by ear,'' he said. American political leaders were alarmed, foreseeing that cancellation could lead to chaos in the Philippines. Senator John Kerry, a Democrat from Massachusetts who was a member of Lugar's observer team, said that if Marcos canceled the elections, ''politically, his credibility with the American people, and the Filipino people, would be so low, the issue is whether he could govern.''

An international team of forty-five observers from around the world was equally disturbed. John Hume, a member of the British Parliament from Northern Ireland, questioned the extent of the irregularities, saying, ''A substantial segment of the Philippines' population distrusts the electoral system as it's being administered.''

As the two opponents fought a war of words, the war of numbers was growing increasingly contentious. Two days after the polls closed, NAMFREL's tally had accounted for 7.7 million votes—nearly a third of those cast—and showed Aquino solidly ahead by nearly 1 million; COMELEC's official count stood at just 2.1 million and had Marcos and Aquino locked in a dead heat.

COMELEC officials knew that the time had come to do something drastic to make Marcos appear the winner, and they decided to alter the accurate data being generated by banks of computers in the Convention Center. Their decision reflected the desperation in the Marcos camp. The tampering would not be an easy matter, but the risk was a calculated one. The technicians and computer programmers were all employed by the government's own National Computer Center, which was run by a former army colonel, Pedro F. Baraoidan, who reported to Marcos. When COMELEC had awarded the contract for the counting to the NCC, Aquino's forces protested bitterly but to no avail. COMELEC officials now reasoned that Baraoidan would be able to control his staff, and even if some were independent-minded, they wouldn't be told what was going on.

Operations at the COMELEC center had gotten off to a smooth start Friday night after the polls closed. The hall housing the computers looked like the very essence of high-tech efficiency, a hushed, brilliantly lit arena dominated by a theater-sized TV screen, to carry live interviews, flanked by white scoreboards listing voting districts. On the broad floor, white-coated operators sat in rows before dozens of desktop computers. Uniformed clerks scurried back and forth, carrying notes and printer tear sheets. Others scampered up and down rolling ladders, writing results on the boards with thick black markers. Crowds of interested bystanders filed in and out of an elevated gallery, cheering when a new number favored their candidate. TV crews, local and foreign, came and went, filming the activity and interviewing COMELEC officials who lounged comfortably in roomy swivel chairs.

By Saturday night, though, the activity had slackened, and few new numbers were being added to the big boards. Some of the computer operators began fidgeting. They sensed that something was going awry but didn't know what it was. The next day, Sunday, some of them began to get a clearer sense. The senior operator, a woman named Linda Kapunan, had gone home that morning to sleep. Late in the day she received a phone call from a colleague who told her that several of the operators believed cheating was going on. By the time she returned to the Convention Center they had figured out that the data generated by their computers were not being written correctly on the board. The figures from the two vote-rich regions of northern Luzon were being changed: Those for Marcos were being added to the tally, those for Aquino were being left off. The computers showed Aquino marginally ahead; the board showed Marcos. The operators realized that this had been going on since midnight and decided to walk out in protest.

At about 10:30 that night, the group's twenty-eight women and two men stood up together, took off their white smocks, and walked briskly out of the hall in single file. Observers in the galleries immediately understood and began chanting, *"Daya! Daya! Daya!"* which means "cheating!" Outside, the thirty were immediately surrounded by a large crowd shouting excitedly, "You are protected, you are protected." Within minutes, two cars and a panel truck appeared and took them to Baclaran Church, three miles away, where they were met by one of the country's leading civil-rights lawyers, a man with the unlikely name of Joker Arroyo, and by Senator Kerry, who applauded them for their bravery.

The smoothness of the walkout suggested that it had been orchestrated by Aquino's organization, but Arroyo, a close adviser to Cory Aquino, denied it, as did Linda Kapunan, who acted as the group's spokesman. Speaking haltingly and with obvious fear to clamoring reporters and TV crews, Kapunan insisted that they were nonpartisans and professionals and had walked out because "we feel that we've been used."

In view of the violence surrounding the elections, it had taken enormous courage for them as government employees to leave their jobs and publicly charge COMELEC with fraud. But, having taken the step, they quickly received protection. Before dawn, they slipped out of Baclaran Church and were taken to a private home that was kept quietly under surveillance by armed soldiers in civilian dress. These were not Marcos's soldiers. They had been dispatched by Defense Minister Enrile, acting on his own.

Kapunan was the wife of air force Lieutenant Colonel Eduardo E. ("Red") Kapunan, Jr., an intelligence officer on Enrile's staff and one of the most active members of the RAM organization. Marcos and Ver detected the link immediately and tried to expose the walkout as a reformist-organized plot. The operators were branded tools of the Aquino camp. By then, though, the president's credibility was such a shambles that he could arouse little sympathy or belief for his allegations, though the association between the Kapunans and Enrile showed that Marcos was close to the mark.

The walkout eliminated the last vestiges of civility between COMELEC and NAMFREL. Christian Monsod, second in command to NAMFREL head Concepcion, charged that the official organization had been dishonest all along and "changed the rules time and again." Commissioner Opinion accused NAMFREL of using "spurious" statistics. His attempt to explain to newsmen why the COMELEC count was lagging so far behind was drowned out by booing spectators in the giant hall. "It's not true that our registrars have adopted delaying tactics," he managed to say before giving up.

At the beginning of the new week, each organization had its favorite leading by a curiously even margin of around 600,000 votes. With the two counts causing widespread confusion throughout the country, commentators on the government-run Channel 4 TV network began reminding viewers that neither tally would be official; the winner would be determined by the National Assembly. In fact, neither count ever was completed.

By now, Marcos was rushing the process so that he would be proclaimed the official winner and, on Monday, February 11, the National Assembly met in the great hall to set the rules for its final tally. In Washington, the Reagan administration, anticipating that the parliamentary body would steamroller a Marcos victory, began transmitting signals that it was prepared to do business as usual with him. A protracted, behind-the-scenes struggle between the professional Philippines-watchers of the State Department and the conservative ideologues of the White House inner circle was now emerging. First, President Reagan told a luncheon meeting of out-of-town newspaper editors that he hoped Marcos and Aquino "can come together to make sure the government works." This astonishingly naive remark, a clear indication that the president saw the deeply bitter Philippine election in the most superficial terms, drew horrified groans from Aquino and her supporters. "I'm gravely disappointed in the United States," said Jimmy Ongpin. "If they can cop out on something like this, we can't depend on them."

On Tuesday, Senator Lugar, who had returned to Washington, briefed Reagan, telling him that the U.S. observer team had concluded that Aquino had legitimately won "at least" 60 percent of the vote and that "despite all the fraud, she may still be ahead." He detailed some of the more blatant cheating—cases where election rolls in pro-Marcos areas had as many as 50 percent more names than voters, cases where NAMFREL workers were locked out of regional counting rooms, and the counts then turned up no votes at all for Aquino. Reagan listened but, it seemed, didn't hear. In Manila, Ambassador Bosworth was showing Cory Aquino's brother Peping Cojuangco a copy of a statement scheduled for release by the White House that supported Aquino's claim that she had been cheated out of victory. But the statement was never released, and just a few hours after being briefed by Lugar, Reagan told a White House news conference that fraud "was occurring on both sides." Furthermore, he said, "we are going to try and continue, as I said before, the relationship regardless of what government is instituted there by the choice of the people."

Most offensive to Filipinos, though, was Reagan's response when he was asked for his position on supporting democracy in the Philippines if it meant risking the future of the U.S. military bases: "One cannot minimize the importance of those bases, not only to us, but to the Western world and certainly to the Philippines themselves."

There was no mistaking what Reagan had said and what he meant—the bases were more important than democracy in the Philippines—and this cut most Filipinos deeply. The president's comment further shook State Department professionals, who realized that without the good will of the Filipino people, the bases would be worthless. Normally, Reagan did not make such blunt statements without first consulting his staff. In this case, though, he just spoke his mind, and the staff was caught unawares. In Manila, the government-controlled media expressed unmitigated glee, concluding that his remarks showed that "Reagan expects Marcos to win."

Aquino was enraged. Ambassador Bosworth, keenly aware of the depth of Reagan's blunder, met twice with Aquino and her brother Peping, urging them "not to do anything precipitous." Bosworth cautioned her that Reagan's comments did not reflect the thinking of the State Department or even of many of his closest White House advisers. But she recognized that, ultimately, the decision on how the United States would react to the election's outcome would be made by the president, and she unleashed a withering attack on him:

"I wonder at the motives of a friend of democracy who chose to conspire with Mr. Marcos to cheat the Filipino people of their liberation. I think not only the Filipinos, but the vast majority of the American people and their Congress would condemn any such action which so flagrantly assists in returning a people to their captivity. I suggest to him that before making further comments on the election itself, he make additional inquiries from his own embassy, the observers, and the media. It would be a delusion of policy to believe that an opposition, whose leaders have been and are being killed, can suddenly settle down to a Western-style opposition role in a healthy two-party system. Too many will be dead the moment the world's head is turned.''

Even as Aquino warned of this grim prospect, one of her most fervent supporters was being gunned down. On the same day as the National Assembly met to work out its rules, Evelio Javier, who had worked as Aquino's campaign manager in the central island region, was shot outside the Antique province capital building in San Jose. The killing was brutal. While passersby watched in horror, six masked men had chased him across the town's broad central plaza, shooting him once and sending him stumbling into a fish pond, then chasing him again and, as he took refuge behind a privy door, finishing him off there with a blast of gunfire.

The murder immediately rekindled recollections of the Ninoy Aquino assassination. Javier was forty-three years old, he'd been elected governor of Antique when he was twenty-nine and had served with distinction for nine years, becoming something of a folk hero. His wife and two young sons were living in Los Angeles, but he'd given up his comfortable life there after Aquino's murder and returned to his impoverished home province to get back into politics.

Those who admired Javier immediately fingered a Marcos crony named Arturo Pacificador. The two men had been bitter enemies. Pacificador ran a private army made up of thugs and moonlighting military personnel, and in May 1984 Pacificador had beaten Javier in the National Assembly elections after seven Javier workers had been shot to death in a gunfight. The enmity between the two had climaxed during the campaign, when Marcos's reelection seemed in doubt and Pacificador feared for his own future. The day after the murder, Aquino's camp released a tape recording made by Javier shortly before he was killed in which he had said, ''Every time I move around Antique, I have to play cat-and-mouse with the goons of Pacificador.''

Javier's body was flown to Manila and, in a smaller replay of the Aquino funeral, put on view in the chapel of Ateneo de Manila University, his alma mater, where thousands came to pay their respect. One among them was particularly notable, Defense Minister Enrile. After being trucked through Manila, past large crowds, the body was flown back to Antique and taken on a one-hundred-mile motorcade before being buried.

The Javier killing, the rush toward proclaiming Marcos winner, the walkout of the computer operators, the sense that President Reagan was turning his back on decency, and frustration over the conduct of the elections finally stirred that most powerful force in Philippine life, the Catholic Church. On Valentine's Day, a holiday fervently celebrated in the Philippines, the country's bishops climbed off the fence they'd straddled for years and officially denounced Marcos in no uncertain terms. After meeting, debating, and praying for two days, the 110-member Catholic Bishops Conference of the Philippines called a news conference and issued a biting proclamation that stated, in part:

"The people have spoken. Or tried to. Despite the obstacles thrown in the way of their speaking freely, we the bishops believe what they attempted to say is clear enough. In our considered judgment, the polls were unparalleled in the fraudulence of their conduct."

The bishops accused Marcos of attempting to seize power through force, thus losing whatever moral basis to govern he might have had, and they called on the faithful to back Aquino in a campaign of civil disobedience. She had visited them during their deliberations and told them she was going to announce a protracted effort to grind Marcos down through industrial strikes, slowdowns, and boycotts of government- and crony-run businesses, patterned on Mahatma Gandhi's independence struggle in India.

Beyond involving themselves in the president's political conduct, the bishops also stated that his immoral behavior had cost him his right to receive Holy Communion, and he was, therefore, subject to excommunication from the Church. Because public excommunication has become rare in the Catholic Church since the Middle Ages, its mere mention carried a mystical, chilling implication, and it shocked many Filipinos. The bishops added inestimable force to their position by saying that Pope John Paul II, who was then traveling in India, had sent them a terse message: "I am with you."

The prelates had not reached their decision easily; some wanted to remain uninvolved; some had been seeking a much tougher stand. A proposal prepared by an American Jesuit at the behest of several of the bishops had recommended that the Church use its influence with the United States to cut off all military aid to the Marcos regime. This document also proposed that the Church involve itself in the anti-Marcos effort in the same way as the Church in Poland had aligned itself with the Solidarity labor movement against the Communist regime.

Before the statement's release, the Marcoses had struggled to head it off. Imelda Marcos had tried repeatedly to contact Cardinal Ricardo Vidal of Cebu, who headed the conference, but was rebuffed. He finally telephoned her at 1:30 in the morning, hours before the announcement was to be made. She was eating a late supper with thirty friends at the Manila Hotel's Italian restaurant and left immediately for the conference's headquarters nearby in Intramuros to plead with Vidal. He promised only that the Church would not support violence. The First Lady had earlier made a similar plea to Cardinal Sin and broke down in tears at his refusal to accommodate her. His suggestion was that she go to pray with a group of contemplative nuns.

When the Church leaders released their statement to the packed news conference, their comments were harsher than what they had written. "Toppling the government is not our explicit goal, but it could come to that," said Bishop Jesus Varela. "As long as the means are peaceful and nonviolent, we couldn't care less."

The bishops' stance took on even greater significance because it happened in conjunction with other rapid-fire developments. Everywhere, the pace was stepping up.

President Reagan had dispatched retired diplomat Philip C. Habib as his special envoy to meet with the principals in Manila. Marcos, determined to present a *fait accompli,* ordered the National Assembly to proclaim him the winner by the time Habib arrived on Saturday, February 15. The KBL machinery in the assembly rolled forward, crushing opposition complaints about improprieties from the country's 147 vote-counting centers. Not a single return was presented for inspection that was not protested by a member of the opposition, but under the baleful eye of Speaker Nicanor Yñiguez, each complaint was cast aside. Just hours after the bishops had issued their statement, the entire opposition walked out of the chamber in protest, and a few minutes before midnight, Saturday, the rump assembly proclaimed Marcos the winner, with 10.8 million votes against 9.3 million for Aquino.

On Sunday, Aquino spoke to a huge, boisterous crowd in Luneta park, announcing her own, self-proclaimed victory and calling for nationwide civil disobedience until Marcos stepped down. In sharp contrast, Marcos spoke to a sparsely attended news conference in Malacañang. Striving to put the best face on things, he brushed aside the huge number of people assembled across town as "normal for a Sunday afternoon" in the park.

But the president knew he had to make a significant gesture to the United States if he was to win backing for the legitimacy of his re-election. So he announced that he was retiring General Ver on March 1 and replacing him again with Lieutenant General Ramos, though, as before, only in an acting capacity. To most Filipinos, especially the military, the move was too little and far too late. Nothing was heard publicly from Ramos. He had confided to Aquino that he was going to resign.

Marcos's bait didn't catch the fish it was intended for in Washington, either. The professionals in the State Department had managed to convince the zealous amateurs in the White House that there was need for damage control. Partly because of this internal pressure and partly in reaction to the bishops' statement, the White House reversed President Reagan's allegation that both sides were responsible for cheating and conceded that the Marcos regime was behind most of it. Then Secretary of State George Shultz told the Senate Budget Committee, "We have a stake in freedom and we have a stake in democracy. Let's put that first, over and above the bases." Aquino was mollified, but not much.

While Aquino and Marcos were both addressing their publics, Habib, a tested troubleshooter who'd established a reputation as a peace mediator in Lebanon, set up shop in Manila. Reagan felt that Ambassador Bosworth and others in the embassy had gotten too close to the anti-Marcos people, and that he needed a firsthand assessment from someone he could trust. Over the next few days, Habib met several times with Aquino and Marcos, and, according to members of both camps, he listened more than he spoke. He also met with Defense Minister Enrile.

A few old hands recalled that as a young diplomat in Seoul in 1960, Habib had played a role in toppling President Syngman Rhee. The autocratic South Korean leader had been accused of corruption and of rigging his reelection to a fourth term, at a time when the country's economy was reeling. The United States helped inspire rioting, and he was forced to flee the country. Rhee went into exile in Hawaii.

16

*T*HE PLOT

Juan Ponce Enrile had become one of the wealthiest and most powerful men in the Philippines through native intelligence, cunning, and a sure sense of timing. Now sixty-two, ruggedly handsome, and urbane, he had grown up as a barefoot peasant, the illegitimate son of a village woman from Cagayan province and a prominent Manila attorney who hadn't known of the boy's existence. In much the same way as Imelda Marcos had been marked by her impoverished youth, Enrile's early deprivation left him insecure about his place in Philippine society.

Enrile met his father for the first time when he was twenty-one and was sent to Ateneo de Manila University, the University of the Philippines, then on to Harvard Law School. He went to work for his father's law firm and moved solidly into the establishment, marrying Cristina Castañer, a striking blonde fashion model of Spanish origin. In 1964, Enrile joined then-Senator Ferdinand Marcos at whose side he would remain for more than two decades.

When, in 1966, the newly elected president settled into Malacañang, Enrile went with him and rose through a number of cabinet posts until taking over the defense ministry in 1970. During his years with Marcos, Enrile became a loyal member of the team, lying and cheating for the president along with the other ministers and cronies. But unlike some of the others, who appeared little more than thugs, blindly obeying the president, Enrile managed to convey an image of relative independence and strength of character. Like the others, though, he went along with the dirty tricks because what was good for Marcos was good for him.

In 1972, Enrile helped the president impose martial law by having his own car shot up in a fake assassination attempt. The little drama was part of a series of actions initiated by Marcos to justify the claim that the country was about to be overrun by violent leftists and rightists. In return for such invaluable services, the president gave Enrile control over the country's lucrative coconut industry by helping him become chairman of the United Coconut Planters Bank. This financial post combined with the defense job firmly established him as the second most powerful figure in the country.

But that wasn't enough for the onetime barefoot boy from Cagayan. His hunger for the top position, once it became known to Marcos, was to contribute to the diminution of his power. Marcos was planning a dynastic succession through his wife and children. Gradually he put the brakes on Enrile by handing over control of the armed forces to his trusted and docile friend, General Ver. Enrile attempted several times to resign, but Marcos, fearful that he could be more dangerous outside the cabinet, refused to let him go.

In this final election campaign, as in previous ones, Enrile had manipulated the balloting for the president in Cagayan, and by his own subsequent admission stole 365,000 votes. But, when ballot tampering throughout the country proved inadequate, forcing Marcos to wring a blatantly fraudulent victory out of the National Assembly, Enrile knew that the time had come. Indeed, he'd been anticipating and preparing for this day ever since he recognized the potential value of RAM.

A few days after meeting with Habib, Enrile began telling friends and colleagues that he was going to resign from the cabinet. At his private law office, which he'd reestablished after many years, he called across the hall to a secretary, asking in a loud voice, "Have you finished typing my letter of resignation yet?" On Tuesday, February 18, he had dinner with two Americans who he knew would report back to Washington and told them that he was going to hand the letter to Marcos the following Monday, the day before the president's inauguration. He also said that if Marcos refused to accept the resignation, he was prepared to remain in the cabinet for two or three months, in order to help "carry out a peaceful transition of power." This broad reference seemed to indicate that he was preparing for the post-Marcos era, but it left unstated who would head the successor government. His own plans, he said, were to travel to the United States with his family. He'd already exchanged his diplomatic passport for an ordinary one and, on the day before he dined with the Americans, had submitted it along with those of his wife and two children to the U.S. embassy for visas.

His timing for this public posturing was excellent. He knew that the Marcos regime was falling, and he wanted to position himself as America's first replacement choice. Enrile knew that the Reagan administration was less than enthusiastic about Aquino. Aside from her questionable positions on the bases and the Communists, there was nagging doubt in the White House that if she did come to power she would have the ability to govern the country. Enrile knew, too, that he didn't suffer from these disabilities as far as the Americans were concerned. He was, as solidly as Marcos, in favor of retaining a U.S. military presence in the Philippines and few Filipinos were as anti-Communist as he. Although the Marcos regime's record against the insurgency was a sorry one under Enrile's fifteen-year term in the defense ministry, most military analysts blamed Ver and other senior officers far more than they did the minister. Several times in the past few years he'd warned that the insurgency was reaching dangerous proportions and made gloomy assessments of the armed forces' efforts to contend with the struggle. These observations had placed him at odds with Ver and helped him appear realistic and forthright to U.S. military strategists. Finally, by nurturing the RAM movement, Enrile had wanted to make the United States believe that he was sincere about cleaning up the military.

In fact, Enrile was already signaling the White House that his reformists would be able to control without bloodshed the civil disobedience that Aquino had called for. Immediately after she issued her appeal, RAM had released an emotional statement to soldiers and policemen: "We implore you to think of your relatives and friends who may be among the millions of Filipinos demanding that their voices be heard. Be involved in the struggle for democracy and freedom by refusing to use force and violence on innocent and freedom-loving Filipinos." Enrile had told his American dinner guests that the military would balk if ordered to open fire on anti-Marcos demonstrators: "They might fire once but the second time the guns would be turned around."

The possibility of bloodshed and violence, as well as civil disobedience opening the way to the Communists, was a nightmare that haunted Washington officials, and by assuring the Americans that he could help avoid such a calamity, Enrile was strengthening his position in the event that Marcos should fall. In reality, his plans were well underway to make the president fall, through a coup d'etat.

The roots of Enrile's plans could be traced back more than a year, to late 1984, when he hired two British mercenaries to provide sophisticated training to about thirty young security and intelligence officers on his staff at the Ministry of National Defense. The training was part of a package Enrile purchased from a shadowy company in London, using his own funds. The two mercenaries, both retired from Britain's elite Special Air Services, brought with them a thousand Israeli-made Uzi submachine guns and high-powered rifles, infrared sniper scopes, and other equipment suitable for defending important figures, countering terrorism, assaulting hijacked aircraft, and rescuing hostages.

The deal was negotiated by army Colonel Gregorio B. (''Gringo'') Honasan and air force Lieutenant Colonel Eduardo E. (''Red'') Kapunan, Jr., whose wife, Linda, was to lead the walkout of irate computer operators. Honasan and Kapunan had considered hiring American mercenaries but decided on the British because their system relied more on the skills of individual soldiers than on high technology. Like many angry young officers in the Philippine armed forces, Honasan and Kapunan believed that their colleagues had lost their sense of professionalism and needed to be taught greater self-reliance.

Enrile had good reasons for having the officers he liked to call ''my boys'' undergo this special training. A few weeks after the Aquino assassination, he had received a report that his own assassination was being planned by General Ver's National Intelligence and Security Authority. According to a member of Enrile's intelligence staff, navy Captain Rex Robles, ''within seventy-two hours, we found the man who was supposed to kill the minister and arranged for his disappearance. He turned out to be a Galman-type of character.'' Another imperative was that two of Marcos's closest confidants were building their own specially trained forces, far more threatening than the private armies common among provincial warlords.

One belonged to Eduardo Cojuangco, who had hired three Israeli mercenaries to upgrade his 1,600-man force. The Israelis trained Cojuangco's men for six months late in 1984 in two locations, on the property of a cement factory in Pangasinan province, located on the west coast of Luzon, and on the tiny southeastern island of Bugsuk, in Palawan province. Particularly ominous to Enrile was the fact that a hundred or so of the men were regulars of the Presidential Security Command, and he foresaw the emergence of a Cojuangco-Ver axis, which could only harm him.

Another private army of sorts was being built within the military establishment itself by Army Commander Major General Josephus Ramas. Considered one of the most ambitious and corrupt officers in the armed forces, Ramas began in 1983 to train a six-hundred-man "Special Action Force," also called a "counter-coup force," at Fort Bonifacio. Enrile and his boys learned that Ramas was laying direct lines of communication to Marcos, circumventing Ver, and they believed that he was preparing to seize power once the president died or became too ill to carry on.

The British package sold to Enrile was counterterrorist in nature, but the training was easily adaptable. As Honasan said, "You can treat anybody as a terrorist. We could very well say Ramas was a terrorist, General Ver is a terrorist." So, while Enrile's initial thoughts when he hired the mercenaries were of defending his personal interests, the urgings of the two young officers gradually turned his thinking toward plans for an armed rebellion against Marcos and Ver.

The training of Enrile's inner circle lasted for about six weeks and took place clandestinely at various remote locations. According to several of the officers who went through the program, it was basically hard, physical work, the kind they had last experienced as cadets, and it left them feeling individually fit and part of a cohesive group. The newly retrained men then began recruiting others from military and police units in central Luzon, Enrile's province of Cagayan, and Manila, and putting them through the same course.

The next important step was taken early in 1985, when RAM was fully formed, and the mercenary-trained hard-core members of Enrile's security unit, particularly Honasan and Kapunan, became the group's leaders. From then on, RAM functioned at a variety of levels. Personable, articulate officers such as Robles operated publicly, speaking to journalists and issuing statements on the need to bring about peaceful reform in light of the recent Agrava board findings. Meanwhile, Honasan and Kapunan worked covertly, pressing within the organization for the need to overthrow Marcos and Ver, assassinating them if necessary. Even within this secret level of the group, cells were formed and remained more or less independent of one another. The thinking behind this partitioning was to protect the organization in the event that any individual was captured. "As long as each of us knew only what we had to know, that would limit the chances of one of us blowing the whole plan," said Lieutenant Colonel Reynaldo Rivera, an officer on Enrile's ministry staff.

At the earliest stages, the dominant view among the RAM officers was much the same as what Robles was saying publicly—to bring about change while avoiding violence. Most feared that a bloody, military-led upheaval would produce instability that would leave the country uncontrollable. But in August 1985, Honasan, Kapunan, and a Philippine Constabularly officer, Lieutenant Colonel Victor Batac, determined that nonviolence would accomplish nothing. They were supported by an older officer, fifty-four-year-old Colonel José T. Almonte, who had worked with Marcos in the 1970s, helping him write several books on Philippine foreign policy. This little group devised a plan to capture Marcos, force him to abdicate, and perhaps kill him.

Honasan and Kapunan reported to Enrile, who responded dubiously: "You think you can really do it?" They assured him that they believed they could, but he wasn't prepared to make a decision. "What will I do with Marcos?" he asked them. "He has been a friend and mentor to me." He told them he would need a week to think it over, then called them and said, "I fully agree with your plans." He told the two men he had convinced himself that the time had come to answer to "a higher loyalty, a loyalty to the country." They took him at his word, at least they said they did, but they also knew, as he did, that by not joining them he risked having no place in the post-Marcos future. In fact, he had already been eased out by Ver, Cojuangco, and Imelda Marcos. "He was no longer in the chain of command. He was bypassed," said Honasan.

It could not have been an easy decision, but once Enrile made up his mind he became fully involved. "He was with us from the planning stage before the election," said Kapunan. "His role was important because he was giving us the political reading. We needed him."

While the boys needed Enrile, Enrile needed the boys. After twenty years at Marcos's side, as "part of the dream," as Marcos once told him, he was preparing to overthrow his boss, to kill him if necessary, and for that he needed not just military expertise but the bold decisiveness of these young officers. He was by nature a cautious man, with the calculating mind of a lawyer, and he was not given to drastic action unless certain that he could achieve his goal. Furthermore, he had an almost mystical tie to Marcos. Although just five years younger than the president, he responded to him much as a young boy might to an elder brother or even a father. People who knew Enrile well speculated that this might have been a result of his growing up fatherless. Occasionally, he told friends that he was incapable of refusing anything that Marcos asked of him. Without the initiative of the RAM officers, he would not have had the nerve to order Marcos seized, let alone killed.

Enrile locked himself into the plot. While the boys devised the raid on Malacañang, with the objective of capturing the president and Mrs. Marcos, Enrile concentrated on the political aspects. Their plan was to turn over ruling power to a civilian-military "committee" (they wanted to avoid the term *junta*), which was to include Enrile, Lieutenant General Ramos, Cory Aquino, Cardinal Sin, retired Lieutenant General Rafael Ileto, who was then ambassador to Thailand, two respected international bureaucrats, Rafael Salas, a close friend of Enrile who was with the United Nations in New York, and Alejandro Melchor, of the Asian Development Bank in Manila, and possibly a few businessmen, including Jimmy Ongpin.

At the time this plan was formulated, Marcos had not yet called the snap election. The plotters were going to move shortly after the regularly scheduled election, in May 1987, figuring that they would build on public outrage over the expected electoral fraud. If things had gone according to this time frame, the plan might have worked. But it seems likelier in the Philippine context, where keeping secrets is anathema, that over such an extended period the entire plot would have become public knowledge. As it was, Marcos's TV announcement in November jolted them. They shifted gears and sped up their operations, and they made errors, most notably by talking too much and drawing in too many people.

Rex Robles described their reaction to the snap elections as "a

Charlie Chaplin movie, with everyone running around like mad.'' But the pressure forced results. A fifteen-man cell calling itself the Movement for National Unity became the hub of RAM, planning tactics. Kapunan spent the period from Marcos's announcement onward meticulously examining what he called "casing reports," including floor plans of the Malacañang Palace buildings, daily routines of key individuals living and working at the palace, guard changes at all of Manila's TV and radio stations, the city's power stations, and the long-distance telephone company. Detailed plans were to be sealed in envelopes and handed to commanders of small units leading the assault shortly before they were to move. Kapunan even devised a shoulder patch, a reversed Philippine flag, to designate the RAM forces, and soldiers using cloth stolen from military supplies cut and hand painted 3,000 of them. "By December, we had a plan all ready," Kapunan said.

Their plan comprised half a dozen elements, all rather fluid and none completely distinct from the others, to be implemented in Manila and widespread provincial locations, the overall scheme being to withdraw increasing numbers of armed forces units from the president until he was isolated. But the triggering element, to be carried out by the hard-core RAM leadership, those with direct personal loyalty to Enrile, was to be the storming of Malacañang. This was to be handled by small, highly trained units, 470 men in all, under the command of Honasan, Kapunan, and two junior colonels, Tirso Gador and Jerry Albano. After toying with dates that included Christmas and New Year's, toward the end of January they settled on Sunday, February 23, at 2:00 A.M.

The leaders were divided over how to treat Marcos. According to Kapunan, "There were strict instructions not to kill him. The plan was to arrest him and put him on trial." Others felt that he should be killed in such a way as to make it appear unintentional. "The main caveat was that he should not be killed by rifle fire, but by explosion or something 'accidental,' " said Colonel Batac. "We were looking into the future, how would you explain it." Honasan, the most swaggering of the RAM leaders, was inclined to kill the president, in one way or another, perhaps sadistically. "What we wanted to do was separate him from his dialysis machine and watch him go," he said. There was no division of views about Ver, however; he would be killed in a bomb blast at his home. Imelda Marcos, her son and two daughters, and Ver's three sons, all officers of the Presidential Security Command at Malacañang, were to be captured.

The coup leaders said they were prepared to be wiped out in the attempt. Kapunan, who was to "neutralize" four battalions of Presidential Security Command forces with 120 assault troops backed by two battalions, estimated that he had a 10 percent chance of survival. But they also believed that their sacrifice would draw in a significant number of other troops, among whom they'd been recruiting for months. Throughout the country, they estimated that they could count on eight battalions, roughly 1,600 men. These forces, if they did in fact come over to the rebel side, would be faced initially by twenty battalions of troops loyal to Marcos and Ver. "So, it was twenty to eight," said Honasan, "but we were confident our boys were better trained than theirs."

The rebels then turned their attention to General Ramos. They recognized that while a significant number of officers and men were prepared to line up behind Enrile, his long political and personal association with Marcos had tainted him in the minds of many more. And this was doubly true among the civilian power structure, the wealthy businessmen who'd emerged as an anti-Marcos force and the large middle class who'd tirelessly marched and demonstrated ever since the Aquino assassination. Ramos's image was much cleaner, so he could be a crucial element in the coup, but he'd been kept only superficially informed because those in the inner circle of plotters were dubious about him. Some remembered that when RAM officers had first approached him in the wake of the Agrava board's implication of Ver he had told them he couldn't do much to meet their demands, and he'd been similarly vague when a few of them sketched their plans for him early in January. "His response was something like, 'You better be careful with all these,' " said Kapunan. "He was noncommittal. He had this complex, you know, that he was willing to suffer for the sake of unity of the country. He was willing to take everything." Once again, the RAM men were disappointed with Ramos, but they also recognized that his involvement in their plot could greatly enhance its chances of succeeding, and so they maintained contact with him.

In a final effort to draw Ramos in, Colonel Almonte went to his office in Camp Crame on Thursday afternoon, February 20, two weeks after the election. It was three days before the coup was to be launched; Cory Aquino's call for civil disobedience and a national boycott of crony-owned enterprises was taking hold, and tension was high in Manila. Almonte assumed the task because although he was much junior in rank, he and Ramos were nearly the same age and were personal friends. During his two hours in the general's office, the colonel provided for the first time considerable detail of their plot. "We hadn't wanted to tell him any sooner because he was working with President Marcos and this could have caused him a crisis of conscience," said Almonte. He made clear to Ramos that the plotters were looking to him and Enrile as leaders. "It was understood in our conversation that we wanted him to lead us," Almonte said. "I didn't ask it specifically, but he knew. None of us had the stature to draw followers. We needed him and Enrile. He understood that." Ramos heard Almonte out and then, looking at him evenly, told him, "Joe, whatever you do, don't make it very bloody."

While Ramos would be important to the military operation, the political success of the coup would rely heavily on Cory Aquino. During the campaign, the election, and since, she'd established beyond doubt that she was the most popular figure in the country, and no coup would succeed without her backing. For that reason, the plotters had kept her informed at about the same level as they had Ramos.

The first contacts between the plotters and the Aquino camp had been made five months earlier, but those involved on both sides were extremely secretive among themselves and with one another, and so there were misconceptions about how much she knew and whether or not she supported the plot. In fact, she knew a great deal, and she was prepared to go along, though with reservations. Because there was considerable distrust between the RAM officers, who were devoted to Enrile, and Aquino, who was seen as an impediment to his ambitions, meetings were carefully arranged through indirect contacts. These included brothers, sisters-in-law, friends, and other members of the convoluted networks comprising Philippine society.

Initial feelers were extended early in September by Colonel Almonte and Dr. Fernando Carrascoso, a physician, a political conservative, and a lifelong friend of Peping Cojuangco's, who had been gathering intelligence for Cory's campaign, and by December, with the campaign just starting, the two men had come to trust each other.

The physician understood that the military man and his colleagues were plotting a coup. Through Carrascoso, Almonte met with Cojuangco, and at this session, two weeks before Christmas, he elaborated further on the plans. He also said the plotters wanted Cory's help in turning out huge numbers of unarmed civilians to act as a buffer between rebel forces and loyalists.

Cojuangco immediately took the information to his sister. "I told her that their plan was to stage a coup," he said. "I told her that it would be at a time of their choosing, and they wanted her support to help bring masses of people out into the streets of Manila. They also wanted her to help get people out in Tarlac, to block the roads against loyalist troops who might try to move into Manila. And they wanted her to help them with radio communications." She agreed.

Over the holidays, life in the Philippines slowed down, as it always does, and the plotters, like everyone else, took a break. In early January, a month before the election, an extremely sensitive meeting was arranged between Aquino and the four key plotters, Honasan, Kapunan, Batac, and Robles. This was the first time that Aquino had met face-to-face with any of them, and it was done without Almonte's knowledge, the younger men being somewhat unsure of the older officer because they perceived, correctly, that he was drifting closer to Aquino and her brother. The four wanted to take Cory's measure before considering her for a place on the ruling committee. This meeting was set up by Ninoy Aquino's sister, Milagrosa Albert, the widow of a naval officer, and took place at the home of a mutual acquaintance, an engineer by the name of Rod Lejano. The atmosphere of secrecy was heightened by their insistence that Aquino come alone while RAM officers provided security outside the house.

The meeting lasted for about two hours, and the four men were blunt. They told her that if their rebellion succeeded, they would not back her as president, that they intended to hand over power to a committee, of which she was invited to be a member, and that the committee would choose a president. They didn't tell her so, but their expectation was that the coming election would be so fraught with cheating that there would be no way to determine with certainty who actually won. This, in fact, turned out to be the case, although they had failed to consider the weight of popular opinion. And although the plotters didn't come right out and say it, they were intent on having

Enrile named president by the committee. He was their leader, this was their coup. "We considered Cory just as a member of the committee, because there was no way the military would know for sure if Cory really won the election," said Honasan. Despite themselves, some of them were impressed by her spirit. "At one point, we told her that we might not vote for her," said Robles. "She said, 'Why not? Marcos has plenty of military who'll vote for him.' I figured then that she'd win."

The young officers also discovered that Aquino was far more astute and capable of subterfuge than she or her advisers wanted the public to know. She simply acknowledged what they had told her and kept it to herself. A month before the elections were to be held, she knew that RAM was planning a coup, that it was likely to be violent, and that the military men did not plan to back her as president but merely install her as a member of a ruling committee. As she stumped the countryside, she continued to call for Marcos's overthrow by the ballot, but she was prepared for his removal by a bullet. Aquino's calm handling of this foreknowledge would show the plotters and Enrile that she was not a wide-eyed ingenue in a Philippine morality play, but an instinctively adroit practitioner of the toughest kind of politics.

One bizarre result of this first meeting was that RAM took over security arrangements for Aquino. A captain by the name of Bing Damian was put in charge, and from then on she was accompanied everywhere by him and other junior officers who had gone absent without leave and now wore civilian clothing. The ease with which they and other military men could slip in and out of uniform was a powerful indicator of how disoriented the armed forces had become. The RAM officers understood the depth of the problem, and hoped to change things, but in this case they took advantage for their own ends. Under their protection, they felt, Cory wouldn't face a repeat of her first campaign rally, in Laurel's home province of Batangas, when her shoulder had been wrenched by an enthusiastic admirer. RAM also wanted to keep her alive in order to assure a real contest in the election. "We heard a lot of threats against her," said Kapunan. "She had to survive the election because things could change, you know." For a similar reason, at a meeting a week later it was decided that all future contacts were to be made through Peping. "I thought it best that she not know too much, so she couldn't be charged with conspiracy" was Cojuangco's explanation.

After the election, as the planned date for the coup drew closer, those involved increasingly began to coordinate their efforts. During the first week in February, Carrascoso quietly called on his medical associates at four Manila hospitals to build up stocks of blood and to be prepared for a sudden influx of wounded patients. Carrascoso also had radio communications equipment delivered to RAM officers, which they used on February 2, the Sunday prior to election day, to broadcast prayer meetings conducted at military bases throughout the country. The broadcast was part of a series of such meetings called *Kamalayan* ("Awareness") '86, which ostensibly was calling on troops to help assure fair elections. In reality, by judging response to *Kamalayan* '86, the plotters were able to assess the mood of the armed forces. The February 2 broadcast tested the communications system that the plotters intended to use during the coup attempt.

As for firepower, the RAM insiders knew early on that they didn't have it, and their intention was to make sure Marcos and Ver lost the use of theirs by employing what in effect would be human shields and barricades. At the same time, they attempted to deprive their enemy of as much armed strength as they could by extracting promises from key units to withhold their fire. Beginning in mid January, they met every night with officers from various Manila-based units, outlining their plans in broad terms. "Once we got a sense of their reaction to the general idea, we recruited them for specific tasks," said Almonte. "This led us to believe that the vast majority, even those we didn't talk to and most of those in the PSC [Presidential Security Command] agreed with us and felt it would be wrong to fire on civilians." Most important, since their human shields would be facing tanks, they began appealing to colleagues in armored units not to run over the people.

They also were in touch with Cardinal Sin, aware that he more than anyone else could cause vast numbers of people to turn out in the streets to support the rebellion. They reasoned that Sin, as head of the Church, could get priests and nuns to be the vanguard and that Filipino soldiers would have great difficulty in obeying orders to fire on the clergy.

The plotters thought of some remarkable, seemingly minor, details. Working with Peping Cojuangco's wife, Margarita, a great beauty who went by the nickname Ting-Ting, Almonte organized what he called "flower brigades"—women and girls who would hand blossoms to soldiers to diminish their hostility, a tactic that had worked well during the improvised anti-Soviet resistance in Czechoslovakia in 1968–1969.

By the middle of February, the Council of Bishops had weighed in heavily for Cory Aquino, and President Reagan had finally conceded that only Marcos's side had committed election fraud. Aquino had called for massive civil disobedience and a boycott of crony-owned enterprises until Marcos resigned. She made public a list, and on February 17, hundreds of thousands of middle-class Filipinos turned against the businesses she named. Aquino and Laurel had made it clear that they were prepared to wait months, even as long as two years, for the effects of the boycott to drive Marcos out of office. But the plotters had a much shorter schedule. The coup was still set for February 23.

That Saturday, February 22, Aquino was to lead a boycott rally in Cebu city. Colonel Almonte tried to get Cojuangco to convince her to cancel the trip, saying only that RAM could better look after her in Manila. But he didn't mention that the assault on Malacañang was to take place while she would be away, and he failed to convince her to change her plans.

Cojuangco learned the exact timing on Friday night from an air force captain named Bodett Honrade, whose father was in charge of security at the Cojuangco's Hacienda Luisita. The young officer was a member of RAM, though not one of the insiders, and his greater loyalty was to his father's employer. When he learned of the impending rebellion, Honrade's immediate reaction was to warn Cojuangco. He was unaware of the regular contact between Aquino, Cojuangco, and the plotters, and he had once asked Dr. Carrascoso how he could trust Honasan and Kapunan since "they are Enrile's men." Honrade said that the coup would be launched at 2:00 A.M. Sunday, and he advised Cojuangco to remain in Cebu with Cory until he sent word. Peping decided not to pass the information on to Cory since he felt she couldn't influence matters anyway.

At about the same time that Cojuangco and Honrade were speaking, Enrile was huddled in his rambling, high-walled mansion in Makati with his press secretary and three military aides, polishing a speech he was to deliver over radio and television early Sunday, immediately after the storming of the palace. It was to be an electrifying announcement: President Marcos has been overthrown and replaced by a committee called the National Reconciliation Council, whose members included himself, Aquino, Ramos, and Cardinal Sin. Enrile was pleased; politically and militarily his plans were complete, and in another thirty-six hours or so it would be all over.

But while Enrile was relishing the moment, the two officers who were to lead the assault, Honasan and Kapunan, were driving around Manila, checking on Malacañang and other locations essential to their plans, and growing increasingly alarmed by what they saw. Troops were massed around the palace and, near a Philippine Refining Company plant upstream from Malacañang on the Pasig River, a battalion of marines was camped. This was a major blow: Kapunan and a 120-man unit were to have staged a diversionary assault from the riverside site. The plan had been firmly agreed on three days earlier, and all details had been settled; now they had to begin scrambling for alternate schemes. "I was shattered because I was in love with that plan," said Kapunan.

Saturday morning, Aquino and her brother flew to Cebu, about three hundred miles southeast of Manila, in a private plane. She and Laurel thanked the wildly cheering throng for voting overwhelmingly for them and, over chants of "Co-ry! Co-ry! Co-ry!" made her appeal for the boycott. It was campaign-time again. Afterward, at the home of a wealthy Cebu businessman, Norberto Quisumbing, Jr., Cojuangco told her that the coup was set for 2:00 A.M. As they discussed what their own plans should be, Aquino received a telephone call from one of her top local supporters, a National Assembly member named Antonio Cuenco. He said that he had gone home after the rally and found a terse telephone message: "Ponce Enrile has been picked up already by Marcos. Monching [the nickname of Ramon Mitra, a prominent opposition assembly member] is included in the list." The information was incorrect. But, as Cojuangco said, "We realized that something must be wrong." Within an hour, phone calls from Manila were jangling in Quisumbing's house. Something was indeed wrong.

That same morning in Manila, Honasan and Kapunan had learned that their plan had been discovered, though they were uncertain as to how much was known. At 9:00 A.M., Ver sent a Metropolitan Command officer, Colonel Rolando Abadilla, to Honasan's office in the Ministry of National Defense at Camp Aguinaldo to try to talk him out of doing anything rash. "He reminded me that Ver and my father were friends, that [Ver's son] Irwin and I were friends," Honasan said. "I told him to tell Ver he can order me to report to him anytime because he is the chief."

Despite his cocky response, Honasan was shaken. As soon as Abadilla left, at about 10:00 A.M., he called Kapunan into his office. They weighed what they had seen on their late-night drive and discussed their options, then decided to freeze operations for twenty-four hours. "We didn't abort our plans," said Kapunan, "just froze." They succeeded in contacting their outlying field units and instructing them to hold off until receiving further orders.

Actually, things were worse than they knew. They'd been unable to get in touch with four officers who were to be instrumental in seizing President Marcos as he slept. What Honasan and Kapunan didn't know was that the four had been captured. One was a Malacañang insider, Captain Ricardo Morales, a member of Ver's Presidential Security Command, whose role was vital. Morales was Imelda Marcos's chief personal security officer. He and the other three had been caught red-handed on Thursday as Morales was quietly leading them on a dry run through the palace, opening doors and showing them the way to Marcos's quarters. The others were infantry battalion commanders, Lieutenant Colonel Jake Malajacan, Major Ricardo Brillantes, and Major Saulito Aromin. The four revealed everything they knew to Ver's son Irwin, including the date and time of the assault on the palace, and said that their mission was to capture Marcos. They also identified as leaders of the plot Honasan, Kapunan, and Major Noe Hong, an aide to Enrile.

That four men with critical tasks could have been held captive for two days and, on the eve of the assault, the leaders still didn't know about it was just one sign of how badly organized the conspirators were. There was an even more serious problem of which they were not aware, one that had enabled Ver and Marcos to penetrate their planning several weeks earlier.

In January, Honasan had pressured an officer on the staff of the Presidential Security Command into acting as an agent within the palace. But thirty-five-year-old Major Edgardo Doromal had been reluctant to take the assignment, and he wasn't up to its demands. In just a few days, Doromal's nerves frayed, and he unburdened himself to his commander, Colonel Irwin Ver, who immediately passed on the astonishing information to his father, the general. The Vers turned the jittery Doromal into a double agent, and he channeled accurate, up-to-date information to them. Thus, when the four officers were captured, Ver and Marcos already knew almost everything about the impending assault.

But the president and his men didn't confront Enrile or the military conspirators. Instead, they spent the next two days frantically building up security in and around the palace. They would allow the raiders in, then fall on them. The Pasig River outside the palace was being mined, and antipersonnel mines were seeded along the riverbank. A sandbagged machine-gun nest was set up, and the entire perimeter of the palace grounds was reinforced with additional guards. Inside the buildings, booby traps were hidden in books and other unlikely locations. Tactically, this concentration on Malacañang's defenses, while a natural reaction, was a mistake. Because of what he'd heard from Doromal and the other four officers, Ver presumed that the plot involved RAM alone and that it was limited to an assault on the palace. He was unaware of the inroads made throughout the military, and as a result he underestimated the strength of the rebels. Thus, both sides were making clumsy errors, each misjudging what the other knew.

Only hours before they were to have launched their assault, the plotters finally caught on. It was Saturday morning and, as was his custom, Minister Enrile was drinking coffee and bantering with other politicians, journalists, businessmen, and hangers-on at a kaffeeklatsch in Makati's Atrium shopping mall that met every day of the year and called itself the 365 Club. It was a splendid cover for a man who was going to lead a coup that night. Some of the newsmen were questioning Enrile about published reports that he was going to resign from the cabinet on Monday, when he was called to the telephone. On the line was Minister of Trade and Industry Roberto Ongpin, who said the soldiers who provided his own personal security had been arrested the night before for "conducting exercises with their firearms." Enrile telephoned his office and had the report confirmed.

What worried Enrile was not that Ongpin's security detail was picked up but that the soldiers in question were closely identified with him. "In the records of the military command, these are defense ministry soldiers, but I assigned them to Minister Ongpin for his own personal security," he said. More to the point, several of those arrested were intimately involved with the coup plot. After the call, Enrile remained calm, even managing to chat with the kibitzers a while longer, and then drove home.

At the same time, President Reagan's special envoy, Ambassador Habib, was flying out of Manila for Washington. The message that Habib was taking back to Reagan was that Marcos no longer had any support. His departure Saturday morning, just a few hours before the dramatic events that were to develop, would bring immediate and widespread suspicion of Habib's involvement. Because he had met with Enrile, among many others of varied political persuasions, speculation arose that he'd given the defense minister a quiet nod to overthrow Marcos. But diplomats who were familiar with Habib's methods doubted that he'd registered approval or disapproval. And Peping Cojuangco, who had spoken with Habib along with Cory, said that the envoy made proposals specifically aimed at sidestepping an upheaval. "He suggested that Cory form a coalition government with Marcos. Of course, she refused."

Certainly, Habib had been briefed by U.S. embassy intelligence officers about the possibility of a coup. During the week that he'd been making his rounds in Manila, one of the colonels involved in the plot had gone to a Central Intelligence Agency official at the embassy and appealed for heavy weapons. The colonel's approach was another blunder; he expected to trade information for arms, but the CIA agent elicited a general rundown of the coup and delivered no weapons. Indications are, though, that neither this agent nor any others in Manila gathered precise foreknowledge of just when the coup was to take place and what was to happen to Marcos and Ver. Other American intelligence officials, among them CIA station chief Norbert Garrett and military attaché Major Victor Raphael, quickly became involved in a studied attempt to make both parties believe that the United States would not take sides if the coup took place. Garrett dealt directly with Ver, who evidently supplied him with some of the information he'd gathered from the double agent Doromal; Raphael spoke with the conspirators. According to some of those who met with him, none revealed the plans. "Never," said Kapunan. "We debated about it.

We all agreed not to get in touch because after the revolution we should face them as equals, not indebted to them.'' According to Almonte, senior officers of the U.S. Pacific Command with whom he spoke had ''analyzed the situation correctly and had a pretty good idea of what was coming. But no one had confirmed it to them.'' After the fact, the Filipinos wanted full credit for the rebellion, and the United States was content to let them have it.

Actually, United States intelligence agencies had a good sense of events and would participate, but at a low level. ''The ingredients were there to let the locals do it themselves,'' said an American intelligence operative. ''The U.S. didn't have to dirty its hands, the Filipinos had all the right instincts. The U.S. also recognized that we had botched things in Iran and in Central America.''

This was a rare instance of the United States staying its hand, though not necessarily through clear direction. Looking at U.S. policy in a positive light, it could be concluded that a judgment had been made to adopt a hands-off attitude and allow the chips to fall where they would. In reality, though, President Reagan's inability to cut off Marcos until—quite literally—the final hours was at odds with the advice of senior foreign-policy experts. This created a conflict with the end result being that the Reagan administration did not have a cohesive policy on the Philippines and would play a very limited role in the rebellion.

Enrile was having lunch with his wife, Cristina, when Honasan, Kapunan, and Major Hong arrived at his home bursting with the disastrous news that their plans were collapsing and they'd ''frozen'' all movement. They told the minister they no longer had the option of attacking Malacañang—they would be walking into a death trap. But they couldn't afford to elaborately revise their plans either because they believed Ver had issued orders to arrest or even kill them and possibly Enrile, Ramos, and a number of others associated with RAM and with Aquino. While they had been meeting at the ministry, a close friend of Honasan's who worked as an intelligence officer for Ver contacted him with urgent information: The younger man had been ordered to ask Honasan to meet Ver at Manila's Bayview Hotel. ''Obviously, Ver will never arrive and somebody else will arrive and spray the room with bullets,'' Honasan concluded. The plotters felt they could wait no longer. They weren't positive that Ver was going to take an initiative, but the signs were clear enough. "When we got information that we were about to be arrested, all indicators also pointed to that," Honasan explained. "So we said, 'This is it!' Whether we were wrong in some aspects or not, we had to bring this to the minister and said there had to be a choice."

In all likelihood, Ver had not yet issued orders for arrests or killings; he and Imelda Marcos were attending a wedding at Villamor Air Base. But Enrile and his boys knew only that their plans had been blown and presumed they would soon be arrested, or worse. Their options, they figured, were either to disperse and be picked off one-by-one or regroup and take their chances. Enrile explained what he had told his men at the time: "I said, 'Well, if we regroup and take a stand, the possibility of an encounter is very high. And that if we will be assaulted, then we will either all perish or some of us will survive. But the other side will also suffer heavy casualties. Or the possibility of a standoff is not far-fetched.' So, I decided that we must regroup." He then issued orders for as many RAM officers as could be reached to assemble at his headquarters at Camp Aguinaldo in suburban Quezon City.

With a military initiative against Marcos now impossible, their number-one priority was to drum up as much public support as they could. To do this, they had to scuttle any impression that they had been planning a coup d'etat. Although the man on horseback is a familiar figure throughout the Third World, where the military often is the best-organized legacy of colonialism, this was not the case in the Philippines. If people realized that Enrile had been planning to stage a coup and then impose a junta, most of them certainly would not have been supportive. As in India, where the British left behind a legacy of an apolitical army, the Filipinos had learned from the United States that once the military takes charge, a country can very quickly degenerate into a banana republic. So Enrile and his men had to cover their plans and portray themselves as victims. That settled, Enrile went to his bedroom, changed into jeans and canvas shoes, and took an Uzi submachine gun out of the closet, one of the weapons that had been part of the package deal he had bought from London.

At the same time, Lieutenant General Ramos was meeting at home with a group of women who worked for Aquino and called themselves Cory's Crusaders. They were Ramos's neighbors and, filled with righteous indignation, were threatening to picket his house unless he investigated the Javier murder in Antique. His wife had just received a phone call from a friend with a rumor that Enrile was about to be arrested. Mrs. Ramos told her husband, who supposedly replied, "Maybe I will be next. But, first, I have to attend to Cory's Crusaders." The phone rang again, and this time it was Enrile, speaking quickly, his voice tense: "Eddie, we are about to be rounded up; will you join us?" Ramos, the professional, first warned the minister not to say too much over the open phone line, then instantly overcame the years of indecision and answered, "I am with you all the way." Enrile told the general he was leaving immediately for his headquarters, and Ramos, whose coolness under pressure would grow to legendary proportions in the next few days, said he'd be along after he'd finished speaking with his neighbors.

As Enrile and his men dashed to their cars, he told his wife to let the local newspapers and TV stations know that his life was in danger and that they should go to Camp Aguinaldo. After reaching his office, the nervous Enrile called Ramos again, asking what was taking him so long, and the unflappable general said he'd be there "as soon as possible." Ramos said good-bye to his wife and the Crusaders, then left, cautiously taking a circuitous route to the camp and arriving at about 6:00 P.M. By then, Enrile had extracted a commitment from the Aguinaldo military police commander that he and his men would remain neutral. This enabled two RAM helicopters to land unimpeded inside the sprawling grounds, bringing supplies of arms, ammunition, and food. At first, Enrile and Ramos had about two hundred men. Later that night there were four hundred, armed with little more than M-16 Armalite rifles and Uzis, barely enough of a force to even slow down the thousands of men, planes, helicopters, and tanks they expected would soon be thrown against them.

17

FLIGHT

As soon as Enrile reached his office, he began using the bank of telephones on the lime-green cabinet behind his desk. The first call was to Ambassador Bosworth. He told the diplomat that he and his men had taken refuge at Aguinaldo, and that they expected to be arrested. He mentioned nothing about the aborted coup. Bosworth, who for the next four days would broker the wildly unraveling situation between Enrile and Marcos, and between Manila and Washington, with skill and sensitivity, knew that Enrile was not telling the whole truth and replied rather coolly. But he immediately sounded the alarm to an around-the-clock task force that had already been set up in the State Department and where, in the words of one of the officials, "all hell broke loose." Enrile then telephoned Japanese Ambassador Kiyoshi Somiya. His reason for calling the two diplomats was to "let the world know what was happening in case we were annihilated." His next thought, for the same reason, was to call local and foreign journalists and ask them to come to Camp Aguinaldo.

The Church and a powerful religious fervor were to play immeasurably critical roles in what lay ahead, and one of Enrile's most important calls was to Cardinal Jaime Sin. "Cardinal, I will be dead within one hour," he told him. "I don't want to die. If it is possible, do something. I'd still like to live." According to the cardinal, he said he'd already heard "the order to smash us." Enrile was again taking liberties with the truth. Then Ramos, a Protestant, got on the line and

279

said he'd just embraced an image of Our Lady of Fatima in Enrile's office, and he appealed, "Cardinal, help us by calling the people to support us." Sin, who had been in contact with some of the rebels and with Aquino's people during the preceding weeks, immediately consented, and at nine o'clock that evening his voice was heard over Radio Veritas, calling on people to "support our two good friends at the camp." Within a few hours, the broad boulevard that runs by the camp, Epifanio de los Santos Avenue, or Edsa, as Manilans know it, was swarming with thousands of cheering people. The poor came on foot or in jeepneys, but most arriving at the suburban camp that first night were middle class, and in their cars they brought hamburgers and chicken, rice, drinks, cigarettes, and cakes, which they passed over the walls to the soldiers. Enthusiasm swept through the crowd, and the feeling was more of a midnight carnival than a last stand.

Reporters, who were among the first to arrive, were allowed inside the gates, and they assembled in the social hall of the defense ministry. As glaring TV lights heated the packed room, Enrile, sweating profusely in an olive-drab windbreaker over a bulletproof vest, explained that he had broken away because, "personally, I think Marcos did not really win this election." He was speaking from firsthand experience, he said, referring to the votes he'd stolen for Marcos in Cagayan province.

Having exposed his own culpability, Enrile then for the first time came out publicly for Aquino. "I believe in my whole heart and mind that Aquino was duly elected president of the republic. She is the rightful owner of the mandate of the people." Out of fear and desperation, Enrile went further in supporting her than he would have liked to, and later he would try to backtrack. Then, in an attempt at bravado that he certainly was not feeling, Enrile called on Marcos to resign "while there's still time."

By his side, Ramos was looking calmer and cooler in a short-sleeved shirt. His remarks echoed those of Enrile: He had come, he said, because "it had been building up in my perception that General Ver and the president are bent on perpetuating themselves in power. . . . It is my duty to see that the sovereign will of the people is respected. I am bothered by my conscience." Ramos complained that Marcos had used his name "as a cosmetic, a deodorant" to create an illusion that the armed forces would provide security for an honest election while secretly distributing weapons to wealthy supporters whose private armies were used to terrorize people into voting for Marcos. "I am making myself available to serve the armed forces of the people," he said. Ramos's remarks and subsequent telephone calls to military commanders throughout the country would prove essential to swinging units behind the rebellion; he enjoyed the respect of officers and men in the field that Enrile did not.

The two spoke to the flabbergasted reporters for two hours but did not mention a word about the coup. As a result, the world was led to believe that Enrile and Ramos had taken refuge in order to avoid being arrested by the willful Marcos and that the subsequent rebellion was almost magically spontaneous.

This belief in an innocent Enrile and Ramos hounded into seeking refuge was the essential element in arousing the sympathy and support of the tens of thousands who poured into the streets outside Aguinaldo as they heard the news conference repeated by Radio Veritas throughout the night. Over the next four nights and days, millions more would take up the cause of the two underdogs, thrilling to the drama in which they themselves were playing a major role, preparing to risk their lives as part of a phenomenon that would quickly become known as "people power." Thus, this most extraordinary, most inspiring aspect of the Philippine rebellion was built on a half-truth.

From Aguinaldo, Cory Aquino's brother-in-law, Butz Aquino, announced over Radio Veritas that he was going to lead a march from the nearby bustling Cubao shopping center back to the camp. People left their homes and joined him, coming from all directions, pouring into Edsa and eventually clogging its eight lanes for miles. Men, women, and children, they were now part of the rebellion. There would be times of tense confrontations between the unarmed civilians and tanks bristling with guns manned by soldiers loyal to Marcos, times of false jubilation and of profound terror. There were to be moments, too, of fiesta, of guitars and singing, of food vendors selling pineapple and ice cream, and whole families sitting cross-legged in the middle of the highway, picnicking, everyone flashing the *laban* L at everyone else. But, ultimately, what transpired at Edsa was an emotional, religious, and patriotic explosion so passionate that few who took part fully understood the ramifications until well after the rebellion was over.

After the news conference, Ramos left for his own headquarters at Camp Crame, diagonally across Edsa from Aguinaldo. Enrile telephoned Cory in Cebu. At this point, there still was no suggestion of the two former Marcos men being the damsel's knights in shining armor, and if the rebellion succeeded, plans still were to turn over power to a committee, though that was not what Enrile had told the journalists. And that was not what Aquino had been working for, but, figuring she'd be better off for supporting the rebels than not, she asked Enrile what she could do. He appealed for her help in getting more people to Edsa, and she went to work, telephoning contacts in Manila, among them her sister-in-law Ting-Ting Cojuangco, who called out her flower brigades.

Aquino had alternatives. At Quisumbing's house, the U.S. consul in Cebu, Blaine Porter, offered sanctuary aboard a U.S. Navy frigate. She declined. She also had been offered refuge by friends in the Mindanao city of Davao; and the king of Malaysia, Ninoy's old friend, had told her she was welcome in his country. But she decided to spend the night at a monastery in Cebu and to return to Manila the next morning.

By 2:00 A.M., Sunday, February 23, the time that RAM was to have invaded Malacañang Palace, its leaders were holed up inside Camp Aguinaldo and Camp Crame with four hundred soldiers. Outside the locked gates, fifty thousand unarmed civilians were protecting them. Across town, Malacañang was an armed fortress, surrounded by some eight thousand marines and troops of the Presidential Security Command. From inside, President Marcos had gone on television at about 11:00 P.M. and called on Enrile and Ramos to surrender. "We can finish this in one hour," he warned, "but it would be a bloody affair." The president then told viewers all about an aborted coup d'etat and assassination attempt he'd discovered. As proof, he produced the captured Captain Morales, who reiterated in detail what he'd already confessed to Marcos and Ver.

His true story went over like a lead balloon. Around the city, people sitting before their television sets laughed. Morales was on the PSC staff and was obviously a Ver loyalist. Who could believe such a confession from such a man? There was bitter irony in this. After years of Marcos's lies, he was telling the truth; there had been a coup plot and Morales was making an honest confession. But Marcos had cried wolf too often. Now no one was listening.

As the night wore on, Ramos worked the phones. One of the more important pledges he won was from Major General Prospero Olivas, one of the top officers who'd been implicated in the Aquino assassination, and who was in charge of the capital's riot police. Ramos succeeded in getting Olivas to turn a blind eye on the crowds massing on Edsa and to ward off orders from Marcos to break up the throng. Meanwhile, businessmen, politicians, and military men who had not been privy to the coup plans pledged their support. Among them was Ver's predecessor as chief of staff, retired General Romeo Espiño. The commissioner of customs and the postmaster general arrived and announced over Radio Veritas, which was broadcasting live from the two camps, that they were resigning from the Marcos government to join the rebels. Soon there would be a flood of such resignations and defections.

Then Colonel Abadilla, Ver's envoy who early that morning had paid a call on Honasan, came to Aguinaldo, this time urging Enrile to telephone Marcos. But Enrile responded, "It is too late for us to talk about this. We have burned our bridges, we have already taken a stand." The emissary left for Malacañang and returned a few hours later, once again saying Marcos wanted Enrile to call. "But I repeated my answer," he said, "knowing that the president has certain ways of dealing with certain situations, always to his advantage." It was as though Enrile knew he would not have the willpower to refuse Marcos, as though he would be mesmerized by his master's voice, and his only choice was to avoid speaking to him.

Abadilla asked if Enrile would be willing to speak on the phone with Ver, and he consented. The conversation turned out to be pivotal, and resulted in the rebels gaining time, during which defections and popular support would tip the balance in their favor. According to Enrile, the conversation went this way:

Ver: "Sir, we were surprised about this turn of events."

Enrile: "Well, I was informed that you were trying to have us all arrested."

Ver: "That is not true. That's not true. There is no such plan. There is no such order."

Enrile: "The only thing I would like to request you, if you want to have a dialogue with us, is not initiate any attack against us tonight."

Ver: "Commit to us that you will not attack the palace tonight."

Enrile: "You have my solemn word that we will never attack the palace. We have no aggressive intention against the palace, and we will confine ourselves in this camp until daybreak and after that we can talk."

Enrile, of course, did not have the capacity to assault the palace, but Ver didn't know it. Ver easily could have overrun Aguinaldo, but because his first obligation was to protect the First Family, the general kept his word to Enrile. Talks of sorts did get underway, with retired Lieutenant General Rafael Ileto, a would-be member of the civilian-military ruling committee, shunting between the palace and Camp Aguinaldo. His calm, mature approach in these early hours helped restrain Ver.

Throughout the tense, sleepless night, rumors filtered in that Ver's forces were positioning artillery pieces at a nearby college, the University of Life. Enrile ordered the scores of newsmen in the building to move from the third floor to the second, in case they were shelled. The bombardment didn't materialize, and Enrile thought this was because Marcos hadn't sensed the rebels' desperation: "I knew that he would not be in a position to assess our state of morale and condition of our defense as long as he could not talk to anyone of us, and they would hesitate to take aggressive action against us."

That hesitation, so uncharacteristic of Marcos, became his undoing. Had he moved at any time during the first night, he easily could have crushed the rebels. Even with vast crowds gathered outside the gates, a few well-placed artillery shells could have ended the upstart rebellion without harming many civilians. By the time he gave the order to attack, it was too late. Enrile and Ramos recognized almost immediately that the president's hesitation was going to be fatal to him. "That was their error," Enrile said. "The first twelve hours of this problem spelled the difference between victory and lack of success."

The president was indecisive that night for a number of reasons:

He hadn't been able to make direct contact with Enrile, a man he'd always been able to talk into or out of anything. If only he could have spoken to his longtime friend and ally, he almost certainly would have wrung a concession from him. He would try again.

He feared for his own safety and the safety of his family inside Malacañang. The four captured rebel officers had confessed the plans for the raid on the palace, and Marcos didn't know if they had been aborted or merely rescheduled.

He was isolated inside the palace and didn't have an accurate picture of events and moods. "The people inside didn't know what was happening outside the palace grounds," said Brigadier General Hermogenes Peralta of the Criminal Investigation Service, who was at Malacañang Saturday night. "It was like a war was on, but it didn't seem that most officers and men knew what was happening."

Ambassador Bosworth had been in touch with Marcos's two sons-in-law in the palace, urging them to influence the president to be moderate, which they did.

Also at Bosworth's urging, the White House had opened regular communication with Marcos, building up pressure against his using force. Although eventually he would reject this recommendation, it unsettled him in the crucial first hours.

He misread the extent of popular revulsion over his manipulation of the elections and, thus, underestimated how popular the rebellion was. Even though he'd seen the enormous crowds turning out for Aquino, he didn't believe they'd ever challenge him and the armed forces. The almost instantaneous response by hundreds of thousands of people to protect the rebels came as a great shock.

So, the president dawdled, and it was not until 2:00 P.M. on Sunday, nearly twenty-four hours after Enrile and "the boys" had run to Aguinaldo, that troops acting on Ver's orders would attempt to put down the rebellion. But then they had to contend with the thousands-deep human barricades of "people power."

By the time the rebels had made it through the first night, it was Saturday afternoon in Washington. President Reagan, who was spending the weekend at Camp David, held a fifteen-minute telephone conference with Secretary of State George Shultz, Defense Secretary Casper Weinberger, National Security Adviser John Poindexter, and Chief of Staff Donald Regan. The four had prepared a statement that said that the charges made by Enrile and Ramos in their news conference "strongly reinforce our concerns that the recent presidential elections were marred by fraud, perpetrated overwhelmingly by the ruling party" and that the fraud had been "so extreme as to undermine the credibility and legitimacy of the election and impair the capacity of the government of the Philippines to cope with the growing insurgency and a troubled economy." Reagan approved the statement. Although it went no further than what Lugar had been saying for two weeks, it was as far as the president was willing to go. He declined to back Enrile and Ramos's call for Marcos to resign, nor would he endorse Aquino. The president was taking his cue from Regan, the adviser he most trusted. Regan was against listening to the urgings of State, Defense, and the embassy in Manila to pull the rug out from under Marcos.

Early Sunday morning in Manila, the protagonists stepped up the pace of their battle of broadcast propaganda. During the damp, chilly night, the crowds had thinned out, and visitors to Enrile's office had gone home, leaving him depressed and anxious.

Shortly after dawn, armed men loyal to Marcos smashed the main Radio Veritas transmitter. This could have been disastrous, but a backup system had been set up by CIA communications specialists just a few miles from Malacañang Palace in the final days before the aborted coup. Over the weak but audible signal, Ramos began announcing deliberate disinformation, claiming that swarms of armed troops, among them members of the Presidential Security Command, had joined the rebellion. He achieved the desired effect. The crowds, bigger than they had been the night before, returned to Edsa, and loyalist troops around the city began wondering if they had the will to fight civilians and their fellow soldiers.

Much of the disinformation campaign, which continued throughout the upheaval, was guided by CIA operatives and communications experts. Although Enrile denied it, a senior U.S. official confirmed that these agents "were in and out of Enrile's offices throughout the period." American experts also helped the rebels tap into General Ver's "secure" radio systems, enabling them on occasion to countermand the general's instructions.

Shortly after noon, Marcos was back on TV, hinting that he might unleash an artillery attack on the rebels and assuring the public that he certainly had no plans to resign "on the say-so of those who criticize my administration." Indeed, the president said, he was going ahead with plans for his scheduled inauguration on Tuesday.

Then he resurrected the previous night's charge that Enrile had been plotting a coup and introduced the three other officers who, along with Captain Morales, had been captured at the palace—Malajacan, Brillantes, and Aromin. Speaking to the Channel 4 camera, Malajacan said that their plan had been "to capture the president and talk to him, force him to resign, or send him to exile and invite some people who we feel are credible to the Filipino nation to lead the country back to democracy." Aromin, who said he had been assigned to infiltrate three trucks of rebel troops into the palace grounds in the guise of reinforcements, said that Honasan had convinced him of "our moral obligation to save our country from a bloody confrontation within the military organization." Despite the candor of the rebel officers, once again, TV viewers brushed off the confessions. The president's credibility was gone.

With circumstances in Manila completely out of her control, Cory Aquino called a press conference before leaving Cebu and attempted to create the impression that the rebellion had been staged to place her in office. Enrile and Ramos, she said, "have made it clear that they are out to support the people's will. For the sake of the Filipino people, I ask Mr. Marcos to step down so that we can have a peaceful transition of government." Then she flew back to Manila, her brother deceptively registering her as being aboard his light plane while she was on another. When Aquino reached the capital, she went into hiding, not only from Marcos, but from Enrile and Ramos, still unsure of how far she could trust them.

In mid afternoon, at Ramos's suggestion that they consolidate, Enrile left his office for Camp Crame, because it was more compact and easier to defend. Nuns in white-and-gray habits, saying their rosaries and carrying images of the Virgin Mary, met him and his heavily armed retinue, led by Honasan, in the hallway. When they reached Aguinaldo's gate, they were engulfed by a sea of supporters, and what was meant to be a simple walk across the street turned into a passionate procession. At first, Enrile was wary. He was still wearing a bulletproof vest under a windbreaker, the Uzi slung around his neck, and he was sweating heavily. "I could hardly squeeze through because of the thickness of the crowd," he said. "My men had to surround me for security reasons. With a crowd like that, somebody can stick a knife in your belly or back." But this crowd was different. People chanted, "Johnny! Johnny!" It was a heady moment for Enrile, a moment when he may have concluded that power was his for the taking.

But, when he finally got to Ramos's headquarters and the general took him out onto the building's fourth-floor terrace, what he saw convinced him otherwise. There may have been a million people packed on the highway. "Oh, my God!" said Enrile. "I was so amazed at the number of people in the area. And they were all chanting, shouting, clapping, laughing, cheering for us.'' They were cheering for Enrile. They were cheering for Ramos, too. But, most of all, they were cheering for Cory Aquino. They were wearing her color. They had voted for her. At that moment, Enrile understood that if the rebellion succeeded, there would be no civilian-military committee, no questions about who would take power from Marcos. Aquino would be the new president.

Aquino's brother-in-law Ricardo Lopa, who had been instrumental in originally promoting her as the opposition's candidate, came to believe that Enrile had been out for himself until he was confronted by that reality. ''He didn't think of Cory when his plan was aborted,'' said Lopa. ''He was thinking only of himself. That's why he called Bosworth. He was in desperation. But then, when he saw the people turned out in Edsa, that's when he realized it had to be Cory. This showed him that he had to pledge his allegiance to her.''

At the same time that Enrile was surveying the enormous crowd from the balcony, a few blocks beyond his field of vision a drama was unfolding that would prove to the world, if not to Marcos himself, that the president's enemy was his own people. Tens of thousands of Manilans, among them several leaders of the political opposition and prominent followers of Cory Aquino, had responded to a Radio Veritas appeal to mass at the broad intersection of Edsa and Ortigas Avenue, about two miles from Camp Crame. They filled the roads and spilled over onto a vacant field. Approaching was a column of oversize marine tanks and armored personnel carriers and trucks filled with combat-armed troops. The marine commander, Brigadier General Artemio A. Tadiar, was in the lead vehicle. He had been ordered by General Ver and the ruthless commander of the army, Major General Josephus Ramas, to attack and seize the rebel headquarters at Camp Crame. As the hulking machines approached the intersection Tadiar saw that buses and trucks had been parked helter-skelter to block their way. Shoving these vehicles aside would have been child's play for the tanks, as would snapping the pine trees that had been laid across the road a few blocks closer to the camp.

But the real contest was between humans and machines, a David and Goliath standoff in the middle of the afternoon on a Manila high-way. Packed tightly together, arm-in-arm, the thousands shuffled tenuously forward, closing the no-man's-land between their ranks and the camouflage-painted tanks, which by now had ground to a halt, their giant engines still roaring, belching black diesel exhaust. In the front lines were nuns and seminarians in white cassocks who dropped to their knees, fingering rosary beads with one hand and touching the hot metal of the tanks with the other, praying aloud, "Hail, Mary . . ."

Left with the unpalatable choice of plowing into the human sea or turning back in humiliation, the marines turned to the right, smashed through a concrete-block wall along the front of the vacant lot, and maneuvered the cumbersome machines into a circle. The troops, bandoliers of bullets crossed over their chests, carried M-16s and fearsome-looking Browning Automatic Rifles. They clambered down from the tanks and glowered at the people, who peered tentatively back. Then, slowly, the crowds began inching forward, using tactics that had been perfected during the years of antigovernment demonstrations, women, girls, and clergy at the front. Many clutched flowers.

One young woman, bolder than the rest, stepped away from the crowd and walked forward across an open place of perhaps five yards. She stopped in front of a slender, grim-faced marine, his fierce weapons failing to diminish his boyishness. Then, taking a deep breath, she held out a bouquet. Unsure of himself, the young man stared at her for a moment, then turned on his heel in a military about-face. But the tension had been broken. Another and then another young woman came forward, holding flowers before them. A teenaged girl scrambled onto one of the towering tanks and rapped on its closed hatch. The round lid popped open and a camouflaged arm reached up, snatched a blossom, and disappeared again. The girl's face cracked into a broad grin, and the crowd burst into laughter, applause, and shrill whistles.

Confused, the marines started up their vehicles several times as the late afternoon light faded. Each time, the crowds surged forward, pressing hands and bodies against the hot steel. Tadiar, dressed in full battle gear, looked sick, fully aware of the dilemma he faced. Pressed by the irritable Ramas, who was calling repeatedly by field radio from Fort Bonifacio, he had set half an hour for the crowd to disperse, and that deadline had long since passed. The marine chief spoke with lawyer Ernesto Maceda and Bishop Federico Escaler, who earlier had been dispatched to the intersection by Enrile, to act as negotiators. The cleric pleaded with the general not to fire on the crowds. "My people only shoot when provoked," Tadiar replied tartly. "I don't want confrontation." Tadiar radioed to army headquarters and explained the situation to Ramas, who barked back at him, "Ram through!" Tadiar was in an untenable situation. He had his orders, but these were people he recognized, people he knew, neighbors, classmates, children. They were not enemies. How could he order the machines to crush them?

At that point, he was contacted by Ver. Enrile had been on the phone with Ver, warning him that if the marines were ordered forward to Camp Crame, "You and the president will both go down in history as butchers of your own officers and men, you'll go down in history as butchers of Filipino people and foreign media men." Ver ordered Tadiar to back off. The tanks pulled back to the edge of the vacant lot and parked for the night.

A man named Ben, an accountant, who had been there all afternoon with his twelve-year-old son, stared, wide-eyed. "This is amazing," he breathed. "Look, they're actually leaving. This means we've won." As he spoke, the sound of victory, not a cheer, not a shout, but something like thunder or an ocean wave, welled up from the people, from deep in their spirits, and rolled out over the field and the street, over the marines and their tanks.

It was not victory, though, not yet. But for millions of ordinary Filipinos, this moment was the turning point. They had gone to the barricades, they *were* the barricades, had stood their ground, and had triumphed.

Still, there was no way to know how Marcos and Ver would react as they saw support draining away. Even at this point, indeed even until the very last, few Filipinos believed that the embattled president and his general would give in. They had had Marcos for so long, they'd seen him pull rabbits out of hats so often, that they could not imagine the country without him. "The only way he'll leave Malacañang is feet first" was common currency as to the way things would end. Watching him at news conferences and on television, listening to his persuasive arguments, becoming infected by his supreme confidence, I shared these views.

Enrile, knowing his former boss better than most, was afraid that Marcos might suddenly lash out in fury, like a caged rat, so, seeking all the assurance he could muster, he telephoned Bosworth. He requested that the White House apply pressure on the president and the general, and Bosworth once again called Washington. It was Sunday morning there, Reagan was still at Camp David, and Philip Habib had just landed in the capital. What a CIA analyst in Manila called "the battle for the mind of Ronald Reagan" now took place.

Secretary Shultz summoned Weinberger, Poindexter, and Armed Forces Chairman Admiral William Crowe to his home in suburban Maryland. They determined that Marcos must be eased out, and that afternoon they met with Reagan and told him so. But Chief of Staff Regan argued that Aquino might be a worse alternative than the dictator and, to illustrate, rehashed the example of Iran and the replacement of the shah by Ayatollah Ruhollah Khomeini. The president then turned to Habib, whose blunt judgment was "the Marcos era has ended."

Reagan ultimately agreed that Marcos must be urged to go, that he mustn't be allowed to "dig in his heels," but said it must be done delicately. Reagan declined to speak to Marcos directly, and presidential spokesman Larry Speakes told newsmen only that the United States would cut off all aid if violence broke out. But, privately, White House aides drafted a message saying that Reagan "looked forward to President Marcos's working out a scenario for a transition government" and that Marcos, his family, and close associates would be welcome in the United States. The message was transmitted to Bosworth, who read it to Marcos.

Shultz and Michael Armacost, the former ambassador to Manila who was now an undersecretary of state, met with Marcos's Labor Minister Blas Ople, who had been sent to Washington after the elections to build support for the regime, and told him that "the time of President Marcos had run out. His life was in danger and . . . if he did not step down the country would be headed toward civil war." Ople telephoned this message to Malacañang.

Following the climactic triumph of "people power" over the marines, Enrile finally felt sufficiently in control to accede to a request from Marcos for a telephone conversation. The president, he said, told him, "I have no intention, really, to punish your men, but they must be tried in order to show the public that we enforce the law. And I assure you that they will be pardoned." Enrile easily saw through this classic Marcos deception and said that he couldn't answer for his men, but would "discuss the matter with them." He did not, but later sent a message to the president, saying that the irreducible demand of the group was for him to "step down in order to prevent a further conflict."

Marcos was enraged. For the first time, he had failed utterly to influence Enrile. At midnight, the president was back on television, pounding his desk, shouting that the traitorous former defense minister had no intention of installing Corazon Aquino in the presidency, but planned to form a junta with himself as its head and Aquino merely a member. "Mrs. Aquino should not delude herself into thinking that she is being supported by Enrile," he said. For the third time, Marcos was telling the truth, and for the third time, people watching their TV screens laughed.

Enrile, after the telephone conversation, could sense the accusation coming, and by the time Marcos went on the air, he'd shifted his position to what he'd realized the day before was inevitable. Calling several prominent pro-Aquino members of the National Assembly, he advised them that they should quickly form a civilian government "to be headed by Mrs. Aquino and Mr. Laurel."

Although "people power" had forced the tanks off the road, the rebel troops in Camp Crame were in the cross hairs of General Ver's guns. By the predawn hours of Monday, the start of the third day, the camp was surrounded by loyalist units—tanks to the north, columns of infantry to the south, mortars installed to the west, two marine battalions across the highway in Aguinaldo, which had been recaptured after Enrile and his men left. Late the night before, despite pressure from Washington, Ver had ordered a concerted assault on Crame. Ramos, monitoring lines of communication, knew it. He didn't know, though, that officers in key positions surrounding the camp were stalling because they had decided to defect. Inside the crowded, sweltering confines of Ramos's headquarters, officers and men had been stretched to the extremes of tension. The air stank of stale cigarette smoke, sweat, and fear. Sleep-starved soldiers, automatic weapons seldom out of their hands, slumped against the walls, drinking endless cups of sour, black coffee. Aquino supporters, opposition politicians, and priests came and went, offering encouragement. Newsmen and camera crews threaded their way through jammed hallways, asking questions of anyone who'd answer. Few realized how dangerous things had become.

When the assault didn't materialize by 3:30 in the morning, Ramos, missing his daily fitness run, put on his jogging shoes and with a few junior officers went loping through cheering crowds outside the gate. But when they returned, so did the foreboding. Some of the men wept and sang the national anthem. Officers sang the military academy's alma mater. Enrile asked Bishop Francisco Claver, the Baltimore-ordained Jesuit who was one of the earliest prelates to speak out against the Marcos regime, to give him absolution.

The attack never came. Instead, government units started defecting. Some simply radioed word. Others marched through the gate of the camp, bringing with them vitally needed weapons and equipment. With dawn came a major development. At about 6:00 A.M., seven helicopter gunships carrying officers from Villamor Air Base clattered down onto the parade ground of Camp Crame and were immediately swamped by cheering, waving soldiers and civilians. The seventeen officers aboard had taken a vote and decided to join the rebellion. At almost the same time, five tactical fighter planes from Sangley Point Air Base defected and were led by their commander to the U.S. installation at Clark.

At about 6:30 A.M., an indefatigable Radio Veritas announcer named June Keithley, who for many had become the voice of the rebellion, reported that Marcos and his family had fled the country. "You are not fighting for anything or anyone anymore," Keithley told loyalist troops. Jubilation swept through Camp Crame and through Manila. At eight o'clock, Ramos and Enrile strode out the front door of the headquarters. Tightly encircled by armed security men, they stood at the top of the building's steps and, with journalists and cameramen swarming beneath them, announced victory. Enrile was still sweating in his bulletproof vest and windbreaker, but, indicating newfound confidence, the Uzi was gone from around his neck. Ramos was so full of joy that he raised his hands over his head, flashing the L sign, and leaped high into the air, as though the carefully cultivated shell of obedience had shattered and the spirit bottled up inside him finally burst out. Enrile spoke: "Never again in the history of this republic will there be a tyrant staying in Malacañang. This day must always be etched in the hearts and minds of all of us. . . . We must remember what happened in the last few days and must thank the Armed Forces of the Philippines for the freedom of the Filipino people." Ramos and Enrile waded out into the tightly massed, shouting throng, climbing onto a tall truck parked outside the gates as someone held an image of the Virgin Mary over their heads.

Aquino, still in hiding, broadcast an appeal for the populace to be "magnanimous in victory" and announced that she would be sworn in the next day as president of the Philippines. Buoyed by her statement and by the report that the First Family had fled, thousands streamed into the city's streets, honking car and jeepney horns, chanting, "Co-ry! Co-ry! Co-ry!"

But the Marcoses were still in the palace.

An hour after Enrile and Ramos had stood on the steps, the president was appearing on Channel 4 again. Gathered around him were his wife, his children, and his grandchildren, Imelda cradling the youngest, a maid holding another. "Don't believe any of these stories," he said. He instructed the camera to pan over foreign correspondents seated before him in the palace's conference room. Their presence would prove that this was a live broadcast and not on videotape. Marcos seemed almost detached from reality. As though he'd been dozing for the past three days, he suddenly branded Enrile and Ramos "rebels" and declared a state of emergency, telling military commanders, "You are now free to use small arms to defend yourselves. . . . You will protect installations against attack." At this point, General Ver, wearing camouflage combat fatigues, stepped up to the president's shoulder and leaned toward him. He asked for permission to bomb Camp Crame. "We are ready to annihilate them, to destroy them," Ver snapped, his breath short, his eyes glistening. Restrained, Marcos turned to him and repeated, "Use small arms." As the general walked away, Marcos looked into the camera and explained, "I have just stopped General Ver from allowing the F-5s to attack."

This televised cameo was nothing more than a charade, the statesmanlike president leashing in his snarling general, and it was staged mainly for the edification of the Reagan White House. The truth was that since the day before, Marcos, who along with Ver and other trusted officers had been studying a detailed drawing of the Aguinaldo-Crame area on a green chalkboard in his study, had ordered ground troops and fighter aircraft to fire on the rebels, but his orders were ignored. And now Marcos and Ver were attempting to salvage diplomatic gain from their military failure.

As the president continued addressing the newsmen, TV screens throughout the capital suddenly went dead. In the palace's conference room, Information Minister Gregorio Cendaña stepped forward and said that the broadcast had been cut off; rebel soldiers had captured Channel 4. "If that's true," said Marcos, "it will be necessary to use extreme force."

It was true. Rebel infantrymen, making their first foray outside Camp Crame, had captured the TV complex in Quezon City, killing two loyalist soldiers. But Marcos wasn't in a position to employ extreme force. Once again, a sea of unarmed civilians flowed into the streets, surrounding the broadcast center, blocking a potential firefight. The rebel seizure of the Channel 4 complex had a critical effect on the final stages of the rebellion, depriving Marcos of the ability to communicate with the country and creating for the rebels an image of being in control.

For millions of Filipinos, Channel 4 had become the symbol of the regime ever since the elections, and one man more than any other represented the essence of that symbol. His name was Ronnie Nathanielsz. The station's chief commentator, Nathanielsz was a native of Sri Lanka who, through the intervention of Imelda Marcos, had been granted Philippine citizenship by presidential decree. Day and night throughout the ballot-counting farce and the start of the rebellion, his obsequious treatment of any matter favorable to the regime and his cold condemnation of the Aquino camp nauseated and infuriated millions. As rebel troops spilled into the broadcast center, the silver-haired Nathanielsz, his professional composure abandoned, was seen clambering over a brick wall behind the compound. By early afternoon, Colonel Mariano Santiago, who had led the attack, was broadcasting from the Channel 4 newsroom along with two Radio Veritas personalities.

At about the same time, Enrile announced from Camp Crame that a provisional government was being formed with Cory Aquino as president. Aquino, making her first appearance since the rebellion began three days earlier, went to the barricades near Crame, where she was swamped by an adoring horde. She led them in the singing of *Ave Maria*.

With the government TV station in their belts, Enrile and Ramos ordered the helicopters that had defected to their side to launch rocket strikes on Villamor Air Base and on Malacañang Palace. The gunships destroyed three presidential helicopters at Villamor, but the three rockets fired at the palace exploded harmlessly on the ground, which, according to Enrile, was what was intended. "The instruction was not to hit the palace itself, because we did not want to harm the president," he said. In any case, the rocket strike had a devastating psychological impact on the Marcoses and the other inmates of Malacañang.

The fact that the helicopter attacks were carried out with utter impunity was a certain sign that the military balance had shifted to the rebel side. Troops with white bands of surrender tied around their arms were filing into a "defection center" that had been set up inside Camp Crame. The elite First Scout Ranger Regiment, under Brigadier General Felix Brawner, was supposed to lead an attack on the camp's perimeter but joined the defectors instead.

The diplomatic balance also shifted dramatically on this momentous third day. At six o'clock in the evening Manila time, White House spokesman Larry Speakes announced that President Reagan had finally asked Marcos to step down. "Attempts to prolong the life of the present regime by violence are futile," Speakes said, reading from a statement that Reagan had approved and already dispatched to Marcos through Bosworth. An hour and a half later, Marcos telephoned Blas Ople in Washington and told the jowly labor minister that he understood what Reagan was saying, but the First Lady was reluctant to abandon the palace. "She is here beside me," he said. "She does not want to leave."

Marcos was holding out until the last possible moment, unable to accept that he was on the verge of becoming a man without power, a man without a country. He went back on television, this time over Channel 9, owned by his friend Roberto Benedicto, intending to put on a show of bravado. The effect was pathetic—he was trying to prove that he still existed. Sitting in an empty room, wearing a gray windbreaker, he held up a newspaper and said: "Here I am, holding up the *Daily Express*. The headline shows it's today. Forgive me my informal dress, but all of us in Malacañang are prepared for any eventuality, either day or night. . . . We have no intention of going abroad, no intention of resigning. We will defend the republic until the last breath of life and the last drop of blood in our bodies."

As in other of his recent TV appearances, Marcos seemed to be lost in a time warp: "I'm going to search for arms. It's time we do this. It's a national emergency." An interviewer then began questioning him, and, incredibly, he lapsed into a detailed description of his health: "I've just finished exercising. I'm fit and strong and quite ready to go to combat if necessary. I'll get back my sniper rifle if necessary to protect my family. I do military presses, lift light weights, I do splits. I brought my weight down from one-hundred thirty-two to one-hundred twenty-six."

Later that evening, he spoke over the radio, and now the attempt at putting up a brave front was slipping. "My family is cowering in fear inside Malacañang Palace," he said. "It's a matter of survival."

In fact, though, Marcos had already decided to leave and was negotiating the details of his and Ver's departure with Bosworth and, through him, with Aquino. Ver had already dispatched his mistress, Edna Camcam, and her children out of the country. After midnight on Monday, the American ambassador telephoned Cory's brother Peping Cojuangco at the home of another sister, Josephine Reyes, where Cory was staying. Marcos was asking for Aquino's permission to go to a home he owned in Ilocos Norte, to "rest." Aquino discussed the request with her brother and with her close adviser, Joker Arroyo, and then called Bosworth back. According to Cojuangco, she said that she would approve if a respite was required to save Marcos's life "because he had given Ninoy permission to leave the Philippines to save his life. Otherwise, to avoid bloodshed, it would be better if he left the country." Bosworth's answer was that it was not a life-or-death matter.

Even more sensitive negotiating was required over General Ver. Because of his implication by the Agrava board in Ninoy Aquino's assassination, Cory was hard pressed to approve of Ver's being allowed to leave with Marcos. But CIA officials convinced Cardinal Sin to intervene with Cory, and after hours of struggling with her conscience she gave in.

While this bargaining was going on, Marcos's two sons-in-law were supervising the packing of dozens of crates of family possessions, including hundreds of thousands of dollars in gold bullion and bonds, more than a million dollars' worth of freshly printed pesos, as well as artifacts and jewels. These were delivered by boat to a bayfront lawn adjacent to the U.S. embassy. Weeks earlier, a number of bulkier items, mainly large oil paintings and other works of art, had been packed and shipped out of the country at the direction of the First

Lady. Nevertheless, neither she nor the president really believed they would ever have to flee, and the decision to abandon the palace was a last-minute one.

There was little sleep in the palace that night as aides scurried from room to room, sifting through cabinets and boxes filled with documents, receipts, letters, many of them incriminating. Imelda Marcos was able to provide little advice to her husband. She seemed dazed, drifting in and out of her private chapel where she knelt and prayed. Marcos's son Bong Bong and General Ver were arguing desperately with him to stay and fight. There was no question of that, but the president was determined to go ahead with his formal inauguration scheduled for Tuesday. He would go out with as much a show of pride as he could muster. And, for practical purposes, as the legally proclaimed winner in the National Assembly, taking the oath might put the law on his side. This could prove useful at some point in the future, perhaps to stage a dramatic return to the Philippines, perhaps in some as-yet-unforeseen court wrangle.

At 2:45 A.M. Tuesday, Marcos telephoned his friend Senator Laxalt, in Washington. It was 1:45, Monday afternoon, in Washington. Laxalt took the call in S-407, a secure communications room in the Capitol building, where secret foreign policy briefings are held. Marcos kept him on the phone for twenty minutes, struggling to find some way he could remain in office until his term expired in 1987, even if it meant sharing power with Aquino. All else failing, he wanted to stay in Ilocos Norte. "He was a desperate man, grasping at straws," Laxalt said. Marcos asked the senator to discuss his situation with President Reagan, and Laxalt consented, then drove the few blocks down Pennsylvania Avenue to confer in the Oval Office with the president, Shultz, and Regan.

At about the same time that the senator was at the White House, Imelda Marcos telephoned there and spoke with Nancy Reagan. Mrs. Reagan expressed her concern for the Marcos family and said they were all welcome to come to the United States.

Nearly three hours later, at 5:30 A.M. Manila time, Laxalt placed a call to Malacañang. Marcos sounded tired. "Senator, what do you think?" he asked. "Should I step down?"

"I think you should cut and cut cleanly," Laxalt responded immediately. "I think the time has come."

The effect was almost as though Laxalt had physically struck the despondent Marcos; there was no sound. The silence seemed so long to Laxalt that he thought he'd been disconnected. "Mr. President," he finally said, "are you still there?"

"I am here, Senator," Marcos answered softly. "I am so very, very disappointed."

Marcos still refused to give up. At nine o'clock in the morning, he telephoned Enrile at Camp Crame, making a last plea. According to Enrile, Marcos offered a proposal: "Why don't we organize a provisional government? I just want a graceful exit. I will cancel the election. I will organize a provisional government and I shall remain as an honorary president until 1987." And Enrile answered: "Mr. President, I do not know about that, but we are not really interested in power. Our mission was not to establish a military junta or military government." Marcos appealed to him to discuss the proposal with Aquino, and Enrile said, "Yes, surely, I will."

Enrile did not bring up the matter. He and Ramos left Camp Crame immediately for Aquino's inauguration at a nearby social club, for which they were already two hours late. The choice of venue represented a small but significant statement of independence by Aquino. While the United States had been negotiating with her over the fate of Marcos and Ver, Enrile was dealing with her adviser, Jimmy Ongpin, in an effort to have her sworn in at Camp Crame. When Ongpin told Cory, she bristled, refusing adamantly to take the oath under military aegis, aware that to do so would heighten the impression that she was wholly reliant on Enrile and possibly strengthen his hand for some future challenge. That was precisely what she didn't want. She did agree, though, to return Enrile to his old post as defense minister.

Not far from Camp Crame, at the gracious old Club Filipino, built by the local elite during the waning days of Spanish rule, the ballroom was packed with two-hundred or so of the newest elite. Most had supported Ninoy Aquino and then Cory for years and finally had gone to the barricades on Edsa. But some were there who had not helped at all, such as thirty-seven KBL members of the National Assembly who had defected during the night. Inviting them to the inauguration was an astute move, showing Marcos and the country that even his staunchest followers were deserting him. A vase of enormous yellow sunflowers was the only decoration on the long table that stretched across the sunlit, airy room, its French doors opening onto terraces and gardens outside. The setting was almost that of a suburban wedding. Bishop Escaler, who two days earlier had pleaded with General Tadiar for the marines not to shoot, now prayed for divine guidance so that Aquino and Laurel could "put the economy on its own feet."

Aquino, wearing a yellow dress with lace sleeves and matching yellow-framed glasses, was ebullient as she placed her left hand on a gilt-edged, red-leather Bible held by her mother-in-law, *Doña* Aurora. Raising her right hand, she took a revolutionary oath of office from Claudio Teehankee, the Supreme Court justice who had refused to allow Marcos to slip out of the elections: "Sovereignty resides in the people and all government authority emanates from them. On the basis of the people's mandate clearly manifested last February 7, I and Salvador H. Laurel are taking power in the name and by the will of the Filipino people as president and vice president, respectively."

This oath, based on popular mandate, was intended to rationalize Aquino's presidency. Her administration was, in fact, illegal.

As soon as Laurel took his oath from Justice Abad Santos, who had also voted to force Marcos to go through with the elections, Aquino issued her first executive order, appointing Laurel prime minister-designate. This was part of the price he had demanded for allowing her to head the ticket. She followed this immediately by reappointing Enrile and promoting Ramos to full general and chief of staff, the appointments he'd been deprived of by Ver.

Aquino gave a short inaugural address, in which she thanked God that "through courage and unity, through the power of the people, we are home again."

At noon, just an hour after Aquino's inaugural, Marcos took his own oath, and the Philippines seemed to have two presidents. Marcos was sworn in at Malacañang by Chief Justice Ramon Aquino. Enigmatic vice president-elect Tolentino did not attend the brief ceremony. Channel 9 was to have carried the event, but just as the oath was being administered the station went off the air, leaving viewers perplexed. The explanation was that a firefight had broken out at the station's transmitting tower, and three pro-Marcos soldiers and a civilian were shot to death. When Channel 9 came back on, it was showing a John Wayne movie. Marcos would not be seen on Philippine television again.

He, his wife, and their children stepped out onto a second-floor balcony, looking down on some three thousand KBL faithful who'd been brought to the barricaded palace grounds that morning and provided with free box lunches. Marcos wore a well-fitting *barong tagalog.* Imelda and Imee were dressed in silky white *ternos,* the puffy sleeved long gown that is formal wear for Filipinas, younger daughter Irene more sedately in a white tailored suit. Bong Bong was in olive-drab combat fatigues. Her face drawn, her eyes soulful, Imelda sang her trademark song in Tagalog, "Because of You," and then told the people below the balcony, "We are sad that you could not all come in." The crowd, waving small paper flags, chanted, "Capture the snakes! Martial law! Martial law!" Marcos, in a brief but fiery speech, vowed to his supporters, "We will overcome these obstacles."

Enrile had gone to sleep after returning to Camp Crame from Aquino's inauguration. During the afternoon, he moved back to his own office at Aguinaldo. "We were already quite secure," he said. "I knew that at that point there was no way by which the president could possibly harm us." At about 5:30, Marcos telephoned him, complaining that troops were firing at the palace. Enrile said they were not his men, but he would have it halted.

There was nothing else to say. Marcos asked Enrile to call Bosworth and have him arrange for the evacuation with Major General Theodore Allen, head of the Joint U.S. Military Assistance Group in the Philippines. "I want to leave the palace," he said. Enrile replied, "Surely, Mr. President." This time, he did as Marcos asked.

At 9:05 on the night of Tuesday, February 25, two U.S. military helicopters lifted off the Malacañang compound's golf course and flew Marcos, General Ver, and their families to Clark Air Base. A U.S. Navy vessel took another group from the riverfront palace to the base at Subic Bay, and others, including Eduardo Cojuangco and his wife, drove themselves to Clark. In all, the United States evacuated eighty-nine people from the palace and, afterward, flew them first to Guam and then to Honolulu, where Marcos would go into exile.

For about two hours after the helicopters lifted off, the last holdouts at Malacañang skirmished with the growing number of Aquino supporters who were flocking toward the palace. Some of the loyalists were stunned. They could not believe that Marcos had fled, even though they'd seen and heard the helicopters take off. Bitter and uncomprehending, they hurled broken bricks at newcomers easily identified by their yellow headbands or T-shirts in the glare of fires set outside the gates. Scattered M-16 shots crackled from inside the tall iron fence encircling the grounds. But by 11:00 P.M., the Aquino crowd had swelled to tens of thousands, and the Marcos loyalists, some of them badly beaten and bloody, simply melted away.

As soon as the fighting ended, young men clambered onto a ten-foot-high gate and dropped to the ground inside. Within minutes, the chains were forced open and thousands flooded in, running across the lawns, past abandoned armored personnel carriers, toward the white colonnaded palace. Most stayed outside the building that for so long had symbolized the Marcoses. They were singing, dancing, shouting, laughing, weeping, and hugging one another, but still somewhat awed to be so close to the center of power. A few dozen young men, the faceless poor of Manila, wearing grimy T-shirts and rubber sandals, went into the palace. They made their way up to the second floor and into the Marcos's living quarters. What they saw amazed them.

Imelda Marcos's enormous, richly paneled bedroom was dominated by a white-canopied, double-king-sized bed on an elevated platform; a half-eaten banana had been tossed alongside it. At the far end of the room stood a gleaming black grand piano. There were no windows. Adjacent was a Hollywood-style dressing room, lined from floor to ceiling with mirrors and rows of light bulbs, its counters filled with spigot-fitted jugs of the costliest French perfumes. It contained closets and wardrobes holding rows of Italian purses and rack upon rack of her clothes—hundreds of dresses and gowns and, most bizarre, piles of underpants, brassieres, and girdles, almost all of them black. (Later, much more would be discovered in a vast ground-floor storeroom, next to the presidential barber shop, the beauty parlor, hospital, and dental clinic.) In the small chapel adjoining her bedroom, devotional candles still flickered on carved images of the Virgin Mary atop a sterling-silver altar and on Hindu religious artifacts the First Lady had brought from India.

Marcos's bedroom contained proof of the secret that he'd been trying to keep for the past three years—a dialysis machine, trays of drugs and bandages, a portable toilet, a hospital bed, and next to it a paperbound volume entitled *A Handbook for Renal Transplant Out-*

patients, from the University of Texas Medical School at Houston.

Left in desk drawers and littered around the polished hardwood floors of the regal apartment were countless papers—deeds, contracts, receipts, and bank records. One showed that on a single day in April 1983, Imelda Marcos had spent the equivalent of $49,000 while antique-shopping in Ilocos Sur province. That was almost exactly the same figure as Marcos claimed was his annual income.

Some of those who entered the palace helped themselves to firearms, silverware, and clothing, and a few young men began tossing some of Marcos's *barongs* out a window, but they were immediately halted by people on the ground, shouting, "Do not destroy anything! That is the people's property." Considering what might have happened, the looting and destruction were insignificant. No one protested, though, when a young man appeared on the balcony where the Marcoses had last been seen and smashed two framed portraits of them. When he hung out paper pictures of Aquino and Laurel, those on the ground went wild, screaming "Cory-Doy! Cory-Doy!" and dancing madly around a blazing rubber tire.

Below the balcony, alongside a towering mimosa tree softly aglow with dozens of electrified mother-of-pearl globes, a middle-aged man in a pale blue shirt looked on quietly, tears trickling down his cheeks. As he watched the jubilation he was having difficulty comprehending that in four days, with almost no death or bloodshed, an era had ended, a new time had begun. It was a miracle, he said, nothing less. His name was Maximo Avendano, and he was a clerk in a shipping company.

"How can I tell you what this moment means to me," he said. "At last I know the meaning of freedom. In 1965, I voted for Marcos because I believed he would help this country. Eight years later, he imposed martial law, and I learned my mistake. I've had that on my conscience ever since. Now this! It's almost too much to imagine. Look at me, I'm crying like a baby. I'm so ashamed. I'm so proud."

*E*PILOGUE

YEAR ONE

Swept into office in as glorious a victory as any national leader could dream of, Corazon Aquino awoke to find herself enmeshed in a political nightmare. By the time the last yellow streamers had disappeared from the streets of Manila, the enormity of the wreckage left by the Marcos regime was apparent, and so was her lack of preparedness for the job ahead. Crises tumbled one upon the other, forcing the country again and again to the verge of anarchy. She faced challenges from the armed forces, the Marcos holdovers, the Communists, and from ordinary Filipinos clamoring for change.

The economy was a shambles. Given the best will and cooperation of investors at home and abroad and a large measure of luck, the country would need at least ten years to return to the shaky financial footing of a decade earlier. But before anyone with money would think seriously of investing in the Philippines, Aquino would have to demonstrate that she was in control of the political machinery. She was not.

Although she held the same dictatorial powers that Marcos had retained from the martial law years, she seemed incapable of exercising them, either vengefully or benevolently. Aquino, totally inexperienced as a leader and a decision-maker, floundered. Sensing her weaknesses, those who'd been tossed aside with Marcos and those who thought they could gain power in the vacuum he left behind went for her jugular. Within weeks of the jubilation at Malacañang, Filipinos were display-

305

ing their propensity for self-destruction. Political intrigue blotted out cooperation for the good of the country, particularly the sacrifices required to institute vitally needed land reform. Her enemies were not the only ones who stood in her way. Many of those closest to her, including her appointed advisers and members of her family, dominated the new president's time with what they unabashedly acknowledged as political gamesmanship. At sea in the world of economics, Aquino stayed away from the hard choices she should have been making. She flailed about, assigning the wrong people to essential jobs, listening to a cacophony of opinions, and otherwise dissipating energy. Marcos had warned of this during the early stages of the campaign when he said that the presidency allowed no time for on-the-job training.

Aquino's advisers were those who'd stood by the family over the years. Many were civil rights attorneys. Their liberal credentials were impeccable, but the same instincts that drove them to fight the Marcos dictatorship for twenty years blinded them to the new realities they had to face now that they were in government.

From the beginning, Aquino's main problem was how to handle her own military. She had a natural bias: Her husband had been railroaded by a court martial and held in a military prison for eight years, and she remained wholly convinced that he had been assassinated by soldiers. Her prejudice was fostered by her most intimate adviser, the man she appointed chief cabinet secretary, attorney Joker Arroyo.

During Ninoy's incarceration, as teams of lawyers came and went, Arroyo had remained loyal, and Cory trusted him beyond questioning. His own feelings against the armed forces were easily explained. For two decades he'd done battle with military men as they arrested and held Marcos's enemies, many of them liberals, leftists, and Communist-sympathizers. A short man with a blocky build and close-cropped gray hair that he wore brushed over his forehead, Arroyo bore a striking resemblance to Napoleon. His cabinet colleagues quickly took to disparaging him as the ''Little President.'' Aquino, who declined to live or work in Malacañang Palace and instead turned it into a museum where the main draws were Imelda Marcos's shoe and dress collections, established herself on the second floor of the palace's guest house. Arroyo worked in a small office on the ground floor from which his access to the president and his influence on her were total.

At the opposite pole in Aquino's estimation was Juan Ponce Enrile.

The man who'd run the defense ministry through most of the Marcos era and who'd led the military rebellion against Marcos had ceded power to her only because he had no choice. He had hardly expected to be back in his old job, as defense minister. Correctly, Aquino was wary of Enrile, his ties with the military, and his frustrated ambition.

She allowed herself to be egged on by Arroyo and other civil libertarians in the cabinet, joking with them about many of the top commanders as benighted Marcos loyalists and fools. The commanders, in turn, came to regard her as a leftist. Or, if they didn't truly believe Aquino was a Communist-sympathizer, they found it a convenient excuse for opposing her.

Frustrated and bitter over their inability to seize power, Enrile and his boys stewed and schemed. Conceding Aquino's undeniable popularity, the military men devised plans to destabilize her government and worked to create discomfiture at home and concern abroad, particularly in Washington, anticipating that they'd be accepted with relief when they came to her rescue. Aquino would be a puppet, and Enrile would pull the strings.

But Marcos, likewise stewing and scheming in Honolulu, managed to create the first stir. Through telephone conversations with his unpredictable former running mate, Arturo Tolentino, the exile arranged for three hundred or so soldiers under the command of officers zealously loyal to him to seize the Manila Hotel on July 6, 1986.

Tolentino, who five months earlier hadn't shown up at Malacañang to be sworn in as vice president, appeared in the lobby to take an oath as acting president. He appointed a six-member cabinet, including Enrile, and solemnly declared the elegant hostelry the true "seat of government." Marcos phoned his congratulations and vowed that he would return to reassume the office he insisted was legitimately his. Bewildered tourists took refuge in their rooms as the band of rebels, casually toting automatic weapons, bivouacked in the marble lobby and carpeted hallways along with thousands of civilian Marcos loyalists who'd swarmed into the hotel from a weekly rally they'd been holding in the adjacent Luneta park.

Aquino and General Fidel Ramos, the new chief of staff, were on the southern island of Mindanao when the hotel *putsch* began that Sunday afternoon. Vice President Salvador Laurel was in Spain, leaving Enrile in charge. The cagey minister appeared on television and, with a show of gracious aplomb, turned down Tolentino's cabinet offer, jolting the older man, who said he'd been assured that Enrile would join him.

Indeed, several of Aquino's ministers came to believe that, at the very least, Enrile had foreknowledge of the coup attempt and kept it to himself, something he subsequently denied in a heated exchange. Whatever he knew or intended, Enrile recognized quickly that without Ramos there was no way to sustain a coup against Aquino, with whom most Filipinos were still blindly in love. And for him to rejoin Marcos would have shattered his credibility. This was not the time for him to strike.

Thirty-eight hours after the hotel siege began, it ended, with a promise of no punishment for the offenders. In a burst of camaraderie, Enrile and one of the rebel officers, Brigadier General Jaime Echeverria, posed, smiling and embracing, for the cameras. Tolentino, crestfallen and confused, went home, and the officers and men returned to duty. The military men were, in fact, punished: Ramos ordered them to do thirty pushups and then joined them in the exercise.

Once again, Filipinos effusively congratulated themselves for resolving a problem uniquely. But the respite was temporary, and the bonhomie a bad precedent. Now there was no deterrent for disgruntled men on horseback. Military participation of that sort in the political process largely defines a banana republic. Marcos, by buying the fealty of the officer corps, had succeeded for twenty years in keeping the Philippines out of that category and himself in the good graces of the United States.

By this time, Washington was locked in to Aquino. But Enrile, perceiving less than overwhelming enthusiasm in the Reagan White House, stepped up his criticism. He zeroed in on her indecisiveness, her orders to investigate alleged human rights violations by military men while ignoring Communist brutalities, and her inclination to resolve the Communist insurgency through appeasement and negotiation rather than on the battlefield. Under other circumstances, Enrile's assessment would have been accurate and his tactics effective. But he went wrong in underestimating the depth of affection for Aquino, not just in the Philippines but in the United States and the rest of the world as well.

Aquino was better abroad than at home. In September, halfway into her first year in office, she delivered an emotional speech in Washington to a joint session of Congress: "Three years ago, I left America in grief to bury my husband. . . . Today I have returned as president of a free people. . . . As I came to power peacefully, so shall I keep it. This is my contract with my people and my commitment to God." Then, focusing a pragmatic eye on the Reagan administration's primary concern, she said that if she were unable to negotiate a ceasefire with the Communists, she would not hesitate to take up "the sword of war."

The Old Testament tenor of her address proved effective. "The finest speech I've heard in my thirty-four years in Congress," said Speaker Thomas "Tip" O'Neill. Three weeks later Congress approved a $200 million increase in aid to the Philippines. For people whose broad-stroke understanding of events in the Philippines had been shaped largely by television transmissions of the elections and the February rebellion, there were no questions: Marcos was evil; Aquino was good, honest, and sincere. Even her shortcomings were considered human and therefore appealing.

The Reagan administration, despite its instinctive predilection for Enrile or someone like him, recognized that it had to keep faith with Aquino. Through Ambassador Stephen Bosworth the White House got word to the defense chief to back off. Normally responsive to the Americans, this time the veteran minister ignored the appeal and continued publicly sniping at her. Assured by Aquino the preceding February that the commission she'd appointed to investigate hidden wealth would not look too deeply into the sources of his fortune, Enrile hinted darkly at corruption among some of her close advisers and members of her family, though wisely leaving the president's own reputation sacrosanct.

As part of his campaign of criticism and innuendo, Enrile brought in his boys to help conduct professional rumor-mongering. Seemingly authoritative documents (one was code-named "God Save the Queen") were leaked regularly to local and foreign journalists. Hardly a day passed that the newly liberated, effervescent, and often irresponsible local press didn't report an imminent armed strike; few questioned why such a move would be publicized in advance. Tension was heightened by a rash of grisly political murders and terrorist bombings.

By the time Aquino traveled to Tokyo in mid-November the impression was widespread at home and abroad that she was on the ropes.

In a very real sense she was but, to continue the metaphor, she had in her corner the man who made the difference, General Ramos. He had pledged his loyalty and assured her of his ability to control the military.

Finally, on the last Sunday in November, with the crisis at a peak, Aquino fired Enrile. To offset interpretations that this was an anti-military move, she fired two other ministers charged by Enrile and Ramos with corrupt practices, then a third who was considered pro-left. In another burst of decision-making, she ordered government negotiators to stop dithering with the National Democratic Front over a possible truce. They did, and worked out a sixty-day ceasefire with the Communists that took effect on November 26. Talks for a lasting peace got underway.

Nine months into her administration, she had at last acted like a president. Most Filipinos were thrilled, and even those who opposed her were impressed.

But the decisiveness didn't last, and she lapsed back into the un-certain ways that had characterized her performance from the start. A pattern of crisis management began to emerge, to be tested next as the February 2 plebiscite for a new national constitution approached.

The new basic law was a mind-numbing, sixty-two-page document that few voters read. Among its key provisions, it limited the extraor-dinary powers of the presidency that Marcos had built into the previous constitution in 1973 and established a U.S.-style bicameral legislature. It required land reform through "just distribution" of property. It also strengthened the president's hand in negotiating with the United States over the future of the military bases once the present agreement expired in 1991. The charter was by any measure a flawed document, but its passage was the best assurance Filipinos had of a return to normality.

The vote would be pivotal. If the constitution were adopted, Aqui-no's presidency would be cloaked with the mantle of legitimacy and she would have the right to serve out a six-year term. But if the charter were rejected, or if it just squeaked by, she would be open to allegations that, after all, she had no mandate and was not entitled to remain in office. Aquino threw herself wholeheartedly into campaigning, just as she had done barely a year earlier. And so did Enrile, now the leader of the right-wing opposition.

The first crisis erupted on the afternoon of Thursday, January 23, a little more than a week before the plebiscite. Seven thousand farm workers and Commuist supporters marched on Malacañang to press their demands for land reform. This was one of the most fundamental concerns of poor Filipinos and one the wealthy, landowning new president had been evading. The demonstrators were blocked at Mendiola Bridge, that symbolic barrier between the palace and the people, by a thousand troops.

What happened in the next few seconds was not certain; someone in the crowd may have fired a weapon or thrown a homemade grenade, or the armed troops may have panicked. But the results were clear. At almost point-blank range, the soldiers opened fire into the tightly packed crowd. Bloodied demonstrators screamed and fell, some dead instantly, others wounded and in agony. As those near the front attempted to turn and run they were blocked by the mob, and hundreds piled on top of one another in hysteria. The gunfire ceased for a few seconds as the troops reloaded. Then they began shooting again. When they stopped, sixteen were dead and a hundred wounded.

Nothing as bloody had happened at Mendiola during the Marcos era. Aquino, who had not been in the palace or in Manila at the time of the demonstration, was held responsible by leftists while Marcos supporters and other rightists joined them in a convenient meeting of interests. The National Democratic Front immediately called off the peace talks, shattering Aquino's proudest achievement.

It seemed that nothing more could befall the harried Aquino, but something did. On the same day as the shooting, a former supporter by the name of Homobono Adaza, who'd been embittered by his exclusion from the cabinet, released a recording of a bugged telephone conversation between Aquino and Joker Arroyo. The tape indicated that the two had meddled with the drafting of the national constitution in order to assure that nuclear weapons could continue to move in and out of the U.S. bases, a vital concern of the United States. The revelation was damaging on at least three counts: Aquino had promised that she would not interfere with the preparation of the charter; she was shown to be, like Marcos, in America's grasp; and, since the phone bug had been placed by the signal corps, the president was once more seen to be at the mercy of the armed forces.

Fresh rumors of a coup raced through Manila. This time they proved real. Before dawn on January 27 seven hundred troops, led by some of the same officers who'd staged the Manila Hotel incident, raided sections of military bases in and around the capital and captured a radio and television broadcasting compound in suburban Quezon City. General Ramos responded quickly, recapturing the military installations by midmorning.

But the scene at the broadcast center, known as GMA 7, was turning into a rerun of the hotel rebellion. A hundred and sixty soldiers, under the command of a paunchy air force colonel named Oscar Canlas, along with a hundred or so Marcos toughs and camp followers, barricaded themselves inside the studios and offices of the block-long concrete compound. Canlas was confused about whether he was there to demand Marcos's return or to demonstrate contempt for Aquino.

Nevertheless, this attempted coup was better-organized than the first try, and it incorporated an elaborate plan for Marcos to return. Hounded by lawyers seeking his hidden wealth, the exile was desperate, believing that once the new constitution was adopted he would face a legitimate government and his chances of ever resuming office would fade.

At about the same time as the coup attempt got underway, Philippine consular officials in Honolulu discovered that Imelda Marcos had gone shopping for $2,000 worth of camouflage fatigue outfits and combat boots. They also found that a chartered Boeing 707 owned by a Lebanese arms trader who was a friend of the Marcoses' dear friend, Saudi Arabian billionaire Adnan Khashoggi, was waiting to fly the former First Couple and their freshly uniformed aides from Hawaii to the Philippines. A few weeks earlier, Marcos had sent a videotape to friends in Manila, showing himself exercising bare-chested, illustrating that he was in good health. The Reagan administration took the circumstantial evidence seriously enough to dispatch two State Department officers to Marcos's home. They ordered him not to travel to his homeland, and the former president protested, "I feel that now I am being treated like a prisoner."

In Manila, Aquino was determined to repair her tattered image. She went on the air, declaring in no uncertain terms that she was going to crush the rebellion. "The full force of the law will be applied to everyone, civilian and military, who is implicated in the crime. I have ordered their arrest and detention. There is a time for reconciliation and a time for justice and retribution. That time has come."

Truly the time had come, but retribution did not. Ramos, fearful that if he ordered soldiers to fire on fellow soldiers they would turn against him, ignored Aquino's order to employ "intensive military operations" against the broadcast center. The result was a sixty-one-hour fiasco, with Ramos and the befuddled Colonel Canlas negotiating face-to-face on TV, the general leading puffing cameramen on a midnight jog around the besieged center, Canlas's weeping, pregnant wife holding his hand and appealing for him to surrender, rebel soldiers propping lifesize portraits of Marilyn Monroe, Clark Gable, and Fred Astaire on the roof, and a onetime movie starlet-turned Marcos loyalist waving delightedly over the compound wall to fans who shouted, "Throw us your panties."

The siege of GMA 7 ended on the morning of January 29, but only after Ramos guaranteed a group of officers brought to his office the night before by Enrile's zealous young turk, Colonel Gregorio "Gringo" Honasan, that he would not use force against the rebels. His concession demonstrated amply that the president did not control her chief of staff and that he did not control the military organization. It also demonstrated Aquino's weakness to any other military groups that might plan to topple her in the future.

Thus, as voters went to the polls four days later, Aquino appeared at her most vulnerable. Ironically, this very frailty jarred a significant number of middle-class Filipinos into realizing that if she did not win a sweeping mandate through wholehearted adoption of the constitution, they faced possible chaos, anarchy, and a military takeover. The middle class, people who'd turned sour on Aquino as she failed to live up to their high expectations, marshaled itself and went out to vote in favor of the constitution.

In the provinces, where 70 percent of the population lived, the poor weighed their fate once again. They had voted nearly a year earlier to depose Marcos and replace him with an untested widow. But they'd seen no improvement in their lives. They were still without work, their children were still hungry, prospects were as bleak as they'd ever been. Yet they, too, pushed aside their doubts.

Voter turnout that Monday was enormous, about 90 percent of the 25 million registered. And the voting was clean, probably the most honest election every conducted in the Philippines. The constitution was adopted by a stunning four-to-one margin. Ordinary Filipinos, whether they were politically inclined in one direction or another, were sending a clear message: They wanted an end to political machinations so that they could get on with their lives. They believed in Aquino's sincerity, they were prepared to take their chances with her, they thought she would grow if she were given the time and the opportunity. Ultimately, they made the kind of choice that confounds political analysts—they voted with their hearts.

Among military men, though, only 60 percent said yes to the constitution and Cory. They, too, voted with their hearts. The military would remain a threat to Aquino's future and to the future of the country.

A year had past since Marcos fled, a year of joy and hope, disappointment, tumult and tragedy. The constitution gave Aquino a new lease on her young political life, yet the antagonism of the armed forces and her own inexperience in the political art of co-opting potential enemies almost certainly would continue to plague her and the Philippines. There would be no shortage of criticism, much of it undoubtedly legitimate.

But as Filipinos continued to pick at their own wounds and to attack one another in self-seeking spasms, it would become all the more important that they remember what they had done only a year earlier. They had created a rare moment in history.

INDEX

315

The Philippines

0 50 100
KILOMETERS

0 50 100
MILES

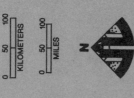

N

Luzon Strait

BABUYAN
ISLANDS

Philippine Sea

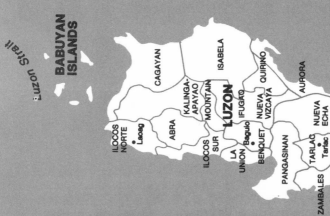

CAGAYAN

ISABELA

ILOCOS
NORTE

Laoag

ABRA

KALINGA-
APAYAO

MOUNTAIN

IFUGAO

QUIRINO

LUZON

NUEVA
VIZCAYA

AURORA

ILOCOS
SUR

LA
UNION

Baguio

BENGUET

PANGASINAN

TARLAC

Tarlac

NUEVA
ECHA

BULACAN

RIZAL

★ Manila

ZAMBALES

Clark U.S. Air Base

Angeles

PAMPANGA

CAVITE

LAGUNA

Olongapo

Bataan

BATAAN

BATANGAS

Subic Bay U.S. Naval Base

CATANDUANES

CAMARINES
NORTE

CAMARINES
SUR

Lamon Bay

QUEZON

MARINDUQUE

MINDORO

South China Sea